PASSPORT TO CHANGE

PASSPORT TO CHANGE

Designing Academically Sound, Culturally Relevant, Short-Term, Faculty-Led Study Abroad Programs

Edited by

Susan Lee Pasquarelli, Robert A. Cole, and

Michael J. Tyson

Foreword by Hilary Landorf

STERLING, VIRGINIA

Published by Stylus Publishing, LLC.
22883 Quicksilver Drive
Sterling, Virginia 20166-2102

Library of Congress Cataloging-in-Publication Data

Names: Pasquarelli, Susan Lee, editor. | Cole, Robert A., 1958-
editor. | Tyson, Michael J., editor.
Title: Passport to change : designing academically sound, culturally
relevant short term faculty-led study abroad programs / edited by
Susan Lee Pasquarelli, Robert A. Cole, Michael J. Tyson.
Description: First edition. |
Sterling, Virginia. : Stylus Publishing, 2017. |
Includes bibliographical references and index.
Identifiers: LCCN 2017015613 (print) |
LCCN 2017042973 (ebook) |
ISBN 9781620365496 (uPDF) |
ISBN 9781620365502 (ePub and mobi) |
ISBN 9781620365472 (cloth : alk. paper) |
ISBN 9781620365489 (pbk. : alk. paper) |
ISBN 9781620365496 (library networkable e-edition) |
ISBN 9781620365502 (consumer e-edition)
Subjects: LCSH: Foreign study--Administration--Handbooks,
manuals, etc. |
International education--Handbooks, manuals, etc.
Classification: LCC LB2376 (ebook) |
LCC LB2376 .P36 2017 (print) |
DDC 370.116--dc23
LC record available at https://lccn.loc.gov/2017015613

13-digit ISBN: 978-1-62036-547-2 (cloth)
13-digit ISBN: 978-1-62036-548-9 (paperback)
13-digit ISBN: 978-1-62036-549-6 (library networkable e-edition)
13-digit ISBN: 978-1-62036-550-2 (consumer e-edition)

Printed in the United States of America

All first editions printed on acid-free paper
that meets the American National Standards Institute
Z39-48 Standard.

Bulk Purchases

Quantity discounts are available for use in workshops and for
staff development.
Call 1-800-232-0223

First Edition, 2018

10 9 8 7 6 5 4 3 2 1

For those who nurture students' appreciation of diverse cultures, religions, and lifestyles.

CONTENTS

FOREWORD

S ince the Middle Ages, when students and professors roamed Europe on academic pilgrimages to gain knowledge, experiences, ideas, opinions, and other perspectives, study abroad has been a part of certain students' personal, cultural, academic, and social development. The importance that institutions of higher education have given to study abroad programs has largely depended on the strength of political and economic winds and the ability of the institution to ride on or resist those winds. Over the past decade, as study abroad programs expanded to reach a greater number and more diverse group of students, the field itself moved toward the center of higher education. Despite the current rhetoric of nationalism and fear of the "other," we have long lived and will continue to live in an increasingly interconnected and interdependent world. One of the best ways for students to learn to successfully navigate this complex world is to engage in a consciously, carefully crafted study abroad program. According to the Institute of International Education's 2016 Open Doors report on international exchange, more than 60% of students who study abroad attend programs of 8 weeks or less, and only 3% study abroad for an entire academic year. These statistics make it all the more important for faculty to develop and deliver these programs in intentional and thoughtful ways.

This book is a much-needed practical guide that covers the nuts and bolts of short-term, faculty-led study abroad programs. The focus is on programs that are academically sound and culturally relevant—those that provide an outcomes-based curriculum in one or more academic discipline and are deliberately designed for a specific cultural context. The framework of all the programs described in this book encompasses experiential learning, specifically the facilitation of such learning prior to, during, and after the study abroad experience.

This book is divided into three parts. Part one carefully details the design and delivery of faculty-led study abroad programs. The contributors are honest in their assessment of the heavy workload and headaches involved in planning and executing successful programs. At the same time, the reader can feel the contributors' passion and conviction of the value of their programs for students' holistic development. Part two features case studies of what I call *habitats of integrative global learning*—environments that provide students with prolonged global learning engagement and opportunities to make connections among their activities, their coursework, their personal lives, and the wider world around them. In their respective chapters in this part, the contributors discuss the ways in which international service-learning; international internships; interdisciplinary study abroad; and, language, culture, and environmental immersion programs open the door for students to connect their classwork with their personal experiences and their learning in communities outside their own. Part three features marketing, preparation of students, and promotion of cultural sustainability—three often neglected but important elements of short-term study abroad programs.

As much as this book guides faculty through the development, delivery, and marketing for short-term study abroad programs, it is also about the student experience— of encountering oneself in another culture, from another perspective, and seeing oneself and others anew. Consider the title: *Passport to Change*. A passport, the official document issued by a government to prove one's citizenship and one's identity while travelling abroad, is juxtaposed with the words "to change." What is the meaning of this title? Does it mean that one needs a passport *in order to* change, or that a passport *facilitates* change? And what is meant by *change*? Is it change in oneself, in one's perspective of the world, in one's view of others? Or does change mean that those who go on short-term, faculty-led study abroad programs learn to collaborate with others to begin to effect change in the world? These are all facets of study abroad that are explored in this informative, thoughtful, and insightful book.

A crucial aspect of this book is that it brings together experts in a diversity of fields, from marine biology, to construction management, to language, literacy and cultural studies, architecture, international and comparative studies, history, psychology, foreign languages, and communications. While all of the contributors share unique stories of the opportunities and challenges of leading study abroad programs in their various disciplines, they are united in their conviction that these programs are of immense value to students' growth as culturally sensitive individuals and responsible global citizens. Short-term, faculty-led study abroad programs are an important high-impact practice for college students, and *Passport to Change* is an indispensable guide for all who believe in long-term student success.

Hilary Landorf
Associate Professor, International & Intercultural Education;
Director, Office of Global Learning Initiatives;
Executive Director, Comparative & International Education Society;
Florida International University

Reference

Institute of International Education. (2016). *Open Doors 2016*. Retrieved from https://www.iie.org/en/Research-and-Insights/Open-Doors/Open-Doors-2016-Media-Information

ACKNOWLEDGMENTS

We would like to thank the following for permission to use their copyrighted material:

Scribner, for permission to use quotes from Anthony Doerr's *Four Seasons in Rome: On Twins, Insomnia, and the Biggest Funeral in the History of the World* (2007). Reprinted with permission of Scribner, a division of Simon & Schuster, Inc.

SAGE Publications, for the use of Figure 2.3, "Process Model of Intercultural Competence," by Darla K. Deardorff, *Journal of Studies in International Education 10*(3), 236. Adapted with permission.

INTRODUCTION

Susan Lee Pasquarelli, Robert A. Cole, and Michael J. Tyson

"International experience is one of the most important components of a 21st-century education, and study abroad should be viewed as an essential element of a college degree," according to Allan E. Goodman. "Learning how to study and work with people from other countries and cultures also prepares future leaders to contribute to making the word a less dangerous place."
("International Students," 2014)

If you have opened this book, then you likely agree with Allen Goodman, president of the Institute for International Education. Goodman's comment is timely as the number of American university students receiving academic credit in study abroad programs has tripled over the past two decades (Farrugia & Bhandari, 2014). In excess of 300,000 students studied abroad for credit in 2014–2015. It is worth noting that about 60% of those U.S. study abroad experiences were short term (Institute of International Education, 2016).

Development and implementation of faculty-led short-term study abroad programs is the trend in the field of international education. A *faculty-led short-term program*, as defined for the purpose of this book, ranges from two to eight weeks in length and is both academically sound and culturally relevant. The market for these types of programs is thriving. As Vande Berg (2003) suggests, the short-term model of study abroad offers flexibility and expands opportunities to students and faculty members who wish to study and work abroad but do not have the resources or time to spend a semester or year abroad.

Purpose of This Book

So what does it take to develop and deliver a faculty-led study abroad program? This volume is intended to answer that question. In these pages, seasoned faculty leaders and administrators describe an overall program development process, identify comprehensive elements for designing an abroad curriculum, and offer advice and solutions to unique challenges inherent in various types of faculty-led short-term programs. Readers will find a substantial focus on practical material for managing program details at home and abroad, information about writing a university proposal, creating a budget, the marketing and recruitment of students, handling abroad logistics, and preparing students for the abroad experience. Most important, readers will come to understand the difference between experiences that are more touristic than scholarly and gain guidance on designing or redesigning their own programs to ensure academically sound, culturally relevant curricula that complements the international field site.

Overview of Chapters

After administering or conducting faculty-led short-term study abroad programs for 10 years, we feel confident that we have captured the intriguing but practical voices of experts who share stories and advice related to the development and delivery of academically sound, culturally relevant faculty-led study abroad programs. Readers will find that the chapters are presented in an accessible voice, not because we do not know how to write in the genres of our disciplinary journals but because we prefer to invite readers to share the intellectual journey of discovery. This is also why the chapters draw on many firsthand examples as we try to bring into relief the larger points being made.

The book is divided into three parts. Part one sets the scene by providing requisite information concerning the overall process of designing and delivering faculty-led abroad programs. From program conception to program implementation, readers will undoubtedly be astonished at the amount of work involved in launching a first-time program. Those who have a framework for an existing program are also likely to find new or expanded ways to enhance the learning experience. Although we do not want to dissuade faculty from developing a program, we are straightforward and candid when establishing the faculty workload associated with these types of programs.

In part two, contributors offer their insights into designing an academically sound, culturally relevant curriculum that takes into consideration research-based theories and pedagogy. Because there are few resources on designing rigorous study abroad curricula, the core of this book is the curriculum section, spanning chapters 2 through 9. In this section readers are introduced to the concept that all faculty-led study abroad curricula consist of three developmental phases: the preparation (before students go abroad), the experience (while abroad), and the return (reentry). The contributors, who focus on outcomes, situate their programs in curricula for service-learning, internships, interdisciplinary study, and language, cultural, and environmental immersion.

Part three takes the reader beyond curriculum development to address other faculty efforts necessary to launch a program abroad. Although numerous tasks are involved in delivering an abroad program, the final section of the book focuses on three significant faculty activities that are critical to a program's success but are often overlooked or underemphasized, that is, marketing the programs, preparing students for the abroad curriculum and experience, and considerations for leaving a small footprint abroad.

In Chapter 1 Robert A. Cole introduces and expands on the iterative program development process. He meticulously explains how faculty developers must negotiate factors among the operational particulars of their campuses, the nature of their proposed field sites, and the preliminary goals of their intended programs. The process presented in Chapter 1 has universal appeal despite differences among institutional procedures for curriculum and international program development and approval.

Through the lens of international and education research, Susan Lee Pasquarelli in Chapter 2 defines what we term an *academically sound, culturally relevant curriculum*. She illustrates research principles with examples from her own study-abroad programs to demonstrate how best practices are realized in a short-term program. Although this chapter is in essence a literature review of curriculum principles, it is presented in an alternative format for readers to visualize their own study abroad curricula and is in keeping with our commitment to reader accessibility.

In Chapter 3 Victor Savicki and Michele V. Price focus on the curriculum element of student reflection. They begin with a comprehensive literature review about guided reflection and provide a rationale for its role in faculty-led study abroad program curricula. Then, using examples of hands-on activities, they offer expert advice to faculty leaders on promoting guided student reflection before, during, and after their experience abroad.

In Chapter 4 Darla K. Deardorff guides faculty developers' understanding of embedding the measurement of student and program effects in the initial curriculum design to determine the extent to which proposed programs contribute to students' growth academically, interculturally, and personally. She expertly leads faculty through a series of exercises and questions to ask themselves to decide on distinctive outcomes-based student and program assessments.

Chapters 5 through 9 are case studies of actual faculty-led study abroad programs. The five chapters focus on designing curricula and course syllabi for various types of faculty-led programs, including interdisciplinary subject matter, field study, global service-learning, internship immersion, and language and cultural study. In these chapters, veteran study abroad leaders contribute firsthand knowledge of how they design and deliver a study abroad curriculum to complement a host country or city. The case studies in these chapters are set in worldwide venues to enable the reader to envision a range of choices when designing new programs.

Although these chapters describe programs in specific countries with specific knowledge learning outcomes, the chapters have universal appeal to readers interested in designing a quality faculty-led curriculum. Each chapter includes information on curriculum design; appropriately related course work; length of program and number of credits earned through the home university; guided experiential learning events, such as walking classrooms, cultural interactions, field trips, expeditions, and independent field work; outcome-based student and program assessments; unique logistical challenges; and provisions for guided critical reflection on cultural experiences.

In Chapter 5 Bilge Gökhan Çelik, Dale Leavitt, and Michael Scully describe an interdisciplinary faculty-led program they designed and cotaught on sustainability studies in Turkey. They describe the challenge of designing and teaching a single sustainability course from the perspective of three professors from three fields of study: construction management, journalism, and marine sciences.

Paul Webb and Brian Wysor describe in Chapter 6 two different field study programs: Tropical Ecology in Belize and Neotropical Marine Biology in Panama. Through interesting vignettes, these professors illustrate the rationale for both programs—immersing students in the diversity of nature to stimulate critical examination of basic patterns of evolution and ecology. Although this chapter is centered on field studies in the water, it has universal appeal to readers interested in designing any field study program in which students explore and research natural phenomena in situ.

Service-learning is the focus of Chapter 7 in which Autumn Quezada de Tavarez and Kerri Staroscik Warren interweave global service-learning principles into the description of the development of their public health program set in El Salvador. In keeping with the literature, these professors designed a program with learning outcomes that cultivate intercultural competency while encouraging historical grounding and demonstration of public health knowledge. This chapter is valuable reading for faculty leaders interested in designing a faculty-led service-learning program.

In Chapter 8 Candelas Gala and Javier García Garrido describe their language and cultural immersion internship study abroad program in Salamanca, Spain. Looking beyond the specifics of a single location and culture, this chapter is helpful to those interested in developing an internship program abroad as they grapple with values, mores, and professional expectations of their intended sites. In addition, the chapter is full of practical advice, including how to identify and secure internship sites.

In Chapter 9 Min Zhou presents a description of her three-week study abroad program on intercultural learning in China. The curriculum she designed centers on the historical, religious, and cultural knowledge of contemporary China. As a guided reflection component, Zhou asks her students to apply their new knowledge to interpreting the behavior of people in the host culture as well as developing strategies for their own behavior in the host culture. Her narrative about the challenge of bringing students to understand the values of a vastly different culture is interesting and thought provoking.

Part three marks a return to program development details. In Chapter 10 Michael J. Tyson, who has substantial experience recruiting students to participate in faculty-led programs, provides a blueprint for faculty leaders to develop marketing plans. This is one of the areas of the short-term program process that is most often overlooked when professors are immersed in curriculum design or managing abroad details. We included marketing in this volume because a faculty member might spend a year developing a program that is cancelled because of a lack of student recruitment. As Tyson says in the chapter title: "No Students, No Program."

In Chapter 11, Susan Lee Pasquarelli shares her own version of faculty groundwork necessary before teaching abroad. The chapter includes preparations to teach all three phases of the faculty led program: student preparations for the abroad experience (pre-), student experiences while abroad (during), and student affirmation on return (after). Her chapter includes guidelines for student orientation as well as ways faculty may prepare themselves for teaching abroad, making this a most practical chapter.

In Chapter 12, a fitting conclusion to the volume, Roxanne M. O'Connell merges her own voice with the voices of faculty and administrators who live and work in locations abroad. Her chapter provides insights into how faculty leaders might leave a small footprint and promote mutual intercultural understanding when they take students abroad. The purpose of this chapter is to encourage faculty leaders to promote cultural sustainability as well as provide ways to immerse students into a new culture.

References

Farrugia, C. A., & Bhandari, R. (2014). *Open doors 2014 report on international educational exchange.* New York, NY: Institute of International Education.

Institute of International Education. (2016). *Duration of U.S. study abroad, 2004/05–2014/15.* Retrieved from www.iie.org/opendoors

International students in the United States and study abroad by American students are at an all-time high. (2014). Retrieved from za.usembassy.gov/international-students-in-the-united-states-and-study-abroad-by-american-students-are-at-an-all-time-high

Vande Berg, M. (2003, February). *Rapporteur report: Study abroad and international competence.* Paper presented at the meeting of Global Challenges and U.S. Higher Education, Durham, NC: Duke University.

PART ONE

UNDERSTANDING THE NATURE OF FACULTY-LED STUDY ABROAD PROGRAMS

SURVEYING THE LANDSCAPE

The Process of Developing Faculty-Led Programs

Robert A. Cole

I t is not difficult to understand the appeal short-term study abroad programs hold for students and faculty leaders alike. As Herbst (2011) indicates in reference to the students he has taken to Istanbul, Turkey, on several occasions, "Unbound by their usual social networks and routines back home, students bonded as a tight-knit learning community in a way that is hardly possible on campus" (p. 224). And for himself, he states, "There has never been a teaching experience so intensely rewarding" (p. 225).

In my role as vice provost for global and international programs at Roger Williams University, I often hear similar heartfelt comments from faculty when they return from a successful short-term program abroad. Perhaps one of the most creative activities in my university role is observing and mentoring faculty as they develop from conception to fruition a broad array of faculty-led programs. This chapter is intended to help a faculty developer shape ideas scratched on a notepad into an organized, thoughtful program ready for launching. For those who already lead short-term programs, the contents may open new ways to think about program design and delivery. Moreover, this chapter provides a preliminary litmus test for faculty members to decide if they wish to forge on with the hard work of developing and delivering an academically sound, culturally relevant faculty-led program or retool an existing program. The topics included in this chapter lend faculty leaders the yardstick to measure their own tolerance for ambiguity, crises management, and program leadership.

Figure 1.1 illustrates our conception of the nonlinear touchpoints of program development for faculty-led short-term programs.

As readers see in the figure, arrows indicate multidirections of where to go after determining the substance of each touchpoint. Because of the nature

Figure 1.1. Touchpoints of program development: The iterative process of creating and implementing a faculty-led study abroad program.

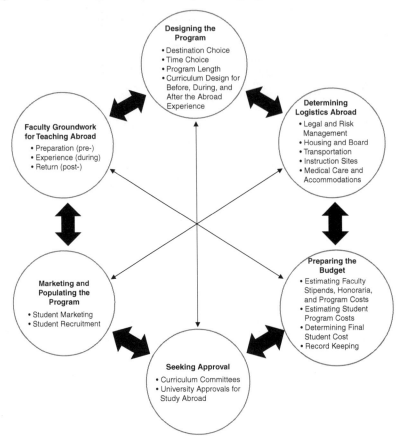

of using an iterative program development process, faculty designers will find it necessary to revise a touchpoint as each design element is added. We found the best approach to our program design is to consider each thematic touchpoint, moving forward, backward, and crossing as each touchpoint is reconsidered in light of new thinking.

Using the touchpoints of program development as a topical outline for this chapter, I begin with the first circle: designing the program.

Designing the Program

Destination Choice
Perhaps the best approach to selecting a faculty-led program destination is a backward design of the study abroad program curriculum so that it

is not forced onto a site. The destination should be an organic or natural choice that fulfills the study abroad program's outcome and, to an extent, stands as the sine qua non of the whole experience. In other words, without that chosen site, the curriculum as designed has little chance of being academically sound and culturally relevant (see Chapter 2 for an in-depth discussion on the fundamentals of an academically sound, culturally relevant curriculum).

So, does backward design mean choosing a content topic and then searching for a field site where students can experience that topic? Or does it mean choosing a field site and then deciding what kind of content to build around that site? Unsurprisingly, the answers are yes and yes. Tacking back and forth between potential field sites and possible topics is one of the many iterative tasks that define the process of program development.

For example, suppose a professor of American studies has expertise in the American themes of liberty, equality, justice, and revolution. He or she might well decide that a powerful experiential curriculum could be built around Paris by developing a program anchored in the concepts of *liberté, égalité, et fraternité*, the national motto of France. Such a program could bring into relief for U.S. students questions about how these concepts are enacted in everyday life after a revolution against the ruling powers.

Alternatively, my colleague Cliff Timpson, a professor of chemistry, and I developed a short-term program titled Beer as Chemistry, Craft, Culture, and Commerce. It is intended to teach students about the recent renaissance that artisanal industries are undergoing, specifically as illustrated by the craft beer movement. Beyond teaching students about the ingredients and processes for making beer, we find it important for them to understand the long history the product has as nourishment, social lubricant, currency, product of trade, and a source of tax revenue. To experience the sensibility in which beer is inseparable from cultural identity, few places abroad engender the type of understanding that is found in Germany and Belgium. Hence, our program moves among the German Rhineland, Brussels, and the Belgian countryside.

An unavoidable consideration for the destination choice is safety. A college or university with a vibrant study abroad office may have hundreds of students away during the course of a calendar year. This means that a university has a great deal of legal exposure at any given time, and if it sponsors faculty-led programs abroad, significant risks need managing. If an institution has a study abroad office, the director assists faculty in matching the school's tolerance for risk with the ever-changing conditions of the field. However, a well-designed program implies that the developer has not only researched and considered the general level of security that prevails at the destination but also has taken into account the degree of risk in the daily itinerary as it relates to transportation, activities, people coming in contact with the students, and so forth.

Time Choice

In May and June the barley fields of the Poperinge district of western Belgium are knee high and getting taller each day. Likewise, the hop bines are inching up the training lines, and the cones are starting to emerge. To smell the agricultural air, to see the grain being malted, to understand beer from its earthy beginnings requires that our program be abroad as summer approaches in western Europe.

The optimum time for a faculty-led program abroad may be quite narrow, as is ours, or more likely open to a range of considerations. The school calendar is the principal driver of when programs can go afield. Typically, short-term programs are confined to the winter period between fall and spring semesters, spring break, or the summer period. Within these school calendar confines, the proposed course itinerary should be laid out tentatively to see if seasonal or weather concerns have an impact.

It might be tempting to imagine warm summer night dinners at the open-air cafés of Europe, or boating on the Thames, but keep in mind that London received more than 31 million visitors in 2015 (Coldwell, 2016). So it could be a long wait to tour the Tower of London, to say nothing of the crowded Tube. Meanwhile, August is when many Europeans go on holiday, so depending on the design of the study abroad program, key people or places may not be available.

Weather is another consideration as temperate conditions might make long hikes more bearable for one program but be the bane of another program that counts on the regularity of a tropical afternoon rain for students to make the observations the curriculum demands. The more flexibility that is built into the itinerary, while still meeting the learning goals, the less encumbered the design of the program will be in regard to the time of year it must be offered.

Program Length

In deciding how long to be abroad with your program, a number of factors need to be considered, including cost and timing. But a program's proposed itinerary drives what is, arguably, the most important determinant for program length—the number of credits to be awarded.

The federal government's definition of a *credit hour* ("Rules and Regulations," 2010) is designed to ensure that students are engaged in the learning process for a period of time commensurate with the number of credits being awarded. The government takes license to define the quantity of learning that occurs because it provides students of most higher education institutions with federal student grants and loans. Meanwhile, regional accrediting bodies translate the government's definition into the standards for colleges and universities to demonstrate that they are in compliance with the so-called coin of the educational realm—the credit hour.

The definition should not be seen as restricting what can be done with study abroad. Instead, it opens pathways to alternative, creative ways of thinking about how, when, and where students might engage in learning. For instance, lecturing for an hour 3 times a week for 15 weeks to students sitting in hard plastic chairs yields 45 hours of student engagement (if you accept that they are riveted to everything we might say during those lectures). Add to each lecture an estimated 2 hours of outside-the-classroom work by the student, such as reading, writing papers, and so on, yields another 90 hours of student academic engagement. Totaling inside-the-classroom to outside-the-classroom time, we arrive at the government's magical number of 135 academic engagement hours to award 3 credit hours. The New England Association of Schools and Colleges Commission on Higher Education assumes a 50-minute hour, therefore the formula for arriving at the required number of engagement hours and days in the field is summarized in Table 1.1.

The government does not bind us to only one approach to teaching and learning, wherein one hour of classroom and a minimum of two hours of out-of-class work over a 15-week semester or trimester earns a credit hour for the student. Shaped in their thinking by the U.S. Department of Education and multiple contributors, the authors of the definition ("Rules and

TABLE 1.1
Credits Awarded for Hours of Student Engagement

Credits Awarded	Clock Hours	Academic Engagement (Adjusted for Accreditor's 50-Minute Hour)	Example for 12-Hour Days	Example for 10-Hour Days	Example for 8-Hour Days
1	45	37.5 hours	3.125 days	3.75 days	4.7 days
2	90	75 hours	6.25 days	7.5 days	9.4 days
3	135	112.5 hours	9.375 days	11.25 days	14 days
4	180	150 hours	12.5 days	15 days	18.75 days
5	225	187.5 hours	15.625 days	18.75 days	23.4 days
6	270	225 hours	18.75 days	22.5 days	28.1 days

Note. From Cole (2016).

Regulations," 2010) recognize that teaching and learning happen in mani-fold ways, with the key quantitative measurement being the amount of time the students are academically engaged. From this perspective, the second paragraph of the definition reads:

> At least an equivalent amount of work as required in paragraph (1) of this definition for other academic activities as established by the institution including laboratory work, internships, practica, studio work, and other academic work leading to the award of credit hours. (p. 116)

With this paragraph, the world suddenly opens up to faculty developing short-term study abroad programs. Anything and everything that can be tied to the learning outcomes of the course are justifiable as student academic engagement in the march toward keeping on the compliance side of the accreditors. Mini lectures on the bus to and from the field site, the readings and journal writing the students do in anticipation of the day's events, their cultural immersion as they independently explore coffee shops and souks, can all be mapped to the program outcomes.

For example, in our own craft beer course, the time spent exploring hop fields, touring malting facilities, visiting breweries, and listening to head brewers discuss their processes are clearly periods of student academic engagement. In addition, though, one of our broad program outcomes is to compare the cultural, moral, and legal attitude toward beer between the United States and that of other countries, with a focus on Germany and Belgium. Thus, the hours students spend on their own in the Altstadt area of Düsseldorf or at the Poechenellekelder Pub in Brussels are the experiential fodder that begins to move them toward analyzing and synthesizing those outcomes. This can only be gleaned from cultural immersion.

One helpful way to determine if a program meets the standard for the number of credits to be awarded is to lay out the itinerary in a grid and attach student academic engagement hours to the total experience, including the hours of learning that are associated with predeparture and postdeparture expectations. In our own course, prior to leaving for Europe, students have already made an independent site visit to a local U.S. brewery and written about it, spent a couple of days with us in the laboratory learning about the chemistry of beer, and brewed a 10-gallon batch of beer that will ferment and be ready for bottling on our return. Table 1.2 provides an example of the first week of our program and how we documented and calculated student engagement hours.

Faculty recognize that quantity of student academic engagement is only one measure of any program's effectiveness. As this book argues implic-itly and explicitly at almost every turn, learning outcomes, prepared in an

TABLE 1.2

Student Academic Engagement Grid

Date	Event	Place	Meeting Times	Student Engagement Hours
Mon. 5/15– Sun. 5/21	Pretrip learning modules and independent field trip	Online via Bridges LMS	n/a	20 hours directed study and field experience
Mon. 5/22	Laboratory brewing session, including identification of raw materials and equipment	Home campus	9:00 am–4:00 pm	7 hours lab experience
Tue. 5/23	Fly to Brussels	Depart Boston	4:00 pm (7:00 pm flight)	1 hour mini lecture
Wed. 5/24	• Double Decker Bus Tour of Brussels • Museum van de Belgische Brouwers (Brussels) • Royal Museums of Fine Arts of Belgium (Brussels)	Brussels	9:00 am–6:00 pm	1 hour mini lecture 3 hours field experience 2 hours homework 3 hours cultural immersion
Thur. 5/25	• Sint Sixtus Abbey of Westvleteren MUSEUM ONLY, NO TOUR AVAILABLE (Westvleteren, Belgium) • Brouwerij St. Bernardus Tour (Watou, Belgium) • 't Hoppecruyt Hop Farm Tour (Proven, Belgium) • Cheese Factory Tour (Passendale, Belgium)	Day trip from Brussels to Poperinge beer district	9:00 am–6:00 pm	1 hour mini lecture 4 hours field experience 2 hours homework 2 hours cultural immersion
Fri. 5/26	• Duvel Moortgat Brewery Tour (Puurs, Belgium) • La Trappe Brewery at the Abbey of Our Lady of Koningshoeven Tour (Tilburg, Netherlands)	Day trip from Brussels to Points North, including The Netherlands	9:00 am–6:00 pm	1 hour mini lecture 4 hours field experience 2 hours homework 2 hours cultural immersion

(Continued)

TABLE 1.2 (*Continued*)

Sat. 5/27	• Castle Malting Plant Tour (Beloeil, Belgium) • Brewery Dubuisson and Hop Farm Tour (Pipaix, Begium) • Brasserie de Blaugies Tour (Dour, Belgium)	Day trip from Brussels to Points South in the Wallonia Region	9:00 am–6:00 pm	1 hour mini lecture 4 hours field experience 2 hours homework 2 hours cultural immersion
Sun. 5/28	• Stella-Artois Tour and Special Tasting (Leuven, Belgium) • Royal Palace Tour (Brussels) OPTIONAL • A La Bécasse Pub (Brussels) • Mannekin Pis Statue (Brussels) • The Poechenellekelder Pub (Brussels)	Day in Brussels area	9:00 am–5:00 pm	1 hour mini lecture 3 hours field experience 2 hours homework 2 hours cultural immersion
			Total Hours week 1	72 Hours

academically sound, culturally relevant manner are the mark of quality. At the same time, quantifying student academic engagement in a manner that maps the experience of those outcomes ensures that a program has the structural integrity to deliver on its promise. Moreover, the administration is assured that the program keeps the institution in compliance with its accrediting agencies, at least in regard to the number of credits students will earn. Such an approach promises that for the students, the world is not only their oyster, but also their credit hour.

Curriculum Design for Before, During, and After the Abroad Experience

Drawing on her experiences of delivering programs in various Latin American countries, Goodrich (2016) notes that "the penchant for frenetic, non-reflexive activity aimed at rendering students' experiences abroad unforgettable, life-changing and action-packed must not replace a well-grounded, goal-oriented, and assessable educational experience" (p. 283).

As readers will encounter in this book, a well-designed short-term study abroad program takes full advantage of the learning opportunities that exist before departure, during the time abroad, and on return. Designing curriculum is well rehearsed in chapters 2 through 9 of this book, starting with a literature review in Chapter 2, which defines an academically sound, culturally relevant program and the rationale for providing three phases of delivery: pre-, during, and post-abroad experience. Since the bulk of this book is focused on curriculum design, I defer to chapters 2 through 9 for description of this touchpoint.

Determining Logistics Abroad

The general rule on my campus is that faculty do not lead a short-term study abroad program by themselves. Some well-practiced programs with a maximum of 8 to 10 students, set in a single urban location such as London, which can foster student independence and mobility, are occasionally allowed to run with a single leader. More standard is two faculty sharing the program direction and either coteaching a single course, or each teaching a course, with students enrolled in both classes simultaneously. The value of two leaders is that the program does not need to stop, for example, when a student needs local medical care. Or if someone gets separated from the group, one leader can go to the prearranged meet-up location while the rest of the group continues on. Additionally, program leaders are not made of iron. They too can be wiped out for a day by the flu or a throbbing knee induced by too many miles up and down cobblestone streets.

Options for managing the logistics of a short-term study abroad program fall under three models: third-party responsibility, full faculty responsibility, or a hybrid shared responsibility. It is important to understand, however, that the contributors to this book believe that for a program to be academically sound and culturally relevant, only the logistics can be bid out or shared, never the curriculum design itself.

Organizations such as WorldStrides' Capstone, Education First, Council on International Educational Exchange, and others work with program developers to create short-term programs for students. These organizations' services are scalable inasmuch as they can be engaged to take care of every conceivable aspect of the experience, including delivering parts of the curriculum, or they can provide for customizable logistical needs, liability policies, medical support, emergency evacuation, and repatriation services, if desired.

Program directors should explore what support systems are already in place at their own institutions and match those to the type of program they are developing. For example, the study abroad office on my campus carries insurance for emergency services, so this feature of a third-party vendor holds little value for our programs. Herbst (2011) describes the proposal bidding process his institution uses for identifying third-party providers for global seminars. Under his institution's model, a single faculty member accompanies 15 to 30 students, and thus needs the third-party provider to free the faculty member to focus primarily on academics. In Herbst's case, he characterizes the use of third-party providers, which were primarily coordinators for logistics and nonacademic problems, as "extremely helpful, but it obviously added an additional layer of cost" (p. 211).

Large worldwide service providers and local in-country service providers are in abundance, although it is time consuming and often difficult to vet and price each for quality and reliability. A posting on a study abroad electronic mailing list asked about providers in Kenya and Tanzania, for example, and the responses revealed more than 16 organizations engaged in some level of program support.

Campuses with a study abroad office often help faculty leaders with researching travel locations, arranging logistics, paying vendors, and building the travel itinerary. With such assistance, those faculty leaders who are committed to the belief that the curriculum and the logistics are part and parcel with their vision of what the program should be will prefer to build the program exactly as they see fit, rather than outsourcing to a third party.

Some institutions may offer curriculum or program development grants that provide financial assistance toward generating new programs. If so, faculty building short-term study abroad proposals are strongly encouraged to take advantage of these. No matter how well one thinks he or she knows the region and the itinerary, it is of immense value to trace the steps, even if at double speed, getting contacts; seeing what might have changed regarding hours of access; and discovering what, if any, aspects are simply unworkable.

For those who cannot go beforehand, the details of the following topics should be worked through by using campus resources such as the study abroad office, colleagues who have successfully led programs abroad, other offices on campus, and one's own research to mine for contacts, logistics, and so forth.

Legal and Risk Management

To begin, any program proposal must have an assurance of security at the most basic level. Program proposers should start with the U.S. Department of State's website to see what legal travel documents are required, what health precautions must be taken, and if any recent travel advisories or warnings have been issued.

Demonstrations, strikes, health outbreaks, elevated terrorist threats, and the like for a targeted country are published electronically as travel alerts. By comparison, travel warnings are issued for more serious situations such as government instability and civil war, high levels of crime or violence, or greater incidents of crime and terrorist attacks.

Program proposers are encouraged to review the U.S. Department of State's website, subscribe to its electronic mailing list, and enroll in the Smart Traveler Enrollment Program (all of which can be accessed from travel.state .gov). Doing so early in the program proposal process allows faculty leaders to have an informed discussion with the staff on their campus, typically those in the study abroad office or office of general counsel, who usually have final authority on weighing student risk. Additional aspects of risk management are covered in the section "Seeking Approvals."

The state department does a good job of laying out the safety risks of travel abroad on a country-by-country basis, but the Centers for Disease Control (CDC) is more authoritative regarding management of health risks for travelers. Current warnings and basic precautions can be found on the CDC website (www.nc.cdc.gov/travel), along with options to subscribe to the CDC electronic mailing list.

Another useful electronic newsfeed for daily alerts about worldwide security and analytical reports is provided at no cost to educators by the Bureau of Diplomatic Security of the Overseas Security Advisory Council. Access to the information from this agency, also a part of the U.S. Department of State, can be obtained from the website (www.osac.gov/Pages/Home.aspx).

If a study abroad office is available, faculty leaders should review with staff what other risk management processes are in place. Usually, the study abroad office, or another group on campus, forms a partnership with program leaders to provide a rapid response to triage and mitigate students' exposure to harm in cases of emergency. This office most likely has a staff member whom faculty can call from abroad when a student breaks a leg or has wandered off and cannot be located, or if the whole group is stranded at the train station because the credit card no longer functions.

When terrorists attacked Paris in November of 2015, killing more than 100 people and injuring hundreds more, staff at the study abroad office on my campus quickly mobilized to locate students and ensure their safety. Throughout that evening, key administrators maintained a continuous string of e-mail communications regarding management of the situation and communicated with concerned parents and the public about the attacks.

For program proposers who do not have access to campus resources that can support them in legal and risk management, third party providers are available, as previously noted. Companies like WorldStrides Risk Management, United Educators, and others can arrange emergency evacuation, insurance, liability protection, and risk mitigation. The study abroad program proposer does not need to be a safety expert but does need to know enough to work as a team, whether through services available on campus or from a provider, to monitor and react to the ebb and flow of travel risk and global crises.

Housing and Board

Program proposers have choices when it comes to housing students and themselves during short-term study abroad experiences. The most common options are standard hotels, apartment rentals, hostels, home stays, and university dormitories. With the powerful reach of the Internet, it is a simple task to research the hotel options, sort them by price, triangulate the reviews from a handful of sites, and decide on the viability of those options. For example, in faculty-led programs to Paris and London, we have cultivated a stock of basic 2.5-star hotels whose key features beyond safety, cleanliness, and affordability are their easy access to underground subway systems. With mass transit nearby, the lodgings do not need to be located in Paris's first arrondissement to be the perfect home base for each day's activities and for the students to relish the experience.

Depending on the curriculum, home stays might be an important venue for student learning in some short-term programs as well as dorm rooms on a vibrant college campus. Again, the power of the Internet is a great aid in locating organizations such as IES Abroad whose more than 30 global locations might fit a program's needs.

An important consideration for program proposers is the lead time needed to arrange accommodations. During peak tourist season, lodgings in popular cities fill quickly, especially if they are clean, affordable, and with nearby access to bus and subway lines.

Affordable housing that includes breakfast is always a bonus because it ensures that no matter how carefully students are managing their discretionary funds, they have access to at least one solid meal. As program proposers develop their itinerary, they should consider how, where, and at what personal cost students will eat each day. If day trips to surrounding areas are called for, what options are available to students for lunch or dinner? In some cases, it might be advantageous to calculate the cost of group meals and some other meals into the overall price of the program. Incorporating this into the program fee means that the student who runs out of a personal allowance will not go hungry for the last few days abroad.

In any case, accurate calculations should be made regarding the cost to eat and other minor expenses during the time the program is afield. It is important to disclose these anticipated costs to students and make sure they understand that these costs are in addition to the quoted program fee (which is discussed in "Preparing the Budget" and in Chapter 10).

Transportation

Shuttles to and from the airport, regional trains, buses, trams, subways, and hired coaches might all be needed at some point, depending on a program's itinerary. For many Western countries, transit schedules are easily retrieved over the Internet, and connections can be planned well ahead of time.

Subway and bus maps are easily saved as PDF files on a smartphone or tablet, and Google Maps allows downloading large areas for use offline. Some in the study abroad group may wish to have small cellular data plans for use abroad so that basic mapping, current location, and navigation features can be accessed without relying on a wireless connection. It is strongly recommended for at least one of the program leaders to have such a plan, not just for navigation but in case of an urgent need for care, data access, or emergency communication.

Using mass transit falls within the acceptable safety risks for a study abroad program and can be an excellent sociocultural introduction to the area for students. However, when using taxis, shuttle services, or long-distance transporters, it is important to avoid unlicensed cabs and individual for-hire services. For faculty leaders designing programs in remote locations, transportation of a large group of students may prove challenging. For example, a river barge or small boats may be needed to transport students during a field course. Whatever the vehicle of transport, program directors are cautioned to hire only established, reputable livery services, preferably those that are insured.

Instruction Sites

Program developers will want to give some thought to how they intend to deliver instruction while abroad. Are formal presentations planned for some of the days, and if so, what kind of space and instructional technology is required?

Many spaces can be pressed into service for an impromptu discussion, student presentation, or similar teaching event. Hotels may have lobby space or a breakout room where 10 students and 2 faculty leaders can easily gather. Museums are full of tour guides instructing small groups of people on their treasures. The same can be accomplished by faculty leaders, with students learning in the museums from well-planned faculty presentations. Day trips on buses might include a period of formal presentation and, weather permitting, parks or other public gathering sites are fine venues for discussions.

Mini lectures can be crafted around walks through the key monuments and markers of a city, thereby returning to a style of teaching first made famous by the peripatetic school of ancient Greece and its walking teacher, Aristotle. Taking their cue from Aristotle, many faculty at my institution call their academic discourse and learning events walking classrooms. If more formal, technology-dependent space is needed, a bit of research will turn up spaces for rent or loan at local schools and organizations.

As program developers work through the particulars, they are well served to keep in mind that experiential education emphasizes guiding students so they do much of the learning on their own. Some heavy lectures might be called for during short-term study abroad programs, but too much suggests an imbalance. Students should be given the intellectual tools to analyze and synthesize what they are seeing and touching, smelling and hearing, and perhaps tasting. That implies ample time for guided reflection and processing in place of passively receiving pedantic instruction.

Medical Care and Accommodations

Like it or not, the students are in large part dependent on the faculty who lead them abroad. That means they may seek comfort and aid for minor medical needs from the program's leaders. We recommend packing a basic first-aid kit to attend to the small cuts and muscle strains that are bound to occur.

For more serious medical needs, on arrival in each location, it is prudent to ask students to memorize the local telephone number for emergency services. It is also wise to have mapped out beforehand the locations of hospitals and pharmacies near the group's lodging. A badly twisted ankle may need an X-ray and ice wrapping by a local medical care provider. In most places, a program leader and the student can call a taxi to quickly deliver them to the local emergency room, but knowing beforehand where one is headed lessens the anxiety. And after the examination, a mild pain reliever is easily obtained if the faculty leader knows where the pharmacy is and how late it is open.

For preexisting medical conditions, faculty leaders should work with the study abroad office to determine which medications can be taken into another country and if a prescription is necessary. For campuses with study abroad offices, students most likely are asked to complete a health disclosure form and indicate if they have a medical condition that may require attention or limit their level of participation. For example, a student may disclose an asthmatic condition, and by working closely with the program leader, everyone is alerted and prepared to respond if the rigors of walking, a food allergy, or pollen trigger a reaction while abroad.

Some students with physical limitations may need accommodations for the study abroad program, and every effort should be made to find ways for them to participate. For instance, if a student in a wheelchair signs up for the program, the faculty leader must ensure that the residence has accessible rooms, train platforms are easily reached, and other elements of the program are designed to provide a substantial learning experience for the student. Consultation with one's campus office of student services as well as an open discussion with the student about her or his needs helps determine the best way to shape the program. In addition, Mobility International USA, a nonprofit organization and national clearinghouse on disability and student exchange, is an excellent resource for information related to studying and teaching abroad.

In summary, my colleague Michael J. Tyson, who works in a university study abroad office, states that one of the most common complaints he reads on postprogram student evaluations is that a program felt disorganized. Although he notes that this is sometimes out of the professor's control, having housing, teaching space, transportation, and site visits organized early mitigates the hiccups along the way and keeps the program running smoothly at a more affordable cost.

Preparing the Budget

Program leaders do not have to be accountants to develop and deliver a study abroad experience. They do, however, need at least the same level of math called for in keeping a household checking or debit account in good working order. Many campuses have an office of finance and a study abroad office that work closely with each other to approve and later reconcile the accounting of a program. But faculty must know enough about pricing a program and managing its finances to gain the confidence of the institution that is entrusting the leader with the authority to spend tens of thousands of dollars on its behalf.

Faculty leaders also need to have a clear sense of what expenses make up the total that each student pays for the experience abroad. If faculty leaders wish to make their proposed programs as affordable as possible, for marketing purposes, they need to know where the expenses are and what can be traded off to maximize the cost-to-benefit calculation. Moreover, knowing what constitutes a program's costs empowers faculty leaders to make flexible decisions about expenses in the discretionary spending category while in the field.

Estimating Faculty Stipends, Honoraria, and Program Costs

A shorthand way to think about the finances associated with a faculty-led study abroad program is in terms of students' direct and indirect expenses. In this discussion we assume that apart from possible scholarship awards an institution does not heavily subsidize students' short-term study abroad, instead passing on the costs of the experience to them.

In most institutions, the salaries faculty receive for teaching while abroad are a significant indirect cost that is borne by the students. Faculty compensation is usually preestablished by the institution and is easily applied to course work abroad. In the case of two (or more) faculty delivering the curriculum, it is usual to split the teaching stipend between the two for a three-credit course. Alternatively, if the program provides students with six credits, it is usual for each faculty member to teach three credits and for each to draw a full three-credit stipend.

The practice on some campuses may be to also provide a modest program director fee in addition to the teaching stipend. Again, with two faculty leaders, this fee could be paid to the individual who assumes this role or shared by the codirectors. Added to the teaching or directing expense might also be honoraria for guest lecturers, tour guides, and other experts in the field. In total, including payroll taxes, these are the labor costs of a program.

Nonlabor costs also get passed on to the students as part of calculating fair pricing for faculty-led programs. The faculty airline ticket, in-country transportation, lodging, and admission to program-specific events are all calculated and included. It is debatable how much if any of a faculty leader's meal expenses should be added to the program's overall costs. Each proposer has to make his or her own determination on this, but there is some soundness to arguments that faculty participation in group meals such as arranged lunches or special, culturally educational dinners contribute to the learning experience of the students.

All these items, plus costs for any group expenses such as renting land transportation, are combined to determine a faculty leader's cost, which I return to in the next discussion on how to arrive at a student's final cost. It is the practice at my campus to also include a program contingency cost from $400 to $800, depending on the total cost of the program. This allows for unpredicted events that might arise and any vagaries in currency exchange rates.

Estimating Student Program Costs

Like faculty, students have program expenses. Setting flight costs aside for a moment, other expenses incurred by students include their lodging, admission to program-specific events, and their individual in-country transportation costs like subway or local train rides. There may also be mandatory group meals, or as in the case of our craft beer program, we include the cost of one substantial meal per day for each student to ensure that if they run out of personal money they have adequate sustenance during the program. In addition, many schools add a small study abroad fee to help the institution cover administrative expenses.

Determining Final Student Cost

It is important to have truth in advertising and not equivocate once students are quoted a price for a proposed faculty-led program abroad. If fliers price a two-week, three-credit program to Paris at $3,525, when students sign on, they cannot be asked two months later for another $200 because the situation has changed.

Faculty developers must therefore establish a reasonable student budget base, which is merely a determination of the minimum number of students needed for the program to happen. The importance of this number rests on the fact that faculty expenses are shared by this unchanging base number of students. For example, suppose the student budget base was set at 10, as it often is on my campus, and the faculty leader's teaching stipend, flight, lodging, events admissions, in-country subway pass, and the group cost for a bus totaled $7,000. Each student would share one tenth of the faculty leader's program expenses, or $700. It is obvious that budgeting on a basis of more students reduces the percentage each student pays for the faculty expense. But if a program sets a high student budget base, it is at greater risk of being cancelled if the larger number of students do not commit.

It is not unusual for a program to be cancelled if the student budget base is not met. In the previous example, if only nine students sign on for the program with each paying his or her portion of the shared indirect costs, then only nine-tenths of the faculty expense would be covered, with no source of funding to cover the $700 program shortfall for the missing tenth student. Having said this, the astute reader is thinking, If I get 11 students, doesn't the university make $700 from the extra student? Well, that is correct, but in the big financial picture that small amount of money can get eaten up by a single desperate phone call from the faculty abroad pleading with the study abroad office to help find upgraded accommodations because things did not turn out quite as promised on the overnight excursion the group is taking.

So to summarize, the program cost quoted to an individual student is the sum total of

- faculty salaries, divided by the student budget basis (e.g., one-tenth);
- faculty's direct costs, divided by the student budget basis (e.g., one-tenth);
- contingency, divided by the student budget basis (e.g., one-tenth);
- student's direct costs; and
- tuition, unless this is included in the faculty salary.

On my campus, we almost always quote program costs without flight expenses because it is impossible to predict where the students are flying from, and it is not at all out of the ordinary for students to travel elsewhere after the program ends and not return home directly.

Record Keeping

The last point on the topic of finances and budget is to emphasize that if a program leader keeps accurate records of expenditures and brings back every receipt, the university finance staff will think she or he is a marvel. In truth, one need not be a financial marvel, just well organized. Many of my faculty members file each day's receipts in separate envelopes. For those who are more ambitious and less inclined to defer the task until the end of the program, it is prudent to take a few minutes each day to enter the expenditures into an expense log. Consistently logging a handful of group receipts over morning coffee is far better than facing the paperwork and the persistent calls from the university finance office after returning to the United States.

Seeking Approval

The vision of a faculty leader's short-term study abroad program is often idiosyncratic and uniquely individual at its inception. But it does take a figurative village to get from the point of the initial idea to the point where everyone is safely back from the field. On most campuses that entails obtaining acceptance and support from one's peers for the academic course work; approval across nonacademic divisions of the institution for the well-being of the students and the program's contribution to the school's mission; and sign-off from the study abroad office, if there is one, for the financial and daily operational aspects. Faculty leaders who follow procedures at every step not only assure each stakeholder that concerns have been met but also generate a forward momentum that inclines the various committees and offices to work with the program proposer to get things right rather than trying to foreclose on the program proposal without attempting to remediate any shortcomings. In short, being well prepared and rehearsed about the particulars of a proposed program is the best defense for obtaining the support and assistance of others.

Curriculum Committees

Obviously, a key element of any faculty-led study abroad program is the curriculum, whose quality and integrity are the purview of those in academic affairs. If a faculty leader has experience with general curriculum development and approval procedures, then preparing the curriculum for a study abroad program is likely to follow a similar path. At many institutions, if a course already exists, a discussion with the department chairperson or dean suffices to inform them of the intention to deliver those outcomes in the framework of a study abroad program. For a course that is new or to be offered under a preapproved umbrella of special topics, it is at the very least a courtesy to discuss the learning outcomes and structure of the proposed course with department colleagues. In many instances, evidence of department approval of the proposed course may be needed to advance the discussion to the stages of overall program design and delivery. On my own campus, the study abroad office will not approve a brand-new faculty-led program if the curricular portion of the proposal has not been approved by the department chairperson on behalf of the department faculty and then approved by the dean.

It is important to consider one's colleagues as resources and sounding boards for curriculum ideas. The faculty member proposing the program should present it in the institution's standard course proposal format so that the syllabus, outcomes, and other elements are readily understandable. If colleagues are viewed as obstacles to a program leader's interest in taking students abroad, then the collective power of thought and experience is lost because the program proposer has preempted the possibility of genuine dialogue and iterative reflection.

University Approvals for Study Abroad

On campuses with study abroad offices, proposal forms that organize the many topics covered in this chapter are common. Provided with evidence that the course work meets the rigor and academic integrity expected by the department and dean, the study abroad office staff will usually gather into a single package the program's details of when, where, for how long, and for how much.

A staff member of a study abroad office is likely to be designated to handle short-term, faculty-led programs. At the front end of the program approval process, this person has the primary responsibility of vetting the proposed field sites for the physical safety, health, and well-being of the students. For example, on my campus we shut down a program intended to take students to a country in the Middle East and moved very cautiously with two other programs to areas affected by the emerging Zika virus. The administrator may also have the lead role in determining the risk level of the proposed itineraries, perform due diligence regarding vendors and other service providers abroad, and in many cases analyze the proposed budgets to ensure their alignment with affordability, value, and student financial access.

Just as one's academic colleagues should be viewed as helpful collaborators, the staff in other parts of the institution should be seen as facilitators, not deterrents or barriers to a proposed program abroad. Administrators and faculty should share a common goal of making programs safe and manageable while not unduly burdening either with too many regulations (Hulstrand, 2015).

To undertake a collaboration implies that program proposers are knowledgeable and cognizant of what they do not know but seek to find out from others. If a campus does not have a study abroad office, the best source of information is other colleagues who have conducted faculty-led programs. New proposers can find out who helped with itinerary, bookings, risk management, and most important, whose approval is needed at the institution. If a campus does not have a central clearinghouse for study abroad, developers can meet with deans, academic provosts, and even vice presidents to ask questions essential to the management and safety of a proposed program. Program leaders must have the assurance that they are indemnified when acting within their scope of responsibilities as an agent of the institution abroad. The corollary to that is that program leaders have an obligation to recognize that leading experiences abroad is a serious matter, and as an agent of the institution, overseeing students in a foreign setting cannot be done in a careless or frivolous way.

Marketing and Populating the Program

After the hard work of developing and getting their program approved, faculty leaders want to ensure there are enough students in the airplane seats. In thinking about the ethics of marketing a faculty-led study abroad program, the question of socioeconomic privilege and colonization is not to be glossed over. Siegler (2015) writes about this in his introductory article to six other articles that offer a similar treatment.

> If the reification of economic inequality and the fostering of a colonist attitude towards the cultural other as an exotic and essentialized object can be said to constitute the main problems with study abroad programs, then these problems surely have no easy solutions, embedded as they are in the marketing of these programs. (p. 40)

However, through the example of teaching a three-week religious studies program in China, Siegler offers the following advice for students and faculty: "Don't look for authenticity, question it" (p. 42). That is, the learning value is in challenging one's assumption that there even exists an authentic experience waiting to be discovered. Therefore, faculty leaders' marketing campaigns should not attempt to take advantage of the exoticism of the other. Program leaders should not betray the integrity of their academically sound, culturally relevant curriculum by marketing the program for its glamour. They have an ethical obligation to avoid exploiting the indigenous peoples of the locations of their programs, and meeting this obligation starts at home with the way one talks about and markets the program.

Because student marketing and recruitment is equally important to the viability of the proposed program, the editors of this book devote an entire chapter to this task (see Chapter 10), where readers will find a clear approach to market and populate an approved program.

Faculty Groundwork for Teaching Abroad

Because the faculty groundwork necessary for teaching abroad is a vast undertaking, Chapter 11 is a comprehensive discussion of everything Susan Lee Pasquarelli prepares and organizes before going abroad, including orientations for students; preparing materials for pre-, during, and postcurriculum delivery; creating guides for packing luggage; obtaining student identification cards; and making logistical arrangements. It is replete with practical and essential activities required to prepare for leading a short-term study abroad program and teaching a course in the field.

Timelines

Designing a new program that pays careful attention to each touchpoint of program development takes at least a year and a half, and often longer. Counting backward from the day of departure, 18 to 24 months should be allocated for creating the curriculum, building a tentative itinerary, and preparing a realistic budget. Depending on the particulars of a campus, another three to nine months may be required for program approval, although some elements of design can happen concurrently. Marketing and recruitment usually need to start at least six to nine months ahead of departure, with some time allowance for making a final selection of students and finalizing class rosters at least a month ahead so that predeparture activities can begin. Finally, on conclusion of the program, taking time to debrief, evaluate, assess the program, and collect notes provides the basis for the iterative redesign needed prior to the next time the program is offered.

A Postscript

Leading a study abroad program means program directors suddenly occupy a never-not-present liminal space wherein they embody the convergence of content authority, travel guide, adviser, travel companion, caretaker, and institutional representative. Once afield, most decision-making swiftly becomes centralized, local, and responsive to the immediate environment. Therefore, program proposers must ask themselves, Do I have the aptitude for managing moderate risk? Am I flexible in the face of uncertainty? Can I improvise in response to the unexpected?

Cognitive flexibility is being able to quickly make a transition from one set of concepts or expectations to an updated belief system in response to incongruent and new information (Stroop, 1935). Oreg (2003) identifies four dimensions connected with willingness or resistance to change: enjoying and seeking stable and routine environments, feeling stress and discomfort in response to imposed change, preoccupation with short-term inconveniences rather than the potential long-term benefits of the change, and a stubbornness and unwillingness to consider alternative ideas and perspectives.

Some people are simply resistant to change, and for those so predisposed to cognitive rigidity, leading a study abroad program can be a trying experience that may undermine the intended student learning outcomes. It is to be expected that in the field things will change, the unpredicted will occur, and the best will have to be made of many situations.

Not long ago I was in Paris evaluating a short-term program led by two faculty members on my campus. The rains were biblical in duration and force that summer, with the banks of the Seine overflowing across roads and rails. A carefully built itinerary had to be rearranged as an otherwise architecturally rich walk from the Place du Panthéon in such a downpour was of little visual value. Meanwhile, in anticipation of serious flooding, the Louvre, like the Musée d'Orsay, was closed to move artwork such as da Vinci's *Mona Lisa* to higher ground.

Adding to nature's disruption of the study abroad program, the high-speed train lines between Paris and Brussels were shut down because of worker strikes. Needing to get back to Brussels to catch a return flight home, I had no choice but to give in to the situation and make the best of it. The result was passage on delightfully slow-paced local trains through the verdant French countryside by way of Amiens and Lille, in place of a functional but dull express line directly to Brussels.

There is a saying: Don't chase planes and trains. This attitude allows one to be flexible in the face of missed connections and unforeseen circumstances. Program leaders are encouraged to seek a mental space that allows them to find the learning value in the changing landscape rather than panicking and chasing after the first solution. The students will follow the lead of the program directors; if they are cool and resourceful, the students will be too. Invite the students to peek behind the veil of the program when things go awry and enlist them to be part of the collaborative effort to discover what there is to learn in every experience.

In the following chapter, we begin part two by defining the design principles of an academically sound, culturally relevant faculty-led program.

References

Coldwell, W. (2016, May 20). London visitor numbers hit record levels. *The Guardian*. Retrieved from www.theguardian.com/travel/2016/may/20/london-record-visitor-numbers-2015-31-5-million

Cole, R. A. (2016). *2016–2017 university catalog*. Bristol, RI: Roger Williams University Printing Office.

Goodrich, S. D. (2009). "City as text"?: Designing curriculum to teach culture onsite in faculty-led study abroad programs. *Hispania, 92*, 283.

Herbst, M. (2011). Building a faculty-led study abroad program: From development to history pedagogy in Istanbul. *History Teacher, 44*, 209–226.

Hulstrand, J. (2015). Best practices for short-term, faculty-led programs abroad. *International Educator*, 58–64.

Oreg, S. (2003). Resistance to change: Developing an individual differences measure. *Journal of Applied Psychology, 88,* 680–693.

Rules and regulations: Part II: Department of Education. (2010, October 29). *Federal Register, 75*(209). Retrieved from edocket.access.gpo.gov/2010/pdf/2010-26531.pdf

Siegler, E. (2015). Working through the problems of study abroad using the methodologies of religious studies. *Teaching Theology and Religion, 18*(1), 37–45.

Stroop, J. R. 1935. Studies of interference in serial verbal reactions. *Journal of Experimental Psychology, 18,* 643–662.

PART TWO

DESIGNING THE CURRICULUM FOR STUDY ABROAD: STUDENT PREPARATION, EXPERIENCE, AND RETURN

2

DEFINING AN ACADEMICALLY SOUND, CULTURALLY RELEVANT STUDY ABROAD CURRICULUM

Susan Lee Pasquarelli

A handbook of best practice delineates the underlying research that supports a given practice. This book is no different. The purpose of this chapter is to define an *academically sound, culturally relevant faculty-led study abroad program curriculum* as well as to provide international education research that supports our definition. Because this volume is intended to be a practical handbook, best practices in curriculum development and pedagogy are illustrated with examples from a faculty-led study abroad program that my writing studies colleague Kate Mele and I designed for our Roger Williams University students, Rome: Art and Culture Through a Traveler's Eye.[1]

After an extensive review of the international education literature and much experience implementing study abroad programs, I have come to understand that if a study abroad program fulfills its student learning outcomes, the participating students' motivations are steered by a desire for deep knowledge gains, transformative cultural experiences, and guided reflection on both (Deardorff, 2015; Engle, 2008; Vande Berg, 2003; Yu, 2008). Therefore, our term *academically sound, culturally relevant* connotes a faculty-led program that delivers a stimulating, thought-provoking, experiential, outcomes-based curriculum in one or more subjects or disciplines designed for a specific cultural context. Before presenting the prevalent thinking from international educators in regard to study abroad curriculum development, it is instructive to talk about what an academically sound, culturally relevant curriculum is not.

Study Abroad Versus Tourism

When students arrive at our international destination, a phrase I routinely impart is the following: This is a study abroad program. The operational word in this sentence is *study*.

Studying abroad is distinct from touring abroad. In our experience with examining faculty-led short-term abroad program curricula, we found several programs that resembled tourism. In describing the results of his doctoral research, Yu (2008) concurs with other international education research-ers that the three significant motivations for study abroad include foreign experience, cultural learning, and academic learning. The tourism literature suggests that tourism may include motivations for foreign experience, but cultural and academic learning is minimal. Aref and Som (2010) reviewed the literature on tourism push-and-pull factors (Baloglu & Uysal, 1996) and compiled prevailing research that supports the following:

> The concept behind push and pull dimension is that people travel because they are pushed by their own internal forces and pulled by the external forces of destination attributes. Most of the push factors, which are origin-related are intangible or intrinsic desires of the individual travelers. Pull factors, on the contrary, are those that emerge as a result of the attractive-ness of a destination as it is perceived by the travelers. They include tangible resources and travelers' perception and expectation such as novelty, benefit expectation and marketed image of the destination. (p. 41)

Caton (2008) advises that unlike tourism, well-designed study abroad programs attempt to ground foreign travel in a critical context. She further suggests that unlike tourism, study abroad programs help to dispel stereo-types while promoting meaningful cross-cultural communications as explicit program objectives.

Perhaps the major difference between tourism and study abroad is rooted in deep academic study of appropriate subject matter goals and cul-tural transformation. As one student who understands the concept of study abroad affirmed,

> When you leave one world and enter another, you are leaving behind familiarity, comfort, and security and must embrace change, distance, and discomfort in order to grow yourself. If you refuse to do this, you are just a

tourist, a passerby who only wants a temporary view into another culture. But when you choose to study abroad, you choose change. You choose discomfort. You choose a new way of living for the sake of learning. And by study abroad, you not only get more out of your education, but your life as well. (Davis, 2014)

This is not to deny that some students may be attracted to study abroad opportunities because of a touristic impulse; however, the task of the educator is to move students from that view toward a more academic understanding of their experiences.

Faculty-Led Short-Term Study Abroad Design Principles

Figure 2.1 illustrates how various learning theories and educational practices dovetail to aid our design of faculty-led study abroad curricula that are academically sound and culturally relevant.

The box at the top of Figure 2.1 specifies where and when curriculum guidelines are best applied for faculty-led study abroad programs. Most international educators agree that study abroad programs are ideally designed along a continuum to include three phases of instruction: before students go abroad (preparation), while students are abroad (experience), and when students return to the United States (return) (Bathhurst & La Brack, 2012; Roberts, Conner, & Jones, 2013; Savicki & Price, 2015).

Three Phases of Study Abroad Programs: Preparation, Experience, Return

In 2005 when I was designing my first faculty-led study abroad program for Siracusa, Sicily, our international study abroad director suggested that my curriculum needed to include learning experiences before, during, and after the program abroad. At the time, I was deeply immersed in the myriad of tasks required to write my first faculty-led study abroad program proposal and did not have the wherewithal to pursue the reason; in fact, I just complied with the director's mandate and produced a curriculum that had three phases of development. After that first study abroad program, I spent countless hours reading books and articles by international educators who informed my further practice in designing curricula for my study abroad programs. I must admit that it is difficult to plan and implement the reentry part of the curriculum, especially if we go abroad in the summer and on returning to the United States, students disperse directly from the airport for two months.

Figure 2.1. Academically sound, culturally relevant curriculum design principles.

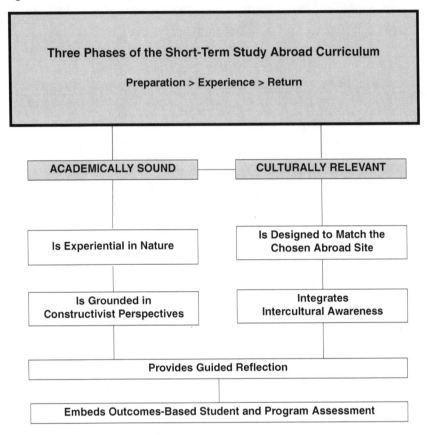

Roberts, Conner, and Jones (2013) state that a pre-, during-, and post-framework for study abroad is an exemplary structure allowing faculty to embed multiple pedagogies across the continuous curriculum as well as augment student learning and transformation. Bathhurst and La Brack (2012), in describing their study abroad programs at the University of the Pacific, state that a "carefully guided, interventionist approach facilitates significant intercultural learning prior to, during, and after the study abroad experience" (p. 261). They further speculate that although most study abroad programs provide predeparture orientations, many programs do not provide a postprogram experience. Their position is supported by the lack of reentry literature as opposed to the abundant publications devoted to predeparture orientation. Mullens and Cuper (2012) suggest that the reentry is an opportunity for faculty to take an assessment of students' gains and help them revisit the program to process their own growth. In Chapter 3 Savicki and Price also use this frame to describe how cultural reflection is optimally embedded into the curriculum before, during, and after the abroad experience.

Next, the terms *academically sound* and *culturally relevant* are separated in Figure 2.1 into two further divisible categories. For the sake of discussion, I review the curricular concepts, academically sound and culturally relevant, separately.

Academically Sound Study Abroad Curriculum

As Huxley (1942) implied, The more you know, the more you see.[2] We envision study abroad programs to be first and foremost, knowledge building. A few years ago, during one of my earlier faculty-led study abroad programs in Siracusa, an English literature major remarked, "Across the water is the site where Archimedes supposedly erected massive mirrors to catch the sun to burn the hostile Roman ships." When I asked her how she knew so much about Archimedes, she quoted Huxley and told her peers that she had been reading well beyond the books and articles selected as program texts. Learning from this astute student, I have relied on Huxley's adage when designing curricula for new programs. For example, our Rome program includes two credits of predeparture study over four Saturdays to ensure that when our students see a Roman mythological creature adorning a corner of an ancient edifice, they are able to recognize the legendary she-wolf nursing twins Romulus and Remus, or when they examine the illustrative carvings of a marble sarcophagus, they recognize the entire text of Homer's *Iliad* scene by scene. As our students walk through the streets of our chosen sites, they only see when they have the knowledge base to support their understanding.

Most study abroad experts agree that faculty-led program curricula need to be grounded in knowledge building, which includes learning the content of the domain being studied as well as the relevant historical, philosophical, political, and sociological aspects of the intended sites.

We can think about our study abroad curricula by using traditional and more current learning theories that have guided curriculum development in the field of education. In the following pages, each of the theories and practices in Figure 2.1 are described in the context of study abroad. In keeping with best practices for short-term international programs, it is beneficial for readers to recognize that the principles presented here are to be embedded in curricula designed for the preparation, the experience, and the return.

Principles of Experiential Learning Theory

Experiential learning theory is regarded as one of the most significant learning models in international education. The theory is somewhat complex and is accompanied by a full body of research and practitioner literature. Those familiar with experiential learning theory will understand why it is included as one of the aspects of an academically sound curriculum. Those who are not familiar with the theory can become acquainted here and refer to a number of exceptional texts for further understanding. Kolb (1984) is of particular importance and a good place to begin.

Experiential Learning Cycle
Although there are many tenets that make experiential education experiential, the ultimate goal of experiential learning is learning by doing. No one will dispute the fact that once abroad, student learning is experiential in nature. The theoretical base of experiential education has its roots in traditional educational theories, including the work of Piaget, Vygotsky, and Freire (Kolb, 1984). Kolb (1984) defines *experiential learning* as "the process whereby knowledge is created through the transformation of experience" (p. 41). Note the word *transformation*. It is not enough to simply have an experience for learning to occur; rather, experiential pedagogical activities ensure that learners are transformed by these experiences. According to Passarelli and Kolb (2012), study abroad programs provide a rich venue for implementing experiential learning theory. They suggest that because students study, live, and work in an unfamiliar environment, they have an ongoing opportunity to learn by experience and transform their ways of thinking about and relating to the world.

To better understand how experiential education principles help us design curricula for our study abroad programs, it is vital to examine Kolb's (1984) learning cycle. This recursive experiential learning cycle includes the following ways of knowing: undergoing concrete experiences (experiencing), observing and reflecting on the experience (reflecting), forming abstract concepts or generalizations about those experiences (thinking), and trying out those generalizations in new contexts (application or acting). A vignette from our Rome study abroad program is provided under each category of the learning cycle to demonstrate how the cycle might occur in an abroad program.

Experiencing
On the first day of our study abroad in Rome, two female students headed to a crowded coffee bar at 1:00 p.m. and attempted to order two cappuccini at the cash register. The cashier shook his head and responded in rapid Italian a phrase the students did not understand. The cashier refused to take their money and continued to repeat what he had said before. In a moment of frustration, he looked over the students' heads and asked the next customer in line what he wanted. The students attempted to catch the cashier's attention again

to no avail. Before the students left, one of them scanned the other customers' tables and observed that everyone was sipping from tiny espresso cups. Feeling ashamed, confused, and a little bit angry, our students left the bar.

Reflecting

The students were understandably confounded while they walked back to our apartments. At first they thought the cashier simply disliked American college students and chose not to wait on them. They quickly dismissed this notion, however, because while reflecting, they realized the cashier was never rude, simply impatient. As they continued to deconstruct and reflect on the episode, they wondered whether they mispronounced the word *cappuccino*, if that particular bar even serves cappuccino (given no cappuccino cups in sight), if they used the correct Italian protocol of ordering, and if there was a major difference between ordering a cappuccino in a coffee shop in America and in Italy. They decided to include the incident in their journals under the required heading of Daily Highlights and share their experience during the afternoon walking classroom.

Thinking

Back at the apartments, both students wrote about the incident in their journals. They also narrated the entire event to their roommates. The other students assuaged their feelings of confusion, but one of them suggested they consult the "Around-the-Town Guide" (see Chapter 11) I had prepared and reviewed with them during one of the predeparture meetings. As the students turned to the section on restaurants and coffee bars, they read the following:

> Never attempt to order a cappuccino after 11:00 a.m. Italians believe that after breakfast, any coffee made with milk interrupts digestion. Unfortunately for the uninitiated, ordering a cappuccino after breakfast usually results in disappointment.

After thinking about the cultural custom and piecing together their observations, reflections, and knowledge (albeit forgotten), the caffeine-deprived students were able to come to an understanding of what took place that afternoon. Learning had occurred. They now knew from their own experience that one can order cappuccino at any bar but not after 11:00 a.m. After 11:00 a.m. and through the evening, one can order an espresso, known simply as *un caffè*.

Acting

The next morning before class at 7:30 a.m., still eager for a taste of that famous Italian cappuccino, the students bravely headed to the same bar and confidently ordered two cappuccini from the very same cashier. He smiled broadly and responded enthusiastically: "*Sì! Due cappuccini, quattro euro.*" (Yes! Two cappuccini, four euros). For good measure, the triumphant students returned at 2:00 p.m. to order two caffé (espresso) with equal success.

As Kolb (1984) points out, not all learning events necessarily require the complete cycle for knowledge to occur. In the Rome vignette, the students might have come to their knowledge application before they left the bar the first time if they had remembered what they learned in their predeparture seminar, or if they deeply reflected on their observation that not one patron in that bar was drinking a cappuccino. Given the fact that it was their first excursion out of their home country, they did not know the language, and they were suffering from jet lag, they deserve credit for even stepping into a crowded Roman bar.

So how does this learning cycle help designers think about faculty-led study abroad programs? See Table 2.1 for suggestions on how to embed experiential education curriculum principles into study abroad programming.

Constructivist Perspectives

What does constructivism mean for learning? Simply put, constructivism is based on the assumption that a learner processes new information based on what is previously known. Several sociocultural learning theories converge to allow us to think about our study abroad curriculum development from constructivist perspectives (Bandura, 1975; Bruner, 1996; Vygotsky, 1987). To begin, we take a look at metacognition.

Metacognition

Whether teaching abroad or teaching stateside, we professors all have the same goal: teaching and coaching students to learn what we teach. We are mindful that the path between teaching and learning is long and complex, so we rely on relevant research to guide our course design and pedagogical approaches to accomplish our goals. When I teach teachers how to teach, I suggest that their most important pedagogical action includes teaching for metacognitive awareness; that is, teaching students to be aware of their own knowledge, thinking processes, and the strategies they are applying for further learning.

The simplest way to conceptualize *metacognition*, or *metacognitive awareness*, is to define it as knowledge about one's own cognition, or to generalize, a learner's ability to think about thinking. Flavell (1985) advises that metacognitive skills are believed to play an important role in many types of cognitive activities, including those related to problem-solving, language and literacy, and social behavior.

TABLE 2.1

Suggestions to Embed Experiential Education Across Study Abroad Programs

Learning Cycle (Kolb, 1984)	Student Engagement Practices
Incorporate the learning cycle across the program	• Use the experiential learning cycle when preparing your teaching events. Build in opportunities for observation, reflection, trial and error, complex thinking, and acting. • Teach your students about the experiential learning cycle. Encourage students to independently seek experiences, observe, and reflect while attempting to make sense about what just occurred in their abroad experiences. • Build in opportunities for independent and group research.
Offer opportunities for experience	• Provide room in the abroad schedule for independent exploration. • Provide students with options for independent field excursions and cultural events. • Teach your students to be careful observers. • Embed observation time in your scheduled learning events.
Offer opportunities for reflection	• Embed guided reflection routinely in your teaching. • Teach students how to reflect on their own. • Encourage the use of journals and diaries to record their encounters, observations, and experiences so students have data to look back on to reflect and learn.
Offer opportunities for complex thinking	• Honor students' thinking, confusion, and trials and errors. • Encourage students to troubleshoot individually or cooperatively as a group. • Embed opportunities for faculty to provide constructive feedback about students' ongoing work on program assessments.
Offer opportunities for action or application of new knowledge	• Build opportunities into the program to have students apply what they know or have learned: metacognitive essays, community forums, experiential events. • Embed free time in your scheduled learning events for students to be on their own to apply new knowledge, skills, and attitudes. • Give students opportunities to write a blog or present their new knowledge, skills, and attitudes, either abroad or on reentry.

Metacognition involves the following elements: (a) knowledge of one's cognitive strategies used when engaged in a cognitive activity and (b) self-regulation of the learning strategies to produce the desired result (Garner, 1987).

Knowledge of One's Cognitive Strategies

Paris, Lipson, and Wixson (1983) describe three types of metacognitive knowledge: declarative, procedural, and conditional. They provide us with a useful framework for thinking about our teaching and our students' subsequent learning. To be metacognitive about learning and ways of knowing, a learner must possess three different types of knowledge: declarative, procedural, and conditional.

Declarative knowledge refers to content (world knowledge), process, and strategy knowledge. It is knowledge about one's self as a learner. If learners are metacognitive about their own knowledge, simply put, they are able to declare and conceptualize the knowledge: "I know how to make ravioli."

Procedural knowledge refers to the ways a learner performs tasks or applies strategies in a learning situation. If learners are metacognitive about what they know, they are able to describe and use their knowledge, such as in the following:

> When making ravioli, the first step is to prepare the homemade pasta. First, I place one cup of flour in the middle of my wooden board, make a little well inside the mounded flour, and crack and drop the egg into the middle.

Conditional knowledge refers to when and where learners apply what they know and includes conditions for success in a given situation: "If the homemade pasta dough mixture is too sticky, perhaps the egg was too large, and I need to add more flour. If the dough mixture is too dry, perhaps I need to add more eggs."

How does this information about metacognition affect designers of study abroad programs? The good news is that metacognitive strategies can be taught if we take time within teaching events to provide students with three clusters of metacognitive knowledge: declarative, procedural, and conditional.

The following is an example of teaching for metacognition from our Rome faculty-led study abroad program. To understand the example, I must provide more information about our interdisciplinary program. Our program design interlaces two courses taught at the university in the spring and during the summer term on site in Rome—Rome: From Myth to Art, intended to familiarize students with Greek and Roman mythology and the art connections found in Rome, and the Art of the Travel Narrative, in which students become familiar with and begin to craft their own travel narratives. I teach the first course that provides students with a broad overview of the literature (Ovid, Homer, etc.) that inspired the art and offer walking classrooms to view and reflect on the corresponding artwork in the great museums and streets of Rome. My program coprofessor, Mele, teaches the second course and provides instruction in the travel narrative genre with much on-site coaching. The mythology and art knowledge, when combined with instruction in the travel narrative genre, is where the two courses merge as students produce a portfolio consisting of a travel journal, two travel narratives (one focused on a myth-art connection and the other focused on a cultural encounter), and a metacognitive essay about their writing.[3]

One of the established learning outcomes in our syllabus states that students will demonstrate understanding of the role journal keeping plays in the production of knowledge. To establish metacognition in regard to journal writing, Mele provides multiple teaching and coaching events prior to the abroad experience and on-site in Rome. Her teaching includes many facets of the travel-writing genre, including the writing processes travel writers use to maintain a detailed journal. While in Rome, I help students maintain the content of the journal by coteaching some of the writing workshop sessions. During these sessions, I provide students with various strategies for recording descriptive details while viewing and interpreting artworks as well as cultural events in Rome. One lesson I teach introduces students to art vocabulary. For students to become metacognitive about the use of art vocabulary in their journals and subsequent travel narratives, I teach a lesson that contains the three clusters of metacognitive knowledge. See Figure 2.2 for a lesson plan that illustrates the three phases of teaching for metacognition.

Teaching for metacognition is a factor in experiential learning theory as well as considered a best practice by constructivist learning theorists.

The Self-Regulated Learner

The second aspect of metacognition has to do with learners' motivations to use and apply what they know. Research tells us that self-regulated learners plan, regulate, monitor, and evaluate their learning situation including their strategy usage (Garner, 1987; Paris et al., 1983). During a learning event, what do learners do to apply and monitor their own cognitive and metacognitive awareness? A good model of self-regulation may include learners developing a plan to learn from an event, self-monitoring their own understanding, using fix-up strategies if their comprehension or strategy use is failing, and evaluating their understanding after the event. This is not unlike what we know from the experiential learning cycle. It does suggest a level of

Figure 2.2. Rome art vocabulary lesson with metacognitive elements.

Lesson Objective: Students will demonstrate understanding of art vocabulary and strategies for applying descriptive vocabulary while writing journal entries and travel narratives.

Declarative Knowledge

1. Tell students they will be learning a strategy to improve art descriptions in journal entries and travel narratives. To conceptualize the strategy, read an excerpt from a published travel story pointing out the descriptive words.

Procedural Knowledge

2. Using a think-aloud approach, model writing a journal entry using the following cognitive processes as applied to various sculptures students viewed the day before:

   - Describe action of main figures. "Cupid is about to get into trouble."
   - Think about the theme of the work. "Love conquers all."
   - Describe facial expressions. "His face describes a wide spectrum of emotions, such as . . ."
   - Describe physical characteristics. "Cupid looks like a chubby, angelic baby."
   - Describe what the character may be thinking or feeling. "I imagine Pluto is thinking of ravishing Persephone once he has her in his lair." "Persephone's face betrays her fear and terror."
   - Describe what is in the background—include descriptions of the other characters, the symbols depicted, the landscape, and so on. "Poseidon must have been angry because the ocean appears tempestuous."
   - Use words to describe the overall artistic style: animate, inanimate, dramatic, earthy, naturalistic, emotional, subtle, dark, light, ethereal, and so on.
   - To help with descriptive art words, search for "art vocabulary lists" on the Internet.

3. Provide students with guided and independent practice in application of the strategy in their journals and travel narratives. Use peer and faculty coaching to help students hone strategy application.

Conditional Knowledge

4. Teach and coach students how to evaluate the effectiveness of the strategy when applied in various rhetorical situations: journal-writing, travel writing, presentations, dialogue, and so on.

Note. From Pasquarelli (1997).

acute awareness on the part of the learner to participate actively in applying newly learned strategies. For example, in regard to our Rome art vocabulary lesson, we often have to prompt and coach students to use their art terminology while writing first drafts of their travel narratives, but with increased coaching, we find that students become more self-monitoring when writing subsequent drafts.

Social Learning

Vygotsky's (1978) work in the area of mediated social experience sets the constructivist view of learning apart from other psychological theories that isolate the individual as the sole constructor of meaning. Vygotsky highlights the role of the social reconstruction of knowledge in human learning. The constructivist approach suggests that learning occurs through interpersonal interactions and intrapersonal examination of behavior and knowledge during a learning event. I have briefly discussed the intrapersonal examination in the earlier sections on metacognition and self-regulation. In regard to human interactions, Vygotsky's social learning theory lends us the skill to think about interpersonal interactions based, in part, on the principle that learning is derived from mediated social activity. It is well known that study abroad programs are the ideal context for group interaction. Opportunities abound in a small group abroad to have community discussions, small- and whole-group dialogues, debates, and community forums to drive us to deeper meanings of what we see, encounter, and experience on a daily basis. These forums are also useful to socially construct rules or regulations within the abroad community. For example, this past summer, Mele and I used a community forum to design protocols for emergencies. Given the state of our world, we found it necessary to conduct a community forum to design a whole-group protocol in case of an act of terrorism, natural disaster, or other all-city or all-country emergency. My colleague and I were most impressed with the students' maturity in designing our protocol and remarked afterward that what they designed had far stricter guidelines for student safety while abroad than we ever would have imposed on them (see Chapter 11 for a longer discussion on student safety).

Summary of an Academically Sound Curriculum

The design principles of our definition of an academically sound curriculum for faculty-led study abroad programs include embedding experiential education principles and using constructivist perspectives, including those related to students' development of metacognition, self-regulation, and the social construction of knowledge. Readers who are familiar with the experiential learning theory body of knowledge know that experiential learning is founded on constructivist perspectives. In the next section, we examine our definition of *culturally relevant curriculum*.

Culturally Relevant Study Abroad Curriculum

Earlier in this chapter, I presented Figure 2.1, which includes design principles suggested by international education researchers to be the most important when designing short-term programs. In the following section, the principles of culturally relevant course work are examined.

Culturally Relevant Course Work

A few years ago, a colleague from another university approached me to discuss his interest in developing a faculty-led study abroad program in Milan, Italy. As this was his first venture in designing such a program, I explained the overall process described by Cole in Chapter 1. My colleague's reaction to the amount of work involved in designing and delivering a faculty-led program was magnified when I presented the principles involved in international curriculum development. He said, "Hmmm, I think I can skip that step. Why don't I just teach one of my calculus courses in Milan so my math majors will elect to participate in the program?" I quickly countered with, "What is the cultural relevance of calculus to Milan, Italy?"

Certainly, curricular connections among the discipline of mathematics and various international locations and venues are easily constructed. The principles of interdisciplinary education assure us that one has opportunities to integrate mathematics curriculum connections with science, engineering, and medicine, not to mention many areas of business. I quickly learned that my colleague was not interested in creating something new, he just set his sights on teaching Advanced Calculus. My question to him was, "So why bother taking the students abroad? You can easily just stay on your home campus to teach this course." Brewer and colleagues (2015) advanced this notion of disciplinary teaching and abroad curriculum when they established the following:

> Research on study abroad is greater in disciplines with obvious stakes in study abroad. The stakes may involve study abroad's potential for adding value to disciplinary learning (e.g., language acquisition) or helping students acquire skills related to practicing the discipline (e.g., engaging with difference as teachers, social workers, or nurses). In disciplines where it can be argued that disciplinary content and methods could just as well be learned at home, there has been less interest in research on study abroad. In part, this may be because commonly understood potential outcomes of

study abroad (e.g., understanding of self) seem peripheral to disciplinary goals. (p. 46)

I asked my math colleague whether there was a more suitable course to alter and offer to teach abroad. Was it possible to teach a discipline-specific mathematics course, for which his students could earn substitute credit, that was more suitable to adaptation on site in Milan?

Once again, I turn to our Rome program as an example of culturally relevant course work. As mentioned earlier, our program interlaces two courses, and, to build our Rome curriculum, I created the course From Myth to Art to teach only in Rome where we could take advantage of the Renaissance and Baroque art depicting Roman and Greek mythology. Mele also designed her course, the Art of the Travel Narrative, especially for our program. Highlighting the idea of art at the heart of the program, Mele created a travel-writing course that focused on the rhetorical and literary arts writers draw upon to communicate moments of transformation prompted by their travel experiences. For the Rome program predeparture seminars, she used travel narratives set in Rome to introduce students to this literary travel genre and to familiarize them with various writers' Roman experiences.

In summary, to build our Rome curriculum, we created two courses exclusively for the site. Chapters 5 through 9 of this volume provide further opportunities to examine how faculty created or adapted courses to their field sites, including how they embedded intercultural awareness into their programs.

Intercultural Awareness

A bright 20-year-old undergraduate student participated in our Rome study abroad program this past summer. When she arrived in my office to submit her application, she told me that she was apprehensive about leaving the country, but she was resolved to participate. When I asked why she was anxious, she responded, "I have never traveled outside of New England; I have never boarded an airplane; I have never studied the Italian language; and you are the only Italian I know." Language differences aside, I knew that there were many cultural experiences she was about to navigate. How do faculty leaders embed intercultural awareness into their curriculum to help students work toward intercultural competence? As in all theories and practices surveyed in this chapter, intercultural awareness with the outcome of developing intercultural competence is a complex domain with a rich body of literature.

Bennett (2004) added to the multicultural literature when he encouraged academics to think about the importance of intercultural education and competence.

As people became more interculturally competent it seemed that there was a major change in the quality of their experience, which I called the move from ethnocentrism to ethnorelativism. I used the term "ethnocentrism" to refer to the experience of one's own culture as "central to reality." By this I mean that the beliefs and behaviors that people receive in their primary socialization are unquestioned; they are experienced as "just the way things are." I coined the term "ethnorelativism" to mean the opposite of ethnocentrism—the experience of one's own beliefs and behaviors as just one organization of reality among many viable possibilities. (p. 1)

In the first research-based intercultural competence framework, Deardorff (2006, p. 256) identified four dimensions of intercultural competence, with attitude as a starting point in her process-based model. Her four-dimension model, with specific intercultural competence elements within each dimension, provides a suitable framework to embed intercultural learning into our study abroad curriculum. Deardorff's model includes the interacting elements depicted in Figure 2.3.

Deardorff (2006) suggests that the degree of intercultural competence is dependent on the degree of knowledge, skills, and attitudes achieved, including as Bennett (2004) described, development of an ethnorelative view. If we think about the four dimensions as a framework for developing our faculty-led study abroad curricula, we can identify learning activities to help students work toward intercultural competence. Table 2.2 is an illustrative example of embedded intercultural learning events in our Rome program.

For a meaningful discussion of intercultural competence research as well as practical applications of building student intercultural competence during short-term study abroad programs, see Berardo and Deardorff (2012). Furthermore, in Chapter 4 of this volume, Deardorff explains the intercultural competence model depicted in Figure 2.3.

Guided Reflection

Guided reflection, another essential curriculum component, is key to the development of a faculty-led study abroad program. The international literature suggests that faculty should build in opportunities for students to reflect on knowledge, skills, and attitudes throughout their experience abroad. In Chapter 3 Savicki and Price examine and present relevant research and practices related to guided reflection before, during, and after studying abroad. Given the broad parameters of their research review along with outstanding examples for study abroad practitioners, I am choosing to focus here on only one important part of the reflection cycle: keen observations and recording those observations in a journal.

Figure 2.3. Process model of intercultural competence.

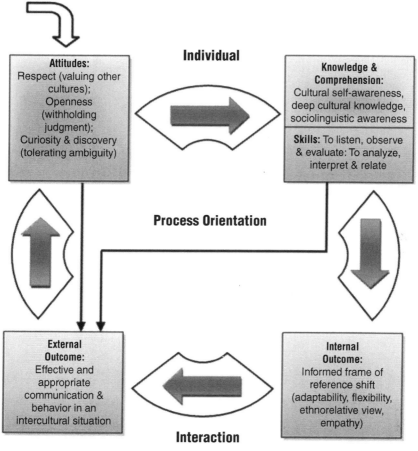

Note. From "Identification and Assessment of Intercultural Competence as a Student Outcome of Internationalization," by D. K. Deardorff, 2006, *Journal of Studies in International Education, 10*(3), 241–266. Copyright 2006 by Sage Publications. Reprinted with permission.

I am taking the liberty to depart from the research literature and instead quote novelist and travel writer Anthony Doerr (2007) on journal writing and the importance of perceptive observations:

> I open my journal and stare out at the trunk of the umbrella pine and do my best to fight off the atrophy that comes from seeing things too frequently. I try to shape a few sentences around this tiny corner of Rome; I try to force my eye to slow down. A good journal entry—like a good song, or sketch, or photograph—ought to break up the habitual and lift away the film that forms over the eye, the finger, the tongue, the heart. A good journal entry ought to be a love letter to the world. Leave home, leave the country, leave

TABLE 2.2

Rome Program Illustration of Embedded Intercultural Learning Events

Deardorff (2006) Four Dimensions of Intercultural Competence	Rome Program Learning Events
Foster in students the attitudes fundamental to intercultural competence	• Experiencing and interpreting day-to-day life in Rome • Observing and interpreting the Roman people in various settings • Journal writing of daily cultural highlights with reflective language • Engaging in reflection and community discussion on various cultural interactions
Improve knowledge and skills integral to cultural competence	• Living in the culture of Rome • Experiencing and interpreting day-to-day life in Rome • Observing and interpreting the Roman people in various settings • Participating in walking classrooms • Journal writing of daily cultural highlights before and after reflection • Socially engaging in reflection on various cultural interactions • Journal writing direct instruction • Receiving direct instruction on writing cultural travel narratives • On-site coaching to improve writing about cultural experiences
Internal outcome: informed frame of reference shift External outcome: includes effective and appropriate communication and behavior in an intercultural situation	• Examining earlier versus later journal entries for intercultural competence outcomes • Self-reflecting in journals to investigate growth or change in knowledge, skills, and attitudes, including behavioral change • Writing cultural travel narratives to identify change in knowledge, skills, and attitudes • Engaging in program evaluation questions and surveys in which students report their growth or change over the course of the program

the familiar. Only then can routine experience—buying bread, eating vegetables, even saying hello—become new all over again." (p. 54)[4]

Here, Doerr aptly describes the importance of observing with a purpose-
ful eye and describing beyond what we habitually *see* to advance observation
to a new level.

In addition to our continual admonishments of "Look up!" while on
the streets of Rome, we also conduct on-site exercises to enhance students'
observation skills. For example, in the previous discussion about metacognition, I describe a lesson (Figure 2.2) in which I attempt to change students'
speaking and writing vocabulary about mythological artworks from benign
words, such as *awesome,* to more incisive words, such as *ethereal.* This lesson
serves many purposes: to encourage students to observe artworks beyond the
emotional; to persuade them to use more descriptive words in their journals
to aid reflection after the experience; and to encourage usage of accurate,
descriptive vocabulary in their travel-writing pieces.

My Rome program coprofessor, Mele, also conducts an observation exercise in which she sends out teams of students to locate iconic street-corner
religious sculptures and to observe and write in their journals what they see
from the top of the icon to the bottom, panning left to right. Doerr (2007)
wrote, "A journal entry is for its writer; it helps its writer refine, perceive,
and process the world" (p. 156).[5] While implementing the Rome program
abroad, my colleague and I often read from Doerr (2007) to encourage students to enact a new level of *seeing.*

So how do these suggestions aid faculty leaders in curriculum and syllabus development? Given that our short-term study abroad students are bombarded with thousands of new images, sights, and sounds over the course
of their programs, the international literature is clear that we need to build
teaching events and exercises into our daily programs where students, without the burden of being graded, have opportunities to hone their craft of
observation and subsequent reflection.

Outcomes-Based Assessment

Another important focus of designing an academically sound, culturally relevant program is to seat the curriculum within the frame of outcomes-based
learning. In Chapter 4, Deardorff describes in detail how faculty leaders
design learning outcomes, teaching events, and accompanying assessments
to evaluate student learning.

One principle in designing an outcomes-based educational program is to
orchestrate the match among learning outcomes, instruction or syllabus topics,

and the student assessment tasks. As an education professor, I am often asked to lead K–16 in-service sessions on outcomes-based assessment. At the college level, the first exercise I conduct is to ask professors to examine one of their syllabi and draw a line between a goal of the course and a student assignment that evaluates the course goal. I have observed some uncomfortable laughter as some participants find that their goals do not match any of the assignments; therefore, there is no measure for how well the goals of the course are realized.

After the exercise, I am poised to make the following points: (a) If the goal is important, the goal should be measured, (b) traditional course goals are easily altered to become learning outcomes, (c) student assignments are easily designed to measure learning outcomes, and (d) to alter syllabi to an outcomes-based model requires a coordination among all components of the curriculum (learning outcomes, syllabus topics, and student assignments).

Table 2.3 includes an annotated diagram demonstrating the alignment of learning outcomes, syllabus topics, and student assessment tasks for our Rome program. This table demonstrates the merger of our two Rome courses to produce one set of student learning outcomes, accompanying syllabus topics, and accompanying student tasks or assignments. In our curriculum planning, Mele and I were careful to address through the syllabus topics our specific learning outcomes and develop student assignments designed to evaluate each learning outcome. In the end, our students receive feedback in the way of a qualitative description of their portfolio artifacts as well as further suggestions for improving their craft.

Postscript

When we conceived this volume as a handbook for study abroad faculty leaders, we determined the substance of the book to include emphasis on the information we deemed salient to the success of a program curriculum abroad. To that end, the next two chapters delve deeply into two aspects of faculty-led curriculum development described in a precursory way in this chapter: how to embed guided reflection into a study abroad curriculum and how to design outcomes-based study abroad programs.

This chapter provides a descriptive definition of an *academically sound, culturally relevant curriculum design for short-term programs* before, during, and after the abroad experience. Only a glimpse of relevant learning theories and practices have been included here. These vast bodies of knowledge have research support for their effectiveness not only in the international curriculum but also in the K–16 curricula, which raises the question, Will faculty leaders be able to integrate all these learning principles and pedagogical practices in a short-term study abroad program? In chapters 5 through 9, faculty

TABLE 2.3

Alignment of Learning Outcomes, Syllabus Topics, and Student Assessment

Learning Outcomes	Syllabus Topics	Student Assessment
1. Students will demonstrate understanding of the role journal keeping plays in the production of knowledge. This learning outcome is intended to focus on the importance of keeping a journal of observations, reflections, and revelations.	Travel Writing and Art and Culture Workshops: How to keep a detailed travel journal while • viewing and interpreting various art works in Rome, • viewing and interpreting the Baroque monuments and sculptures, • investigating and interpreting the ancient ruins of Rome, • experiencing and interpreting day-to-day life in Rome, • observing and interpreting the Roman people in various settings, • living in the culture of Rome, and • participating in walking classroom workshops on Renaissance/Baroque artists. These syllabus topics are focused on the events in which journal writing is taught and coached.	A writing portfolio that contains the following: A reflective metacognitive essay that explains the writing process, specifically how their travel narratives emerged from their various journal entries. This assignment matches the learning outcome because students' assignments reveal their understanding of the role that journal keeping plays in their knowledge building.
2. Students will demonstrate knowledge about the writing process, specifically the travel narrative.	Travel Writing Workshops: Instruction in drafting, revision, peer review, and editing, with attention to the genre and rhetorical features of an ethical travel narrative	A writing portfolio that contains the following: Two travel narratives that demonstrate the students' experience of Roman art and culture and their knowledge of storytelling. One narrative is focused on an intercultural experience and the other on a literature-to-art connection.

(Continues)

TABLE 2.3 (*Continued*)

Learning Outcomes	Syllabus Topics	Student Assessment
3a. Students will demonstrate understanding of various aspects of the art and culture of Rome through their writing. 3b. Students will demonstrate understanding of various Greek and Roman myths and the link between the stories and the art seen in Rome.	Art and Culture Workshops: Student "expert" presentations on mythological stories created in the spring course work, mythology workshops, walking classrooms to museums and cultural events, community discussions and personal reflection on the artists, the Roman culture, the literature-to-art connection, and the art-to-culture connection as experienced	A writing portfolio that contains the following: Two travel narratives that demonstrate the students' experience of Roman art and culture and their knowledge of storytelling. One narrative is focused on an intercultural experience, and the other on a literature-to-art connection. Proper references and in-text citations required.

Note. From Pasquarelli & Mele (2012).

program leaders describe their study abroad curricula in great detail. Readers will find that these programs embed some but not all of the curriculum design principles presented in this chapter. Embedding best practice pedagogies depends on multiple variables including the practitioner's established teaching styles and familiarity with pedagogical practices, the content of the course work intended for the proposed site, the length of the programming, the logistics of the site, and cultural interactions predicted or planned.

The next chapter presents an extensive research review on guided reflection and expert advice on how to embed this practice before, during, and after a short-term, faculty-led program.

Notes

1. I would like to acknowledge my Roger Williams University writing studies colleague Kate Mele, cocurriculum developer of the study abroad program Rome: Art and Culture Through a Traveler's Eye. I was more than fortunate to have such an able and trusted faculty member with whom to team-teach in the glorious setting of Rome.

2. Although Huxley is widely quoted for saying, "The more you know, the more you see," I was not able to find this direct quote in Huxley (1942). Instead, on page 19, Huxley implies these words when, among other examples, he describes how a naturalist's knowledge provides him with the opportunity to see more in a forest than a layperson is capable of seeing.

3. When designing their program Travelblogging Ireland, O'Connell and Mele used a unique curriculum structure having two courses leverage a single set of learning outcomes, which we adapted for the Rome program. See Mele (2011) for more about the Ireland program and Chapter 12 in this volume for vignettes from the Ireland program.

4. Reprinted with permission of Scribner, a division of Simon & Schuster, Inc., from *Four Seasons in Rome: On Twins, Insomnia, and the Biggest Funeral in the History of the World* by Anthony Doerr. Copyright 2007 by Anthony Doerr. All rights reserved.

5. Reprinted with permission of Scribner, a division of Simon & Schuster, Inc., from *Four Seasons in Rome: On Twins, Insomnia, and the Biggest Funeral in the History of the World* by Anthony Doerr. Copyright 2007 by Anthony Doerr. All rights reserved.

References

Aref, B., & Som, A. (2010). An analysis of push and pull travel motivations of foreign tourists to Jordan. *International Journal of Business and Management, 5*(12), 41–50.

Baloglu, S., & Uysal, M. (1996). Market segments of push and pull motivations: A canonical correlation approach. *International Journal of Contemporary Hospitality Management, 3*(8), 32–38.

Bandura, A. (1975). *Social learning & personality development.* New York, NY: Holt, Rinehart & Winston.

Bathhurst, L., & La Brack, B. (2012). Shifting the locus of intercultural learning. In M. Vande Berg, R. M. Paige, & K. H. Lou (Eds.), *Student learning abroad: What our students are learning, what they're not, and what we can do about it* (pp. 261–283). Sterling, VA: Stylus.

Bennett, M. J. (2004). Becoming interculturally competent. In J. S. Wurzel (Ed.), *Toward multiculturalism: A reader in multicultural education.* Newton, MA: Intercultural Resource.

Berardo, K., & Deardorff, D. K. (2012). *Building cultural competence: Innovative activities and models.* Sterling, VA: Stylus.

Brewer, E., Shively, R., Gozik, N. Doyle, D., & Savicki, V. (2015). Beyond the study abroad industry. In V. Savicki & E. Brewer (Eds.). *Assessing study abroad: Theory, tools, and practice* (pp. 33–56). Sterling, VA: Stylus.

Bruner, J. (1996). *The culture of education.* Cambridge, MA: Harvard University Press.

Caton, K. (2008). *Encountering the other through study abroad.* Retrieved from ProQuest Dissertations and Theses database. (UMI No. 3314739)

Davis, C. (2014, June 19). Studying abroad vs. tourism [Web log post]. Retrieved from soleducationblog.com/2014/06/19/studying-abroad-vs-tourism

Deardorff, D. K. (2006). Identification and assessment of intercultural competence as a student outcome of internationalization. *Journal of Studies in International Education, 10,* 241–266.

Deardorff, D. K. (2015). *Demystifying outcomes assessment for international educators: A practical approach.* Sterling, VA: Stylus.

Doerr, A. (2007). *Four seasons in Rome: On twins, insomnia, and the biggest funeral in the history of the world.* New York, NY: Scribner.

Engle, Lilli. (2008). *Study abroad program elements.* Retrieved from forumea.org/resources/outcomes/outcomes-assessment-toolbox/position-papers

Flavell, J. H. (1985). *Cognitive development.* Englewood Cliffs, NJ: Prentice Hall.

Garner, R. (1987). *Metacognition and reading comprehension.* Norwood, NJ: Ablex.

Huxley, A. (1942). *The art of seeing.* New York, NY: Harper & Brothers.

Kolb, D. A. (1984). *Experiential learning.* Englewood Cliffs, NJ: Prentice Hall.

Mele, K. (2011). Travelblogging Ireland: An old genre in a new landscape. In R. O'Connell (Ed.), *Teaching with multimedia: Pedagogy in the websphere* (pp. 153–165). Cresskill, NJ: Hampton Press.

Mullens, J. B., & Cuper, P. H. (2012). *Fostering global citizenship through faculty-led international programs.* Charlotte, NC: Information Age.

Paris, S. G., Lipson, M. Y., & Wixson, K. K. (1983). Becoming a strategic reader. *Contemporary Educational Psychology, 8,* 293–316.

Passarelli, A. M., & Kolb, D. A. (2012). Using experiential learning theory to promote student learning and development in programs of education abroad. In M. Vande Berg, R. M. Paige, & K. H. Lou (Eds.), *Student learning abroad: What our students are learning, what they're not, and what we can do about it* (pp. 137–161). Sterling, VA: Stylus.

Pasquarelli, S. L. (1997). What is strategic reading instruction? Addressing the Rhode Island English language arts frameworks. *Rhode Island Reading Review, 14,* 8–13.

Pasquarelli, S. L., & Mele, K. (2012, November). *Rome: Art and culture through a traveler's eye.* Paper presented at the annual meeting of the International Journal of Arts and Sciences, Rome, Italy.

Roberts, T. G., Conner, N. W., & Jones, B. L. (2013). An experiential learning framework for engaging learners during study abroad experiences. *North American Colleges and Teachers of Agriculture Journal, 57*(3a), 28–35.

Savicki, V., & Price, M. V. (2015). Student reflective writing: Cognition and affect before, during, and after study abroad. *Journal of College Student Development, 56,* 587–601.

Vande Berg, M. (2003). Rapporteur report: Study abroad and international competence. Paper presented at the conference of Duke University Global Challenges and U.S. Higher Education, Durham, NC.

Vygotsky, L. S. (1978). *The mind in society.* Cambridge, MA: Harvard University Press.

Yu, H. C. (2008). *An examination of the effects of participation in a college study abroad program.* (Unpublished doctoral dissertation). Pennsylvania State University, University Park.

3

GUIDING REFLECTION ON CULTURAL EXPERIENCE

Before, During, and After Study Abroad

Victor Savicki and Michele V. Price

Reflection is the heart and soul of student learning in study abroad. Reading a book about another culture or even being physically present in that culture does not guarantee that students will learn important things about themselves, cultural patterns, and how the self and culture interact (Bennett, 2008). The key to such learning is students thinking about how they are thinking. That is, the process of observing, reviewing, and analyzing cognitive content and past, present, and even future experiences leads to an understanding and ownership of ideas. Students construct meaning rather than regurgitate facts or ruminate about experiences. According to Freire (1998), "To teach is not to transfer knowledge but to create the possibilities for production or construction of knowledge" (p. 30). As study abroad practitioners, we can guide students to find such meaning and develop a strategy for learning about learning that will benefit them during and well beyond their study abroad sojourn. In this chapter, we offer rationales and theoretical support for reflection, context for using reflection in short duration study abroad programs, research relevant to reflection in study abroad, and ideas on how to guide students through the reflection process.

Why Reflection Is Important

Based on a constructivist view (Bennett, 2012), reflection supports students' transforming their perspective regarding study abroad experiences in ways that allow them to be active construers of those events. "Moving from simply recording experiences to actively changing and designing them is a major factor in assessing learning" (Zull, 2012, p. 175). Experiences gain significance to the degree that students can ascribe meaning to them. Unexamined experiences do not rise to the level of learning that will result in meaningful outcomes; "our experience of reality itself is a function of how we organize our perceptions" (Bennett, 2012, p. 103).

Paige (2015) states that "virtually every program identified in the research literature as being effective in helping students develop their intercultural competence embraces reflection as a key principle of learning" (p. 566). Likewise, Engle and Engle (2003) name "guided reflection on cultural experience" as a key feature used to evaluate study abroad programs.

Thus, reflection emerges as a central factor in student-centered study abroad learning (Vande Berg, Paige, & Lou, 2012). Students are active participants in their own learning and development. Some will already have the skills necessary to use reflection effectively, and others will need to be guided. In any case, reflection serves as a key that unlocks the process of transformation.

What Is Reflection?

Although study abroad professionals tout the importance of reflection, the process itself has been largely assumed. Homan (2006) attempts to define this concept in the following: *Reflection* "refers to the process by which an individual builds meaning by analyzing an experience, evaluating its worth, and conceptualizing its relevance through the synthesis of additional viewpoints and information" (p. 9). Another path to understanding what reflection is is to know what reflection is not. Table 3.1 shows examples of what reflection is and is not.

TABLE 3.1
What Reflection Is and Is Not

Reflection Is Not	Reflection Is
Rumination	Shifted perspective
Overgeneralized	Disaggregated, well differentiated
Universal, unchangeable	Contextual
Unidimensional, intellectualized, disconnected	Integrative (emotion, behavior, cognition)
Purely visceral	Descriptive

Our examination of student reflection essays and blog posts revealed these contrasts, although there may be more distinctions. We also draw on guidelines for critical incident reflections such as those from Bennett, Bennett, and Stillings (1977) and Deardorff (2012) as well as descriptions by Taylor (2009) to find characteristics illustrative of what reflection is.

Thinking about an experience over and over again with no change (rumination) is not an example of what is usually thought of as reflection. Rather, reflection requires a shift of perspective (Mezirow, 1991; Pagano & Roselle, 2009). Most often such a shift comes from being able to step away from the event by looking at it at a different time or by virtue of having recorded it (e.g., a journal or a photo) that allows the event to be encapsulated in time rather than ongoing. Other perspective-shifting possibilities are explored later.

Overgeneralizations lack the detail necessary for a more nuanced consideration of experiences on which students may be reflecting. Rather, reflection is aided by disaggregating events into well-described, well-differentiated parts. The more detail available, the more possibility to find aspects that pique interest and offer threads of narration leading to alternative interpretations that delve beneath initial, simplistic impressions.

In a similar fashion, language that presumes that events are universal and unchangeable (e.g., "That's just the way I am or they are.") detaches contextual influences from the events that are being discussed. It is difficult to reach an alternative explanation of events when one's language presumes they cannot be different. Rather, a focus on the context of the experience presumes that events may be changeable depending on the situation. A description of the external conditions in a study abroad setting also increases the probability of capturing cultural factors.

Descriptions of experiences devoid of emotional content (feelings, values, attitudes) lead to intellectualized, disconnected, and unidimensional statements that lack the full richness of human response. According to Ward (2001), the acculturation process during study abroad has an impact on affect, behavior, and cognition. As Zull (2012) suggests, "We gain knowledge through feelings that come with the sensory information" (p. 173). Strong reflections link the students' responses to the experiences they are writing or speaking about. Those events do not happen in a vacuum. Integrating oneself into reflections increases the probability of the meaning-making, potentially transformational, process (Hunter, 2008). Experiences can be evaluated, interpreted, acted on by the reflector.

On the flip side of the coin, an emotions-only report ("It was awesome!") does not aid in an integrated, meaning-making process. Clearly, all aspects of the self need to be addressed to enhance the construction of meaning; that is, a goal of reflection.

Additionally, various brain capacities may be involved in reflection (Zull, 2012). "Reflection does not exclusively engage any brain function or anatomic area of the cortex. However, processing our experiences engages the integrative regions of the cortex" (p. 173). New study abroad experiences without mental processing can lead to "a shallow experiential base" (p. 183).

In another conceptualization of reflection, Hubbs and Brand (2010) offer a typology based on two dimensions of reflection content (see Figure 3.1).

In this approach, the dimension of level of reflection is paired with the contrast between content versus process focus. From the point of view of this chapter, we hope that we can guide students to engage in the reflective process in the lower right quadrant of Figure 3.1: an integration of content analysis and self-awareness.

Overall, we have some ideas about the mechanisms that undergird effective reflection. Cognitive and affective components contribute. Cognitive complexity sets the stage for reflection in terms of describing in detail distinctions observed and in terms of integrating all aspects of the self.

Figure 3.1. Reflection dimensions and typology.

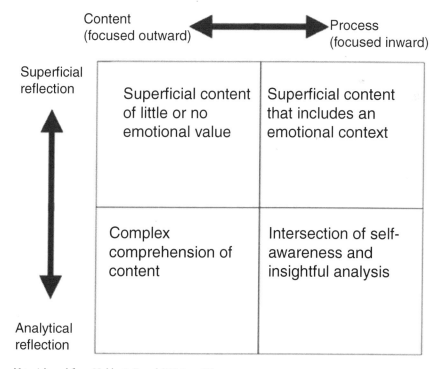

Note. Adapted from Hubbs & Brand (2010, p. 69).

Theoretical Underpinnings

Two popular theories of learning place reflection at a key juncture in the learning process: experiential learning theory (Kolb, 1984) and transformational learning theory (Mezirow, 1991). Meaning-making lies at the heart of both theories, and reflection is pivotal in the process of meaning-making.

In experiential learning theory, observation and reflection bridge the gap between concrete experience that launches the learning cycle and forming new knowledge that supplies meaning (Savicki, 2008). The observations need to be sufficiently detailed and described to allow the reflections to ponder a relatively complete picture of the concrete experience. At this point learners can experiment with *constructive alternativism* (Maher, 1969) to generate an array of possible explanations for why the experience played out the way it did, and how the learner's values, beliefs, attitudes, and emotions might have influenced the meaning they initially ascribed to the event. Clearly, in this theory of learning, reflection offers a means to shift perspective.

In transformational learning theory, a specific disorienting dilemma sparks the need to understand an experience that is different and unexpected. One choice is to try to cram the disorienting event into the student's existing meaning framework. However, reflection can be employed to think about the event in an unconventional manner, thus paving the way for the student's meaning frame to expand, which is the definition of *transformation* (Hunter, 2008). This type of change in meaning perspective requires reflecting on the student's premises, presuppositions, and assumptions regarding the event (and the host culture). This is a deeper, more engaging level of reflection.

The theories of Kolb (1984) and Mezirow (1991) provide a framework to consider how reflection might be designed for shorter duration study abroad sojourns.

Reflection in the Short-Term Study Abroad Context

If we assume that reflection on study abroad experiences presupposes contact and even immersion in the study abroad culture as the experiential base, then shortening the duration of that contact and immersion raises questions concerning the methodology best used in that context. Concrete experience à la Kolb and disorienting dilemmas à la Mezirow form the content for reflection in each theory. Regardless of the shortened duration, there should be enough content for effective reflection. Everyday mundane events such as riding public transportation, greeting host nationals, reacting to the pace of life, and noting differing personal space expectations will yield grist for reflection.

The key, we think, is applying an effective reflection process. To begin that process students must have opportunities for reflection. Protected times and places for students to step out of the flow of ongoing events are necessary. Immersion in the host culture is like standing in the stream of a fire hose of events, many of which carry emotional reactions and can be surprising, scary, and certainly disorienting. How do we capture some of these events for the reflective process?

An important aspect of reflection, shifting perspective, may be promoted by use of media (journals, critical incident reports, photos, videos, etc.) that capture and hold an event still so that it can be examined. Likewise, shifting of time can be helpful. Reflection does not happen only at the end of a sojourn on reentry (looking back). Rather, current experiences and even anticipated future events (looking forward) provide a one-step-removed opportunity for reflection (see Savicki & Price, 2015a). In fact, we have found that discussion of predeparture anticipations and expectations helps students form a point of reference for self-examination that can be drawn from during and after actual exposure to study abroad cultural experiences. Also important is the effort of speculating about the thoughts and feelings of other people in student interactions and observations. For example, what could a host national be thinking and feeling when he or she cut in line in front of a student? The student was angry and thought the line cutter was rude, but maybe the host national was being efficient in the use of personal space because the student stood too far back to be perceived as being in line. Empathy and taking the perspective of others allow a different view of events. We discuss more methodology for reflection later in the chapter.

Research Findings Related to Reflection

Research on reflection in study abroad is relatively sparse. Much of what has been done relies on qualitative methodologies. For example, Brewer and Moore (2015) and Gillespie, Ciner, and Schodt (2015) scored student essays and responses to specific reflective prompts using rubrics adapted from the Association of American Colleges & Universities (2010). Such rubrics address issues such as critical thinking, intercultural knowledge and competence, global learning, and 12 others (Association of American Colleges & Universities, 2010). The adapted rubrics were focused on the needs of the unique institutions in the studies. Especially interesting was the following reflective prompt that students found most helpful: "Discuss experiences abroad, small or large, that were especially meaningful and memorable. Explain why and how these will have a lasting effect on you. (500 words)" (Brewer & Moore, 2015, p. 152). This prompt embodies a request for components of reflection as described earlier in this chapter.

In another qualitative study, Bosangit and Demangeot (2010) used the Hubbs and Brand (2010) four-part typology of reflection to evaluate reflective learning from travel blogs. Interesting conclusions focused on the useful, salutary impact of negative experiences (e.g., disorienting) and highly positive experiences. Routinely modest positive experiences were not as effective in prompting reflection. Also, a focus on the difference between the host and home culture set the stage for deeper reflections. We might expect similar findings in study abroad research.

One quantitative approach to reflection in study abroad studied how students reflected rather than what they reflected on. Savicki and Price (2015a) used a content analysis software program, Linguistic Inquiry and Word Count (Pennebaker et al., 2007) to measure types of language students used to respond to specific study abroad topics at three time periods: predeparture, during the sojourn, and after return. Findings indicate that students felt unfinished processing cultural expectations on reentry, and that psychological issues (emotions) showed a high level of change across the three time periods. A second study using the same methodology measured language usage in student blog entries longitudinally across seven time periods (Savicki & Price, 2017). Results indicated that students had a difficult time reporting their own values, beliefs, and attitudes (process variables) while immersed in the study abroad experience, but they had no problem at predeparture or on reentry (see Figure 3.2 for examples of reflection prompts for each time period). These results illustrate the need for protected opportunities for reflection as well as a need for feedback and guidance for reflection during the sojourn.

Although not focused specifically on reflection, research on coping mechanisms and adjustment in study abroad students adds support for components of reflection as described earlier. The coping strategy of positive reinterpretation was significantly correlated to psychological health in study abroad students. This mechanism exemplifies a shift in perspective in that it employs a cognitive shift to reconstrue a seemingly negative event into one that has positive implications. In contrast, the coping mechanism of venting emotions, or ruminating about events with no attempt to resolve them, was significantly correlated with lower psychological adjustment (Savicki et al., 2004).

As we see in the next section, a plethora of ideas exist about methodologies to enhance student reflection, but there is a dearth of research to assess the effectiveness of the methods.

Figure 3.2. Prompts for student blog posts at specific time periods.

Predeparture post:

Describe what you think your host culture will be like and how you see yourself interacting with your host culture. Are you excited, apprehensive, uncertain? Why?

Arrival post:

Describe the scene that greeted you upon arrival in the airport and recount the behavior you observed. What bewildered, delighted, interested, amused, or frightened you? Why?

While abroad posts:

1. Post at least once a week.
2. These posts are open-ended and give you the opportunity to observe your new culture at a deeper level, using all of your senses—sight, sound, taste, smell, touch—to explore your environment. What do you observe that stimulates your curiosity? Use DIVE in these posts; **D**escribe what captured your attention; **I**nvestigate to see if you can discover the meaning, history, or purpose; **V**erify what you find out by talking to locals, going to the library, researching the Internet, and so on; **E**xplain what you discovered to the rest of us. Include links that you found helpful and that will help us as well.

Prior to coming home:

Refer back to your earlier predeparture post. Has your host culture turned out to be what you visualized before departure, and have you interacted with your host culture as you thought you would at the beginning of your journey? Why or why not? Now that your program or internship is ending, how do you feel about returning home?

Return home:

1. Refer back to your earlier post about arrival in your host country. How does your arrival in the United States compare with how you felt arriving in your host culture?

Note. Adapted from Gothard, Downey, Gray, & Butcher (n.d.).

Application

As we explore various methods to aid our students to reflect deeply, we must keep in mind that however intriguing the stories they tell may be, the way they deal with the content of their stories will demonstrate their skill at reflection.

> Reflective learning is not what happens to a student, it is what the student does with what has happened. When we assess reflection it is important that we do not assess the content of an experience, but, rather, that we assess what the student has done with the content. (Bourner, 2003, p. 270)

It is worthwhile to note that reflection is a skill that can be learned and polished. It does not magically appear but rather increases in increments and through repeated iterations. The dramatic a-ha moments usually occur at the end of a trail of questioning and discovery that may span several attempts at understanding.

In the following, we present a number of methods to elicit deep reflections from students. But first, there are several general principles that apply to all these methods.

General Principles for Reflection

Feedback
There is no guarantee that student reflections will result in intercultural competence, global awareness, or any other positive result that we may be hoping for. Unfortunately, sometimes reflection can lead to ethnocentric conclusions. For this reason, and because reflection is not a usual pattern of thought in daily life, study abroad practitioners need to provide feedback about student reflections as described in the excerpt from Bourner (2003) at the beginning of this section. Feedback may be individual, such as faculty to student, or it may be offered in a group setting where others may benefit by observing feedback and discussion. In any case, feedback should be benign, not judgmental, with suggestions for how to think more deeply about the experience being reflected on. Feedback can often take the form of Socratic questioning rather than instructor pronouncements such as, "It seems that this experience was confusing to you. Why do you think that was the case or what did you find most confusing?" Also, opportunities should be offered for confidential reflection and feedback should the student request it.

Iterations
Although, as coaches for reflection, we may wish students to move quickly to realizations that we see clearly, students have their own pace and their own

previous experiences, values, beliefs, and attitudes that may hinder them. It may be difficult in a short duration program to be patient, but rushing students to conclusions may backfire. Multiple iterations may be necessary for them to come to what seems to us an obvious conclusion. Remember to breathe.

Metacognition

Very early in this chapter we raised the concept that reflection is thinking about thinking, or metacognition. This is the point at which we encourage students to consider themselves as part of the reflection process. What values, beliefs, attitudes, presuppositions, assumptions, or expectations do they bring to their observation and evaluation of the experience on which they are reflecting? None of us can be absolutely neutral in observing an event because we have a history that shapes our perceptions. Clearly, for students to think deeply about an event, they need to think about their own contributions to how they construe an event. Raising these issues will help students integrate the experience and their perspective with the chance that they see alternative ways of thinking about the experience. "The reflective process entails bringing students to a point where acquiring new information and building meaning around it involves examining their perceptions and challenging what they currently understand to be true" (Homan, 2006, p. 13).

Integration

None of us are sliced into disconnected pieces of thinking, feeling, and behaving. We are integrated, holistic beings. Thus, when students reflect, our task is to help them consider all the parts of themselves that may be effective in deep reflection. Reflection is not a pristine, rational, purely cognitive activity. All of our selves are involved. So noticing and asking for clarification about aspects of self that might be missing in an initial reflection may help students round out their thinking.

Intercultural Sensitivity Development

In study abroad, one of our goals in a general sense is to increase students' intercultural sensitivity. We want them to move from ethnocentrism toward ethnorelativism. The developmental model of intercultural sensitivity provides a theoretical base for this movement (Bennett, 1993). Student reflections are likely to bounce around on the developmental scale offered by this theory. Our task is to help them move in an ethnorelative direction. It is sometimes difficult to find that students rant about their host culture in an ethnocentric way. That is to be expected. Our task is to coax them to an alternate perspective that allows a more ethnorelative view.

Gradualism

Deep reflection that examines one's cultural beliefs, values, attitudes, and assumptions may tread on parts of personal identity. For many students, reflecting on cultural differences may be the first time they have thought about what their culture is and who they are in relation to it. It pays to approach these issues gradually. People tend to feel threatened and uncomfortable in cross-culture interactions (Frey & Tropp, 2006). They may experience these feelings during interactions with host culture members because they are worried about being rejected, embarrassed, ridiculed, or exploited, which is intergroup contact anxiety (Stephan & Stephan, 1985; Voci & Hewstone, 2003). Particularly in a study abroad setting, the day-to-day foreign encounters with the host culture may elevate threats to self-identity through symbolic anxiety (Stephan, Stephan, & Gudykunst, 1999). Lou and Bosley (2008) offer a model for feedback and guidance to students concerning their reflections. They suggest helping students move only one step along the developmental model of intercultural sensitivity continuum rather than jumping immediately to the most ethnorelative stage. This step-by-step movement tends to allay fears of overwhelming challenges to student cultural identity.

Methods

Most of the methods for eliciting student feedback listed next may be applied at any time while the student is involved with study abroad—before, during, and after. Our experience evolved from a single, generalized postreentry essay through specific prompted questions before, during, and after the host culture contact to frequent blog post requests (specific and nonspecific) with instructor feedback and group sharing (Savicki & Price, 2015b). Our impression is that to maximize host culture contact time, students need to be prepared prior to immersion, coached during immersion, and debriefed after immersion. Although longer duration student sojourns allow a more leisurely pace of reflective, meaning-making activities, shorter duration sojourns require more careful attention and can capitalize on naturally occurring opportunities.

Journals

Journals are the most popular mode of requesting student reflection. "A broad body of research has identified the benefits of journal writing as an instrument for promoting critical reflection as pivotal to all areas of education" (Power, 2016, p. 239). Yet journals can yield superficial travelogues and unanalyzed narrations of daily life. Careful guidelines for the structure of journals are necessary to encourage deeper reflection, and feedback requesting more integrated involvement is usually necessary, especially at the

Figure 3.3. Questions as tools for reflective thinking.

1. What happened that most surprised you?
2. What patterns can you recognize in your experience?
3. What was the most fulfilling part? And the least fulfilling part? What does that suggest to you about your values?
4. What happened that contradicted your prior beliefs? What happened that confirmed your prior beliefs?
5. How do you feel about that experience now compared with how you felt about it at the time?
6. What does the experience suggest to you about your strengths?
7. What does the experience suggest to you about your weaknesses and opportunities for development?
8. How else could you view that experience?
9. What did you learn from that experience about how you react?
10. What other options did you have at the time?
11. Is there anything about the experience that was familiar to you?
12. What might you do differently as a result of that experience and your reflections on it? What actions do your reflections lead you to?

Note. From Bourner, T. (2003). Assessing reflective learning. *Education+Training*, *45*(5), p. 270.

beginning (see Figure 3.3 for examples of questions faculty can ask to elicit deeper reflection).

The key is asking the right questions—that allow integration of experience and self-perception. For short-term programs, the turnaround for feedback should be quick so that multiple iterations can occur. Journals have the advantage of keeping faculty informed of ongoing issues with students. As a disadvantage, students initially think of journals as a place for superficial reports. Faculty have to work diligently to make journals a place for deeper reflection.

Free Writing

Free writing, as illustrated by Dirkx and Smith (2009), is usually a short quiet period for students to write during a group meeting. Students take a brief time (e.g., 5–10 minutes) to write about a significant, emotionally tinged event that happened to them or that they witnessed in a specific time period. Then they are asked to "identify the themes that are present within their free write and elaborate on what these themes might suggest to them with regard to the meaning of the emotion laden images" (Dirkx & Smith, 2009, p. 63). The faculty and other group members can query about the cultural import of the themes and student emotional reactions. This method has several advantages. It provides a protected time and space for reflection, it requests an integration of experience and abstraction of themes triggered by emotions, and it uses multiple sources of feedback.

Temperature Check
At the beginning of class or a small group meeting, the instructor asks something like, "What interesting thing have you noticed about the host culture since last we met?" Often students respond with emotion-laden gripes, frustrations, surprises, epiphanies. Usually student responses illustrate a culture clash, misunderstanding, or ethnocentric view that becomes a topic of discussion. The advantages to this method are that the incidents brought up are usually hot—in that they are current—and so are the student reactions. After a while students feel safe in expressing these reactions, and the faculty can immediately move toward integration and shifted perspective.

Photos, Videos, Art
Sometimes the entry into reflection comes not from words but from images. Some students will be much more fluent with graphics and the technology available to them on their smartphone than they are with spoken or written words. The key is for them to not only describe the image but also clarify the meaning they perceive. Digital storytelling can lead to deep reflection, especially in the scriptwriting process and ultimately in the production of the video presentation (Lambert, 2006).

Structured Critical Incident Reporting
Students may be asked to find a specific critical incident that has meaning for them and disaggregate the event into subparts. The description, interpretation, evaluation framework (Bennett, Bennett, & Stillings, 1977), for example, asks first for a nonemotional description of the critical incident that is as objective as possible. Then students are asked for their interpretation of why the event unfolded the way it did. Usually students supply an interpretation from their own perspective and are also asked for an interpretation from the host culture's perspective. Some educators request not two but three perspectives to illustrate that there are many ways to view the event (Pusch & Merrill, 2008). Finally, students report their own feelings about the event, hopefully from a more integrated viewpoint. The advantage of this method is that students choose situations that have intensity for them emotionally or in regard to cultural issues (Arrúe, 2008; Minucci, 2008; Savicki, Adams, & Binder, 2008).

Role Play and Theater Games

A dramatic way for students to begin to understand another's point of view may be to act as if he or she were that person in a role play or structured theater game. The game of Alter Ego, for example, asks students to play the key roles in a cultural incident while others act as alter egos saying what they think the person in the role may be actually thinking (Binder, 2008). It is entertaining and requires a bit of empathy to verbalize thoughts, values, and attitudes that have been silent during the original interaction. Other students can step in as alter egos or role players. Discussion flows from the players and the audience and during the role play. Alternative actions and thoughts can be plugged into the situation as what-if scenarios to see how they may have changed the outcome. The playfulness of this approach permits an openness that produces freer creative thinking than sometimes results from other methods.

The methods described in this section are only a sample of how to engage students in reflection. The key is the willingness of the faculty to mobilize students in expanding and exploring their ideas about themselves and study abroad following the general guidelines discussed at the beginning of this section.

Final Thoughts and Conclusions

We have several thoughts that may help faculty and study abroad practitioners to maximize their effect in using reflection.

In the best of situations, reflection needs to be incorporated into the curriculum for the study abroad course. Making it subject to academic grading provides extra student motivation. It also provides academic legitimacy. Although experiential learning and transformational learning theories are well established through research, they may not be well known as rigorous approaches in an academic setting that values pure cognitive content and grades. Putting reflection in the study abroad course provides support for an important piece of learning that we hope our study abroad students will achieve.

As the title of the chapter suggests, reflection is not limited to reentry only. Reflection needs to begin before the sojourn and continue after the sojourn. Especially in short duration courses, preparation, coaching, and support for reentry transitions will help ratify learning in the course.

Overly general questions as prompts for reflection do not elicit the detail and emotional integration required for deep reflection. Creating appropriate prompt questions at various points throughout the course will lead to deeper personal reflection—thinking in terms of I, the integration of self as observer construer.

Most short duration faculty-led study abroad courses are relatively small. Therefore, faculty-led programs offer a unique opportunity for continual discussion and debriefing of the prompt questions and responses. The intimacy of the student-faculty contact in such situations provides a safe context for deeper reflection.

Faculty have a bias toward the academic content of their courses. That is only natural. However, academic assignments and academic considerations of the experience, readings, and content focus are important, but personal reflection opportunities need to go hand in hand with these more cerebral tasks, and reflection requires different kinds of questions. If all faculty want to do is convey academic content, then they may be better off staying home. The study abroad environment offers a richness of experience with academic content, the host culture, and the growing self-understanding of students.

Regarding the notion of more complete involvement of faculty, we believe that faculty can be involved in predeparture orientation and reentry activities so that students have a stronger sense of the complete span of the study abroad experience. Certainly faculty have a role in the facilitation of discussion around the reflection prompts for their course.

In conclusion, we hope this chapter gives guidance for shorter duration and faculty-led study abroad courses in regard to incorporating reflection into the student experience. The chapter was brief; the resources available are many. We hope readers will check out the books, articles, and websites listed in the references. We believe that reflection is the key to students integrating what they experience in study abroad into their belief systems and identities. Reflection opportunities require forethought, luck, in-depth questions, proposing alternative perspectives, support, and challenge. The results, when they emerge, are intensely gratifying for students and for faculty.

References

Arrúe, C. (2008). Study abroad in Spain viewed through multi-cultural lenses. In V. Savicki, (Ed.), *Developing intercultural competence and transformation: Theory, research, and application in international education* (pp. 236–258). Sterling, VA: Stylus.

Association of American Colleges & Universities. (2010). *VALUE rubric development project*. Retrieved from aacu.org/value/rubrics/index_p.cfm?CFID=6634177&C FTOKEN=40351583

Bennett, J. M. (2008). On becoming a global soul: A path to engagement on study abroad. In V. Savicki, (Ed.), *Developing intercultural competence and transformation: Theory, research, and application in international education* (pp. 13–31). Sterling, VA: Stylus.

Bennett, J. M., Bennett, M. J., & Stillings, K. (1977). *Description, interpretation, and evaluation: Facilitators' guidelines.* Retrieved from intercultural.org/training-and-assessment-tools.html#DIE

Bennett, M. J. (1993). Toward ethnorelativism: A developmental model of intercultural sensitivity. In R. M. Paige (Ed.), *Education for the intercultural experience* (2nd ed., pp. 21–71). Yarmouth, ME: Intercultural Press.

Bennett, M. J. (2012). Paradigmatic assumptions and a developmental approach to intercultural learning. In M. Vande Berg, R. M. Paige, & K. H. Lou (Eds.), *Student learning abroad: What our students are learning, what they're not, and what we can do about it* (pp. 90–114). Sterling, VA: Stylus.

Binder, F. (2008). Action methods for integration of experience and understanding. In V. Savicki, (Ed.), *Developing intercultural competence and transformation: Theory, research, and application in international education* (pp. 195–214). Sterling, VA: Stylus.

Bosangit, C., & Demangeot, C. (2010). Exploring reflective learning during the extended consumption of life experiences. *Journal of Business Research, 69,* 208–215.

Bourner, T. (2003). Assessing reflective learning. *Education+Training, 45*(5), 267–272.

Brewer, E. & Moore, J. (2015). Where and how do students learn abroad? In V. Savicki & E. Brewer (Eds.), *Assessing study abroad: Theory, tools, and practice* (pp. 145–161). Sterling, VA: Stylus.

Deardorff, D. K. (2012). Framework: Observe, state, explore, evaluate (OSEE) tool. In K. Berardo & D. K Deardorff (Eds.), *Building cultural competence: Innovative activities and models* (pp. 58–60). Sterling, VA: Stylus.

Dirkx, J. M., & Smith, R. O. (2009). Facilitating transformative learning: Engaging emotions in an online context. In J. Mezirow & E. W. Taylor (Eds.), *Transformative learning in practice: Insights from community, workplace, and higher education* (pp. 57–66). Hoboken, NJ: Wiley.

Engle, L., & Engle, J. (2003). Study abroad levels: Toward a classification of program types. *Frontiers, 9,* 1–20.

Freire, P. (1998). *Pedagogy of freedom: Ethics, democracy, and civic courage.* Lanham, MD: Rowman & Littlefield.

Frey, F. E., & Tropp, L. R. (2006). Being seen as individuals versus as group members: Extending research on metaperception to intergroup contexts. *Personality and Social Psychology Review, 10,* 265–280.

Gillespie, J., Ciner, E., & Schodt, D. (2015). Engaging stakeholders in assessment of student learning in off-campus programs. In V. Savicki & E. Brewer (Eds.). *Assessing study abroad: Theory, tools, and practice* (pp. 262–276). Sterling, VA: Stylus.

Gothard, J., Downey, G., Gray, T., & Butcher, L. (n.d.). *Bringing the learning home.* Retrieved from ozstudentsabroad.com

Homan, A. (2006). Constructing knowledge through reflection. *The Cross Papers, Number 9.* Phoenix, AZ: League for Innovation in the Community College.

Hubbs, D. L., & Brand, C. F. (2010). Learning from the inside out: A method for analyzing reflective journals in the college classroom. *Journal of Experiential Education, 33*, 56–71.

Hunter, A. (2008). Transformative learning in international education. In V. Savicki, (Ed.), *Developing intercultural competence and transformation: Theory, research, and application in international education* (pp. 92–107). Sterling, VA: Stylus.

Kolb, D. (1984). *Experiential learning as the science of learning and development.* Englewood Cliffs, NJ: Prentice Hall.

Lambert, J. (2006). *The digital storytelling cookbook.* Berkeley, CA: Digital Diner Press.

Lou, K. H., & Bosley, G. W. (2008). Dynamics of cultural contexts: Meta-level intervention in the study abroad experience. In V. Savicki, (Ed.), *Developing intercultural competence and transformation: Theory, research, and application in international education* (pp. 276–296). Sterling, VA: Stylus.

Maher, B. A. (1969). *Clinical psychology and personality: The selected papers of George Kelly.* Huntington, NY: R. E. Krieger.

Mezirow, J. (1991). *Transformative dimensions of adult learning.* San Francisco, CA: Jossey-Bass.

Minucci, S. (2008). Every day another soulful experience to bring back home. In V. Savicki, (Ed.), *Developing intercultural competence and transformation: Theory, research, and application in international education* (pp. 215–235). Sterling, VA: Stylus.

Pagano, M., & Roselle, L. (2009). Beyond reflection through an academic lens: Refraction and international experiential education. *Frontiers, 18*, 217–229.

Paige, R. M. (2015). Interventionist models for study abroad. In J. M. Bennett (Ed.), *Sage encyclopedia of intercultural competence* (pp. 563–568). Thousand Oaks, CA: Sage.

Pennebaker, J. W., Chung, C. K., Ireland, M., Gonzales, A., & Booth, R. J. (2007). *The development and psychometric properties of LIWC2007* [Software manual]. Austin, TX: LIWC.net.

Power, J. B. (2016). Has this begun to change the way they think? Moving undergraduate learners' level of reflection from where it is to where it needs to be. *Teaching in Higher Education, 21*, 235–248.

Pusch, M. D., & Merrill, M. (2008). Reflection, reciprocity, responsibility, and committed relativism. In V. Savicki, (Ed.), *Developing intercultural competence and transformation: Theory, research, and application in international education* (pp. 297–322). Sterling, VA: Stylus.

Savicki, V. (2008). Experiential and affective education for international educators. In V. Savicki, (Ed.). *Developing intercultural competence and transformation: Theory, research, and application in international education* (pp. 74–91). Sterling, VA: Stylus.

Savicki, V., Adams, I, & Binder, F. (2008). Intercultural development: Topics and sequences. In V. Savicki, (Ed.), *Developing intercultural competence and transformation: Theory, research, and application in international education* (pp. 154–172). Sterling, VA: Stylus.

Savicki, V., Downing-Burnette, R., Heller, L., Binder, F., & Suntinger, W. (2004). Contrasts, changes, and correlates in actual and potential intercultural adjustment. *International Journal of Intercultural Relations, 28*, 311–329.

Savicki, V., & Price, M. V. (2015a). Student reflective writing: Cognition and affect before, during, and after study abroad. *Journal of College Student Development, 56,* 587–601.

Savicki, V., & Price, M. V. (2015b). Continuous improvement in a small study abroad office using outcomes assessment. In V. Savicki & E. Brewer (Eds.), *Assessing study abroad: Theory, tools, and practice* (pp. 230–245). Sterling, VA: Stylus.

Savicki, V., & Price, M. V. (2017). Components of reflection: A longitudinal analysis of study abroad student blog posts. *Frontier: The Interdisciplinary Journal of Study Abroad, XXIX*(1).

Stephan, W. G., & Stephan, C. W. (1985). Intergroup anxiety. *Journal of Social Issues, 41*, 157–176.

Stephan, W. G., Stephan, C. W., & Gudykunst, W. B. (1999). Anxiety in intergroup relations: A comparison of anxiety/uncertainty management theory and integrated threat theory. *International Journal of Intercultural Relations, 23*, 613–628.

Taylor, E. W. (2009). Fostering transformative learning. In J. Mezirow, E. W. Taylor, & associates. *Transformative learning in practice: Insights from community, workplace, and higher education* (pp. 3–17). San Francisco, CA: Jossey-Bass.

Vande Berg, M., Paige, R. M., & Lou, K. H. (2012). Student learning abroad: Paradigms and assumptions. In M. Vande Berg, R. M. Paige, & K. H. Lou (Eds.), *Student learning abroad: What our students are learning, what they're not, and what we can do about it.*, (pp. 90–114). Sterling, VA: Stylus.

Voci, A., & Hewstone, M. (2003). Intergroup contact and prejudice toward immigrants in Italy: The mediational role of anxiety and the moderational role of group salience. *Group Processes and Intergroup Relations, 6,* 37–54.

Ward, C. (2001). The A, B, Cs of acculturation. In D. Matsumoto (Ed.), *Handbook of culture and psychology* (pp. 411–446). New York, NY: Oxford University Press.

Zull, J. E. (2012). The brain, learning, and study abroad. In M. Vande Berg, R. M. Paige, & K. H. Lou (Eds.), *Student learning abroad: What our students are learning, what they're not, and what we can do about it.*, (pp. 162–187). Sterling, VA: Stylus.

4

DESIGNING AND ASSESSING OUTCOMES-BASED FACULTY-LED STUDY ABROAD PROGRAMS

Darla K. Deardorff

Faculty involved in study abroad programs have numerous roles in areas that are addressed in this book, including student care, logistics, academic teaching and learning, and intercultural teaching and learning (Goode, 2007). An often underaddressed faculty role relates to student outcomes assessment. Although study abroad administrators may measure study abroad outcomes using a pre- and post- measure (administered before the program begins and again after the program ends), this approach is insufficient in assessing the actual outcomes of student learning during a study abroad program. Why is one pre- or post- assessment insufficient? Simply using one assessment instrument in a pre- and post- fashion is capturing only indirect evidence outside the learning experience itself and provides an incomplete picture of the actual student learning that occurs during the experience. Thus, it falls to faculty to engage in the key aspects of outcomes assessment *throughout* the study abroad experience.

What should faculty know about designing and assessing an outcomes-based learning experience in study abroad? This chapter provides an overview of the key points of outcome design and assessment in study abroad so that faculty will be able to determine the extent to which the program is contributing to students' growth academically, interculturally, and personally. In addition, and more important, faculty will be able to use the collected evidence from stated outcomes to continue to guide students in their own intercultural and personal development.

Overview: The Importance of Why

Why do students participate in study abroad? (And conversely, why do faculty lead study abroad experiences?) What are the larger purposes of study abroad, and how do those align with the institutional mission and goals? What are the desired changes in students who study abroad? Why assess student outcomes?

These bigger questions are fundamental to consider when designing outcomes-based learning programs, and in particular, addressing student outcomes assessment, which is "information collected from individual learners as evidence that stated course goals and objectives were achieved" for the purpose of improving individual student learning (Deardorff, 2015b, p. 7). It is important to note that this is quite different from program assessment, which is learner cohort information collected in aggregate and reported at the program level usually for the purpose of program improvement. In fact, as international education assessment continues to develop and mature, a new paradigm is emerging that requires educators to change their thinking about assessment as something that is done *to* learners (efforts that primarily benefit administrators, who too often conflate outcomes assessment with program evaluation—two very different processes) to assessment as something done *with* learners. This chapter describes that changing paradigm, how this affects the design process, and the central role that faculty have in student learning by providing some guiding questions that faculty can use in the design and assessment of their study abroad programs.

This is the reason assessment questions should be examined first before delving into the what or how of design and assessment. Too often staff may push for easy-to-use assessments without giving much thought to why or to what extent the measure may even align with the outcomes of a particular study abroad program. It is important to recognize that there is no one-size-fits-all assessment tool in any program, especially in study abroad. Faculty should resist succumbing to a one-size-fits-all assessment approach because each program or course has tailored goals and outcomes and students are at different places in their own learning journeys. So why assess? Educators most often respond that outcomes assessment is about deepening students' learning, as well as improving teaching and learning.

Student learning is arguably at the core of any study abroad program. A fundamental question for faculty to ask is, What should students know and be able to do as a result of their study abroad experience? Beyond gaining content knowledge of a course (academic outcomes), other often mentioned student outcomes of study abroad experiences include intercultural outcomes (e.g., increased development of intercultural competence), language outcomes, and personal growth outcomes (e.g., increased self-confidence).

Increasingly, learner-centered assessment (and design) attempts to involve students in their own learning by

- promoting high expectations of learning,
- respecting diverse talents and learning styles,
- promoting coherence in learning,
- synthesizing experiences and concepts,
- fostering collaboration, and
- providing prompt feedback, including through the use of peer feedback. (Huba & Freed, 2000)

Engaging learners in the design and assessment process ultimately empowers them to take more responsibility for their own learning and subsequent outcomes.

A Changing Paradigm

This focus on the learner is leading to a shifting paradigm in outcomes assessment in education abroad (see Table 4.1).

This changing paradigm focuses more centrally on the learner, as opposed to focusing on the course or program, and means ensuring that assessment measurements are relevant to the learners by involving the learners more collaboratively in the design and assessment process; thus assessment is a process done with learners and not to learners. Often in study abroad,

TABLE 4.1

The Changing Paradigm of Outcomes Assessment in International Education

From	To
Program or course centered	Learner centered or engaged
Traditional evidence	Authentic evidence
Self-perspective	Multiple perspectives (including self)
One approach	Multiple pathways
Separate	Holistic
Results	Process

Note. Adapted from Deardorff (2015b).

this means comingling intercultural and personal development outcomes as learners cocreate their experiences (see Baxter-Magolda et al., 2010). In making assessment more relevant, this also means the context itself is changing in collecting evidence in real-world, authentic settings through observations (moving beyond self-perspective), teamwork, relationship development, and so on, instead of the more traditional route of data collected through contrived instruments in forced, disconnected environments. Furthermore, given the different pathways and personal developmental levels in acquiring global, international, or intercultural outcomes, today's learners need a more tailored approach to assessing short-term outcomes, which could include individualized feedback and coaching. Given the complexities of study abroad outcomes for students, it is important to consider the holistic, lifelong learning *process* for learners (as opposed to results) and recognize that the study abroad experience is part of the much bigger picture of a student's overall growth and human development.

Design questions about this changing paradigm include the following:

1. How do the stated outcomes of the study abroad experience address not only the academic (and language) learning but also the intercultural and personal growth dimensions of the student's experience?
2. To what extent and how are students involved in the identification of outcomes of the study abroad experience?
3. To what extent do the stated outcomes focus on results versus the process (of learning and meaning-making)?
4. What is the evidence that students have achieved these outcomes? From a student's perspective? From an employer's perspective?
5. How are students being individually coached to continue their growth and development, based on the results of the assessments?
6. What are the most effective ways to document unanticipated outcomes of the study abroad experience?
7. What are the limitations of focusing exclusively on outcomes?

Getting Started With Outcomes-Based Design and Assessment

From the outset, it is important for faculty to return to the pivotal question of what students should know and be able to do as a result of participating in this study abroad experience that they wouldn't be able to accomplish if they had stayed at the home campus. To answer this question, it is important for faculty to consider three key dimensions in terms of short-term, intermediate, and even long-term outcomes of the initial study abroad experience: academic, intercultural, and personal.

Academic Dimensions

Academic outcomes are related to the discipline and are best determined by the faculty involved in teaching the courses. As the course is being designed, though, it is important to consider the unique cultural context of the course or experience and ways to maximize the resources that may be available to the instructor and learners in the host country.

When possible, academic and intercultural domains of outcomes can be interwoven. For example, faculty can consider the following questions in determining the appropriate intercultural dimensions in a content, discipline, or knowledge domain:

1. How are respect, open-mindedness (including nonjudgmentalness) and curiosity incorporated concretely into the discipline?
2. Where is cultural self-awareness addressed in the discipline?
3. Do students recognize the ways they view the world, issues, and solutions as culturally bound, and can students clearly articulate the multiple ways others view these same issues?
4. How is knowledge of different populations (age, gender, culture, religion, indigenous beliefs, etc.) in the disciplinary context taught and from whose perspective?
5. Are the historical, social, economic, political, and religious contexts of different populations included in the curriculum when appropriate?
6. Do the disciplinary materials reflect different perspectives? Whose voices and perspectives are missing, and how can those be included?
7. How are communication styles being addressed in the disciplinary context?
8. Are students able to reflect regularly and intentionally on the process of developing their intercultural competence, and do they recognize the lifelong nature of developing such a competence?
9. Are students able to display empathy and humility in approaching and working with others?
10. Can students communicate and behave appropriately and effectively with those from different backgrounds, especially when working in groups and teams?
11. Whose knowledge is being privileged and how is the knowledge conveyed?
12. How does the material go beyond content knowledge to intentionally include and address intercultural skills and attitudes as well as the process of learning? (Deardorff, 2015a, 2015b)

These are just a few of the questions to explore in relating discipline-specific knowledge in a short-term study abroad program to intercultural learning outcomes. Although these questions can certainly be used in any course, either at the home institution or abroad, they are particularly essential to include in study abroad experiences to maximize the opportunities available by being in a different cultural context.

Intercultural Dimensions

Many short-term study abroad programs note intercultural competence development as one of the main goals. Intercultural competence is a lifelong process of learning how to communicate and behave appropriately and effectively with those from different backgrounds (including people of different ages, religions, gender, etc.).[1] Here *appropriateness* means that such communication and behavior meets others' expectations of what is acceptable, whereas *effectiveness* means that the individual has met his or her goals in the interaction.

Given that this particular competence is a lifelong process, it is important to keep in mind the following considerations when designing a short-term study abroad experience:

1. No one training, course, or experience (even study abroad) can result in achieving intercultural competence.
2. Every individual is at a different place in his or her intercultural journey, so a one-size-fits-all approach to developing intercultural competence will not work.
3. Intercultural competence development, in the end, is more about the process of learning interculturally about oneself and the world than about achieving results.

Thus, the focus should be much more on the process itself, including how one's intercultural competence continues to develop over time; which intercultural dimensions of knowledge, skills, or attitudes are improving (and how and why); and which ones need to be strengthened further. In addition, a focus on process requires thoughtful reflection on what went well in an actual intercultural interaction, what could be improved, and what lessons were learned on further reflection (see Chapter 3 for more on reflection). To what extent is critical reflection integrated into the experience before, during, and after? Often this is demonstrated through blogs or online journals. However, it is very important for students to go beyond simply what was learned to why this learning was important and what students will do as a result of this learning academically, interculturally, and personally. Another part of a process focus is stepping back to reflect and identify areas of individual strength and areas that need further work academically, interculturally, and personally.

In designing intercultural activities and experiences, it is helpful to explore some definitions of *intercultural competence* (see Spitzberg & Changnon, 2009, for more than 20 different definitions) and prioritize which intercultural elements or dimensions should be addressed through a specific activity or overall study abroad experience. Even though no one activity or experience can result in intercultural competence, a helpful starting point is often having learners engage in learning activities that increase their own cultural self-awareness and identity, such as who they are in the world, how they have been culturally conditioned to respond to others, what their own worldviews are, and how they make meaning of their identities, especially given the complex world we live in. Research has shown that starting with one's own cultural identity is very helpful as a first step in improving interactions with others. Several of these types of identity activities can be found in resources such as Beaven and Borghetti (2015), Council of Europe (2015), Berardo and Deardorff (2012), and Stringer and Cassiday (2009).

When including learning activities with students to work on intercultural dimensions of the experience, it is important to review the following design considerations in a study abroad program:

1. Meet learners where they are (i.e., what are their needs, recognizing these will vary throughout the group.).
2. Go beyond knowledge and include skills and attitudes as well as the process of learning.
3. Incorporate active learning.
4. Involve the learners in the design process. (How will learners' needs and ideas be incorporated and addressed?)
5. Provide authentic intercultural engagement opportunities that go beyond transactional interactions.
6. Integrate assessment for and as learning and transformation instead of assessment of learning.
7. Go beyond a one-time intercultural activity, reading, or discussion.
8. Build in critical reflection as crucial to intercultural development. (Deardorff, 2015c)

Moreover, the following are some questions to answer when integrating intercultural activities and experiences into a short-term study abroad program:

1. How is *intercultural competence* being defined? Based on what?
2. Which elements or dimensions of intercultural competence need emphasis or strengthening?
3. What is the purpose of the activity, and how does it align with learners' needs?
4. How does this activity meet learners where they are?
5. How does this activity help enhance learners' intercultural competence development?
6. How does this activity go beyond knowledge?
7. How does this activity include multiple perspectives?
8. How does this activity avoid reinforcing stereotypes?
9. What kinds of active learning are incorporated into the intercultural learning experience?
10. How will learners be included in designing the activity?
11. Does the activity provide opportunities for authentic engagement?
12. Does the activity include critical reflection so learners can step back and reflect on their own learning in the activity?
13. Does this learning go beyond a one-time activity or discussion? In other words, how will learners continue to develop their intercultural competence?
14. How is assessment integrated into this learning activity (beyond a pre- or postmeasure)?
15. How are learners being connected with the unique study abroad context outside the classroom and in their informal and nonformal interactions with the local community, and how can these be integrated into the classroom?
16. How does this intercultural learning connect with other learner development academically and personally? (Deardorff, 2015c)

Exploring these design considerations and questions will aid faculty in developing appropriately guided intercultural interventions in the study abroad experience that will help enhance learners' intercultural competence development.

Personal Growth Dimension

Beyond academic learning in a disciplinary context and the intercultural learning that occurs in and beyond the classroom during the study abroad experience, an overarching dimension for learners is that of personal growth, whether manifested in increasing self-confidence; developing greater resilience in the face of inevitable challenges and adversities; or acquiring a tolerance for ambiguity, meaning that learners are more comfortable with the unknown. Learners may have other specific areas of desired individual growth while abroad (e.g., emotional intelligence, self-authorship, or moral development), which underscores the importance of connecting directly with the learners in identifying their specific needs in this area.

A learning contract can be used to work with learners in helping them identify their own desired outcomes in the study abroad experience, especially in regard to the intercultural and personal growth dimensions. Learning contracts have been used at all levels of education (Knowles, 1991) and are formal agreements negotiated between learners and instructors on what will be learned, how it will be learned, and how the learning will be assessed and verified. (For more on this, as well as a learning contract template, see Deardorff, 2015b, pp. 163–165.) Learning contracts, or variations thereof, such as having students include two or three of their own outcomes in the syllabus, is one way to address the changing paradigm of outcomes assessment in study abroad.

More on Outcomes-Based Assessment in Study Abroad

Once faculty have identified responses to the key question of what students should know and be able to do (especially in regard to processes), the next step is to create realistic goals that are achievable within the parameters of a short-term study abroad experience and aligned learning outcomes in each of the three dimensions: academic, intercultural, and personal.

Writing Realistic Goals and Aligned Learning Outcomes

The goals and aligned outcomes of the study abroad experience drive everything else in terms of content, activities, and assessment, so faculty need to invest adequate time in developing them, ideally in collaboration with students through focus groups, conversations, preexperience needs assessments, and so on to ensure relevancy to the learners themselves.

Start by considering the desired changes in the learners within the time frame of the short-term study abroad experience and then asking, What would be evidence of these changes? Well-written outcome statements often start with a specific action verb, include a time frame, are relevant to the learners, and are realistic (achievable) within the parameters of the learning experience. To articulate desired changes in learners, Bloom's (1956) taxonomy of learning outcomes, updated by Anderson and Krathwohl (2001), is a classic reference for developing outcome statements. For more on outcomes-based assessment, see Driscoll and Wood (2007). The following are action verbs aligned with the levels of learnings:

- Remembering: recognize, list, describe, identify, retrieve, name
- Understanding: interpret, exemplify, summarize, infer, paraphrase, compare, explain
- Applying: implement, carry out, use
- Analyzing: compare, attribute, organize, deconstruct
- Evaluating: check, critique, judge, hypothesize
- Creating: design, construct, plan, produce (Green, 2012, p. 12)

Once outcomes, ideally within the academic, intercultural, and personal growth dimensions, have been developed for a study abroad course, it is often helpful to receive feedback from students, study abroad administrators, and colleagues in order to further refine the outcome statements. A key question to ask at this point is, Are the stated outcomes the most significant and meaningful outcomes of the overall experience? From the point of clearly developed outcome statements, faculty can then work backward to design the study abroad experience to determine the most effective activities and materials that support the outcomes, as well as identify the evidence that demonstrates achievement of the outcomes. (See the following section for more on evidence and the following chapters for concrete assessment examples, as well as Deardorff & Arasaratnam-Smith, 2017.) Mapping goals, outcomes, activities, and evidence is an excellent tool for determining how closely all are aligned with each other.

Principles of Outcomes Assessment in Short-Term Study Abroad

What are the underlying principles that are important in designing and assessing learning outcomes in short-term study abroad programs? Five key principles are foundational to designing and assessing student outcomes and can serve as first steps in developing an assessment protocol, which can then help inform the overall study abroad program design from the outset.

Define

Define ambiguous terms and concepts used in stated goals and outcomes. Of the three areas of learning (academic, intercultural, and personal), the most ambiguous is often the intercultural dimension. Often, terms related to intercultural competence are used but rarely adequately defined. So one principle is to define these ambiguous terms or concepts in the stated outcomes, such as *intercultural competence* or *global citizenship*, in a programmatic or institutional context, based on existing literature. So, for example, how exactly is *intercultural competence* (or a related term) being defined in your context? According to whom? In some instances, it may be important to take into account different perspectives, including disciplinary or geographic perspectives. For example, in defining *intercultural competence*, it may involve using more than one definition or framework, as many of these can be complementary, and by adapting a variety of definitions and frameworks, a more holistic definition of *intercultural competence* can be developed for a particular context. To illustrate further, the frequently used intercultural knowledge and competence (Association of American Colleges & Universities, n.d.) rubric uses Deardorff's (2006) and Bennett's (1993) definitions of *intercultural competence* to inform the development of the rubric, which must be adapted to each specific course instead of being applied directly).

Prioritize

Prioritize specific elements of academic, intercultural, and personal development within the learning context, in this case, in the specific study abroad program in accordance with its particular participants. What are the specific needs of the participants in regard to academic, intercultural, and personal learning? What are the most significant desired changes in each learner in the program? For example, intercultural competence is often a stated goal in study abroad programs. However, this goal is too broad and complex to address and assess as a whole, and furthermore, it is not realistic to achieve in the parameters of a short-term study abroad program. Therefore, it is helpful to prioritize specific elements of intercultural competence by asking learners what key elements they feel should be emphasized in the program based on their needs and what changes are desired by the learner from the learner's perspective as well as from the instructor's perspective. Usually two or three intercultural elements are sufficient and manageable to assess, especially within a short, time-delineated study abroad program. These elements can then be developed into specific measurable learning outcomes statements indicating the desired change.

Align

Align learning outcomes with the goals, learning activities and interventions, and assessment measures. This kind of alignment is central to the overall study abroad program design, known as a backward design approach, which starts with the selection of the goals and outcomes before determining activities and assessments. For example, given that intercultural competence as a goal is too broad to assess, the prioritized elements, such as increased cultural self-awareness or perspective taking or empathy, become key and are aligned with the broader goal of intercultural competence development. In turn, specific learning activities or experiences can be mapped to these more specific learning outcomes to ensure not only a close fit but also that these outcomes are actually supported through intentional activities. Alignment also needs to occur through collecting evidence that fits the stated outcomes (see the next section, "Identify Evidence," for further explanation). If generic intercultural competence assessment measures most closely aligned with collecting the evidence (there are more than 140 ICC instruments; see Fantini, 2009), it is crucial to understand exactly what the tool measures and how closely it aligns with the learning outcomes. If there is little to no alignment between the stated outcomes and the purpose of the measurement tool, then the evidence collected will be invalid, no matter how valid and reliable the tool.

Identify Evidence

Identify direct and indirect evidence of changes in the learner to indicate that the stated learning outcomes have been achieved to some degree. Instead of seeking particular assessment measures to use, it is more helpful to think about what kinds of direct and indirect evidence can be collected to indicate that learners are making progress toward achieving the stated learning outcomes in the study abroad program. This evidence can be collected in the following ways.

Direct Evidence of Learning

This is often defined as evidence of actual student learning collected during the learning experience, meaning the evidence collected regularly, even daily, throughout the study abroad experience and usually based on learning assignments and formal learning activities in the classroom. Examples of direct evidence can include course assignments, reflections throughout the experience, projects, tests, observations of interactions (from instructors, host families), peer assessments, and so on.

Indirect Evidence of Learning

This involves perceptions of student learning with evidence being collected often outside the learning experience, such as through pre- and postmeasures. Indirect evidence can also be collected through interviews and focus groups.

It is important to use direct and indirect evidence for a more complete picture of the learning that has occurred. Such evidence is ideally collected through multiple means and should involve multiple perspectives such as peer assessments and observations by others. This multimeasure, multiperspective approach to study abroad outcomes assessment is essential not only in providing a more complete picture of the changes that occur but also in more adequately addressing the complexities of academic, intercultural, and personal growth for learners in this kind of experience. With any evidence collected, it becomes important to analyze the information, ideally from more than one perspective as there can be different interpretations, identifying emerging common themes and issues.

In addition to collecting direct and indirect evidence of the achievement of stated learning outcomes, faculty and learners may also want to consider and explore evidence of unintended and unstated outcomes as part of the overall learning experience. This often occurs through careful analysis of reflections submitted throughout the study abroad experience.

Use

Use the collected information for learner improvement. Use of assessment information (data) is crucial and relates directly to the purpose of assessment. Why was the assessment undertaken? How will the collected information be used, especially for learner feedback? Will this information be meaningful to the learner? How will this benefit the learner? In assessing elements of intercultural competence, for example, it is crucial to provide feedback to the learner to further develop the learner's intercultural competence. For instance, what are the areas of intercultural strength? Which areas are growth areas, and what are some ways to continue to grow in those areas? Given the changing paradigm of outcomes assessment, providing such feedback directly to the learners is essential for their continued learning. Too often, the use of outcomes assessment results is overlooked. If outcomes assessment results are not used, then it is inefficient to undertake assessment efforts. Having a plan to use the assessment results from the outset is key to ensuring use.

Using Learning Outcomes Assessment for Program Evaluation

To reiterate a point made earlier in this chapter, outcomes assessment is a different process and purpose from program evaluation. Often, administrators will use satisfaction surveys when evaluating programming, which have obvious limits. At other times, pre- and postmeasures are used inadvisably to evaluate the effectiveness of a program, often using measures not even aligned with the specific goals and outcomes of the program itself. In the end, however, outcomes assessment, as a more direct measure of student learning, can also be used for program improvement by quantifying the qualitative. This means that outcomes assessment can be reviewed in the aggregate to report percentages of students who achieve specific learning outcomes. Mapping these percentages can indicate areas program administrators need to improve in terms of learning interventions such as with content or delivery, for example. These percentages can be communicated to a variety of stakeholders, including parents and partners, as well as institutional leadership.

Beyond aggregating learner outcomes to identify areas for program improvement, other aspects of program evaluation need to be taken into consideration, such as an evaluation of the program logistics, partner and host relationship, overall support and care of students in the program, quality of teaching, quality of the facilities, and so on. In the end, program evaluation can benefit from external input from experts well versed in the intricacies of designing and implementing a short-term study abroad program.

Summary

Beginning with the end in mind is a classic adage that works quite well in designing an outcomes-based study abroad program. This chapter discusses the necessity of starting at the end, namely, starting with the goals and aligned outcomes in the three key dimensions of a study abroad program—academic, intercultural, and personal growth—and building a program based on outcomes that are developed in consultation with learners to ensure relevancy. Because there is no one-size-fits-all approach for designing and assessing an outcomes-based study abroad program, this chapter includes several series of questions, as well as five principles that faculty can use to guide the design of their programs. In the end, learners are central to the bigger question, Why study abroad? Thoughtful engagement in outcomes-based learning can result in a meaningful learning experience for all involved.

Note

1. There are many different definitions and terms used to describe *intercultural competence*. The first research-based definition and framework of *intercultural competence* is from Deardorff (2006, n.d.).

References

Anderson, L., & Krathwohl, D. (Eds.). (2001). *A taxonomy for learning, teaching, and assessing: A revision of Bloom's taxonomy of educational objectives.* New York, NY: Longman.

Association of American Colleges & Universities. (n.d.). AAC&U VALUE rubric for intercultural competence. Retrieved from www.aacu.org/value/rubrics/intercultural-knowledge

Baxter-Magolda, M., Creamer, E., & Meszaros, P. (Eds.). (2010). *Development and assessment of self-authorship: Exploring the concept across cultures.* Sterling, VA: Stylus.

Beaven, A. & Borghetti, C. (2015). *IEREST: Intercultural education resources for Erasmus students and their teachers.* Primorska, Slovenia: University of Primorska.

Bennett, M. J. (1993). Towards ethnorelativism: A developmental model of intercultural sensitivity. In R. Paige (Ed.), *Education for the intercultural experience* (2nd ed., pp. 21–71). Yarmouth, ME: Intercultural Press.

Berardo, K., & Deardorff, D. K. (2012). *Building cultural competence: Innovative activities and models.* Sterling, VA: Stylus.

Bloom, B. (1956). *Taxonomy of education objectives: Handbook 1: The cognitive domain.* New York, NY: David McKay.

Council of Europe. (2015). *TASKs for democracy: 60 activities to learn and assess transversal attitudes, skills, and knowledge.* Strasbourg, France: Author.

Deardorff, D. K. (2006). The identification and assessment of intercultural competence as a student outcome of internationalization at institutions of higher education in the United States. *Journal of Studies in International Education, 10,* 241–266.

Deardorff, D. K. (2015a). A 21st century imperative: Integrating intercultural competence in Tuning. *Tuning Journal for Higher Education, 3,* 137–147.

Deardorff, D. K. (2015b). *Demystifying outcomes assessment for international educators: A practical approach.* Sterling, VA: Stylus.

Deardorff, D. K. (2015c, September). *Exploring intercultural competence as a key competence in the 21st century.* Presentation at DARE+. University of Groningen, The Netherlands.

Deardorff, D. K. (n.d.). *Theory reflections: Intercultural competence framework.* Retrieved from www.nafsa.org/_/File/_/theory_connections_intercultural_competence.pdf

Deardorff, D. K., & Arasaratnam-Smith, L. (2017). *Intercultural competence in international higher education.* New York, NY: Routledge.

Driscoll, A., & Wood, S. (2007). *Developing outcomes-based assessment for learner-centered education: A faculty introduction.* Sterling, VA: Stylus.

Fantini, A. (2009). Assessing intercultural competence: Issues and tools. In D. K. Deardorff (Ed.), *The Sage handbook of intercultural competence* (pp. 456–476). Thousand Oaks, CA: Sage.

Goode, M. (2007). The role of faculty study abroad directors: A case study. *Frontiers, 15,* 149–172.

Green, M. (2012). *Measuring and assessing internationalization.* Retrieved from http://www.nafsa.org/_/File/_/downloads/measuring_assessing.pdf

Huba, M. & Freed, J. (2000). *Learner-centered assessment on college campuses: Shifting the focus from teaching to learning.* Boston, MA: Allyn & Bacon.

Knowles, M. (1991). Introduction: The art and science of helping adults learn. In M. Knowles (Ed.), *Andragogy in action: Applying modern principles of adult learning* (pp. 1–21). San Francisco, CA: Jossey-Bass.

Spitzberg, B., & Changnon, G. (2009). Conceptualizing intercultural communication competence. In D. K. Deardorff (Ed.), *The Sage handbook of intercultural competence* (pp. 2–52). Thousand Oaks, CA: Sage.

Stringer, D. M., & Cassiday, P. A. (2009). *52 activities for improving cross-cultural communication.* Yarmouth, ME: Intercultural Press.

5

DESIGNING THE CURRICULUM FOR INTERDISCIPLINARY STUDY ABROAD

Sustainability Studies in Turkey

Bilge Gökhan Çelik, Dale Leavitt, and Michael Scully

On a sunny June day, students and faculty from Roger Williams University (RWU) gathered at Istanbul Bilgi University, situated at the confluence of Alibeyköy and the Kagithane rivers, at the headwaters of the Golden Horn (Haliç). The purpose of the site visit was to initiate the discussion of sustainability issues related to the reclamation of the Haliç, a once highly contaminated urban estuary.

The property where Istanbul Bilgi University currently sits was once the location of a coal-fired electric generating plant, which the government retired in 1983. From 1914 to 1983, it was the primary power station for the city of Istanbul. After sitting idle for 20 years, the property was reconditioned to host the university, which opened in 2007 (Düzgün & Aladag, 2013). Today, the property is called the Santral Istanbul Campus of Bilgi University, which is home to architecture and engineering programs as well as a modern art museum located in the former main power plant.

We would like to acknowledge a number of Roger Williams University and Istanbul Technical University faculty and staff for their leadership and contribution to the development and implementation of the Sustainability Studies in Turkey program, especially their contributions to the initial program proposals and syllabi, parts of which are included in this chapter. A special thanks to Ulker Copur, Lonnie Guralnick, Patrick Charles, Charles Thomas, Loren Byrne, Marybeth MacPhee, Charles Hagenah, Kate Greene, Marcy Farrell, Aslihan Tavil, and many graduate and undergraduate Istanbul Technical University students, guest speakers, lecturers, and site hosts in Istanbul.

Our tour of the Haliç started with a tour of the campus, demonstrating the creativity that can be applied to the repurposing of former state-owned facilities. Here Dale Leavitt began his two-day lecture series about the reclamation efforts of the Haliç as he led a dozen students along the waterfront at the headwaters of the waterway that is 7.5 kilometers long.

We chose to focus on the Haliç because, at its peak, the estuary was one of the most polluted bodies of water in Europe. The causes were many. In the 1950s the waterfront was saturated with 696 industrial plants that engaged in metal smelting and manufacturing consumer electronics and textiles. There were also numerous shipyards, slaughterhouses, and food processing facilities (Coleman, Kanat, & Turkdogan, 2009). Because the city was lacking in sanitation and runoff standards, the Golden Horn became an easy receptacle for industrial waste. In addition to the industrial waste, in the 1980s Istanbul discharged an estimated 100,000 cubic meters of raw sewage daily into the Haliç. Compounding the problem was the fact that the Galata Bridge, installed initially as a floating bridge in 1912, acted as a plug bottling up the natural flow of the Haliç, further pooling the industrial and human effluent in the estuary. It did not take long for the pollution to affect the city and its inhabitants; many living along or near the Haliç suffered from diseases related to environmental contamination (Coleman et al., 2009).

In 1984 the Istanbul Water and Sewage Administration, formed three years earlier, began reclamation efforts targeting the Haliç. This included purchasing or expropriating 620 factories and 1,200 shops situated along the estuary, which were relocated to a new industrial site 15 kilometers away. The agency cleared the land, removing illegal settlements, buildings, and factories, replacing them with parklands. It repurposed some of the buildings, with the Istanbul Bilgi University as an example of that effort, and the Galata Bridge was altered to allow the natural flushing of water and waste to evacuate the estuary (Coleman et al., 2009).

Today, 35 species of fish—including a seahorse that was once thought to be extinct—now call the Haliç home (Coleman et al., 2009). The shoreline is a thriving green space filled with parks and other recreational facilities, and a commuter ferry service remains active up and down the riverway. The Haliç reclaimed its role as the Golden Horn of Istanbul, whose value lies in the success of reversing years of environmental insult to make it a place of attraction and activity.

During our walking classroom with Leavitt, the students not only had an opportunity to experience Turkish efforts to preserve historic architecture and muse over the engineering efforts to dredge the riverway, but also were stunned to hear about the former industrial profile of the Haliç, which stood in stark contrast to the parklands and waterways they were now visiting.

Leavitt's educational message was clear: It is entirely possible to transform even the most polluted of spaces, reclaiming them and restoring them to their once natural beauty. Furthermore, that transformation does not have to be at the expense of sacrificing the architecture, engineering, industry, culture, and other valuable aspects of a country and a society.

This is just one of the many lessons presented during the 3-week Turkey program. The program is directed by 3 RWU faculty members and hosts up to 12 students from a broad array of academic majors, such as architecture, business, communication, construction management, engineering, journalism, and marine sciences. The disciplines of the faculty leaders are likewise diverse, representing construction management, journalism, and marine sciences.

So how did we get here?

In this chapter, we discuss the development of a study abroad program offered at RWU, Sustainability Studies in Turkey. The details of the program rationale, multidiscipline experience, site selection process, syllabus and content development, target audience and student admissions process, program learning outcomes, and the overall logistics are some of the areas we explore in further detail in this chapter.

Developing a study abroad program is quite different from developing traditional college courses. Making a study abroad program an interdisciplinary one is even more intimidating. We believe a study abroad program is enhanced by an interdisciplinary approach combining a diverse group of faculty as well as students who bring in a variety of disciplinary perspectives that add to the overall experience. Although many topics offer intersection opportunities from one discipline to another, we concluded that the issue of sustainability offered the maximum potential toward accomplishing the following goals:

- immerse students in the history of an international culture,
- talk about sustainability issues in a dense urban environment,
- demonstrate an appreciation for issues related to the natural sciences in a dense urban ecosystem,
- explore the influence the building industry has over the environment, and
- discuss communication issues related to sustainability in an emerging global media market.

Program Rationale

While planning our faculty-led study abroad program, we were fortunate to have an existing relationship with our Turkish partners from Istanbul Technical University (ITU) through a previous Fulbright grant, followed by a pilot study abroad program that enables RWU to build capacity for study abroad programs in Turkey. Building on the coordinated efforts of Turkish and RWU faculty and administrators, we wanted to use our relationship with ITU to not only address some of our logistical concerns but also build a lasting relationship between American and Turkish students. We believed that the long-term impact of this program could easily include more tolerance, empathy, and sincerity between two nations so far from each other. This long-term ideal contributed to the selection of sustainability as the center of attention in the development of the program, which we understood from a United Nations' statement to be meeting "the needs of present without compromising the ability of future generations to meet their own needs" (UN Documents, 1987, p. 43).

Given what we knew about sustainability studies from the professional literature, and given our own points of view from our individual disciplines (marine sciences, journalism, and construction management), with support from a number of other faculty at RWU and ITU, we decided to offer the interdisciplinary program. Fortunately, it was not too difficult to find a home for this program as RWU requires all undergraduate students to take a Core Interdisciplinary Senior Seminar, which unites studies in the liberal arts and sciences; integrates knowledge; and involves sophisticated analysis, synthesis, and defense of original ideas. Consequently, we were able to design our program to provide students with opportunities to fulfill their core requirement while traveling abroad to consider themes and issues relating to sustainability in the context of Turkey, a fascinating nation bridging two continents: Europe and Asia.

Site Selection

Turkey is one of the rare locations where American students can experience a variety of intriguing contrasts between modern and traditional, urban and rural, and twenty-first-century technology and ancient crafts. The Sustainability Studies in Turkey program focuses on issues from a variety of points of views including, but not limited to,

- built environment (architecture, urban planning, construction management);
- natural environment (marine science, biology); and
- politics, people, culture, and communication (political science, history, anthropology, sociology, journalism, communication, and media studies).

A major focus of the program is how to effectively communicate sustainability challenges and opportunities to a diverse audience of majors. Given the breadth of the disciplines represented by our participating faculty and the area's intersection of urbanization and ecology, our selection of Istanbul and the greater Bosphorus area as a platform for the study of sustainability issues was an easy decision. Although many other locations may have fit the bill, the history and current state of Istanbul provide an array of intriguing sites that can be used as specific examples of adapting a long-term history to a modern solution (or failure).

Istanbul is a fitting site for sustainability discussions. Its origins date from the third century BCE, and the peoples who populated this city participated heavily in the core disciplines that defined Western culture, namely the development of architecture, government, industry, publishing, science, trade, and theology. As for historic value, the Romans lived here, as did the Ottomans; in each case, these societies built atop one other, creating a complex cultural heterogeneity. Searching for examples, the Basilica Cisterns were built by the Byzantines, all but forgotten by the Ottomans, and rediscovered by the modern Turks. The Hippodrome was constructed by the Byzantines, expanded by Constantine the Great, and forgotten by the Ottomans; today it lies under two meters of sediment since being abandoned. Both of these early structures of Constantinople (the Byzantine name for the city) served an important purpose for the city but have evolved into something different. Now mostly tourist attractions, they provide numerous teaching moments as we tour the locations with the students.

Turkey is a country bridging two continents not only geographically but also culturally and politically. It offers a dynamic perspective on how Europe and Asia meld into one another and the impact of this shift on a variety of sustainability efforts in social, economic, and environmental progress. Inspired from the United Nation's definition of *sustainable development* as a focus on the present with an eye on future generations (UN Documents, 1987), Turkey as a program site allows us to illustrate decisions made in the past and how they affect our world today. For example, it provides us with an opportunity to ride the ferry through the Bosphorus to the Black Sea, where a future bridge over the Bosphorus connecting the European side of Istanbul to the Asian side will be constructed. During this walking classroom, students are exposed to a controversial issue in Istanbul, questioning the role the third bridge may play in furthering the development of a forested area to the northwest of the city. Often regarded as the "Lungs of Istanbul," because of the high level of vegetation in the area, many citizens of the region are concerned that the additional expansion will cause an overdevelopment of the area, thereby exceeding the projected carrying capacity of the urban area to support the quality of life envisioned by the existing populace as well as the city planners. Knowledge of this future project's potential provides a strong education opportunity for discussion and illustration of how our actions today have an impact on future generations.

Another reason for selecting Turkey as the learning site for this program was our preexisting relationship with ITU, one of the oldest universities in the world with a wide range of resources. Established in 1773 during the Ottoman Empire, ITU (then called Royal Naval Engineering) had the responsibility to educate shipmasters and shipbuilders. ITU's architecture school was founded in 1847 and has been the main partner of RWU's in the delivery of this program. ITU helps by

- arranging a variety of faculty members and graduate students for guest lectures and guidance during site visits,
- identifying a group of Turkish undergraduate students to attend lectures and site visits with RWU students to have an opportunity to participate in multicultural and interdisciplinary discussions and debates regarding sustainability,
- providing local transportation to some of the sites where public transportation is not the most convenient option,
- providing dorm rooms for RWU students and faculty to stay on campus, and
- providing classroom space when needed by the RWU or ITU faculty to deliver traditional in-class lectures.

In short, Turkey's geopolitical significance as a bridging nation between Europe and Asia; its extensive and unique historic sites; and its proximity to many natural sites such as the Bosphorus, the Golden Horn area, and the Prince Islands, all combined with a strong local academic partner were the overriding factors in choosing Istanbul as the main site for this program.

Interdisciplinary Program Development

As part of our intention to offer this program with an interdisciplinary core, we separated the underlying philosophies of sustainability into the following categories: science and technology, history, human behavior, and aesthetics. Once we identified the interdisciplinary categories, we continued to develop them into a syllabus that was relevant to the city and the program goals. Some of the thoughts underlying each segment that when combined offer a unique interdisciplinary senior seminar experience for students are presented next.

Science and Technology

Our Turkey program has a strong technical and scientific basis, specifically in regard to ecology, the environment, and sustainability issues. The construction management component, a series of lectures at ITU, investigation of the Golden Horn urban estuary remediation, and visits to renewable energy sites demonstrate ancient development of these technologies and contemporary applications. Intertwined with the science are numerous side trips investigating the local culture of Istanbul. For example, the faculty and students spent a full day on the Haliç ferry, traversing the estuary through eight ports of call. At each stop we disembarked, so students were exposed to not only the history of the Haliç and the science of its reclamation but also the characteristics of each urban village we visited. We went exploring for the site of a fifteenth-century synagogue built in Haskoy by displaced Majorcan Jews, walked a large street market in the conservative Muslim neighborhood of Ayvansary, drank Turkish tea at the Pierre Loti Café overlooking panoramic views of the Haliç from the hillside, and stopped at a dockside fish market alongside the Haliç at Karakoy. With each stop, the students interacted with the diverse culture of Istanbul as they walked, talked, and observed the daily life of the city. Throughout the day, we presented the roles of science and technology through the perspective of the part they played in the evolution of modern Istanbul.

History

It is impossible to visit Istanbul without experiencing its history. As previously mentioned, Istanbul and Turkey have layers of archeological sites from diverse cultures and the heritage of major world civilizations such as Hittite; Greek; Hellenistic; Roman; Byzantine; Ottoman; and the traditional, vernacular environments that are representations of traditional lifestyles. The association between vernacular architecture and modern sustainability efforts offers an alternative way of integrating science, technology, and design with history. The students are provided a rare opportunity to explore the sustainable traces of these cultures throughout Istanbul's 2,500-year history. Site visits focus on the history of Istanbul and Anatolia including museums, but more important, highly preserved sites such as Hagia Sophia, the Blue Mosque, the Basilica Cistern, Grand Bazaar, Spice Bazaar, Galata Tower, and many other sites around the city. The exposure of students to the history of Istanbul includes discussions about its development as a capital city of numerous states and empires throughout time. These developments are discussed in the context of urbanism, culture, and politics to better understand sustainable development and how it relates to our history.

Human Behavior

The program is designed to expose students to significant social-psychological dimensions of public awareness about sustainability. This is accomplished through predeparture seminars as well as activities while abroad. The students spend time exploring municipalities' and universities' initiatives on sustainability, renewable energies, deforestation, environmental health, recycling, behavioral patterns in regard to environmental initiatives, and their positive and negative impacts, perceiving and understanding them in the context of Turkish and global cultures. All of these aspects of sustainable development are instrumental to achieve the learning outcomes of this program. RWU students have opportunities to communicate with Turkish students who join the group for a number of site visits. We find that much of our students' experience is tempered by their discussions with participating ITU students, who share their own perspectives on issues. Many hours over group dinners are spent discussing and contrasting the attitudes and experiences of the RWU students to those of their ITU counterparts. Often the discussions evolve from what they had immediately experienced that day to how culture, science, technology, or communication in the United States contrasts with the same in Turkey, particularly when observed from the perspective of the students. This allows RWU students to explore the local behavior toward sustainability issues while developing a better understanding of the Turkish culture and tradition.

Aesthetics

Representation and investigation of sustainability in an aesthetic manner on location is witnessed in a variety of ways, such as through examples of public art, architecture, and landscape environments. While exploring the Hagia Sophia, the Blue Mosque, and the Roman Cisterns, students are led to consider not only the historical but also the vernacular environment. Visiting such locations where functionality and aesthetics coincide is instrumental in defining *environmental aesthetics*.

For example, we visit the Hagia Sophia, a World Heritage Site that served first as a cathedral, was later converted to a mosque, and is today a primary tourist destination because of its beauty and historical significance. It now serves as a secularized museum. During our visit to the site, the faculty members spoke about the Byzantine architecture as well as Turkey's restoration efforts. Given the size and age of the site, there were ample opportunities for discussions related to architecture, history, theology, aesthetics, and so forth. As students moved through the site, Michael Scully began an impromptu discussion about the rule of thirds, a photography practice, which the students began employing immediately.

Later, as one of the construction management students looked about, he said quite innocently, "I really appreciate all of this old stuff, I really find it interesting, but I don't see how it relates to my major." To this, Scully said, "The staircase you're standing on: is it to spec?" (i.e., does it meet construction specifications?) The student responded by stepping off the stairs to study them and then turned with a look of amazement on his face. "The building specifications for staircases may have been established by a Greek engineer centuries before this building was built," Scully said. That student, and his peers from his major, spent the remainder of the trip evaluating the construction elements of a series of historic buildings with that same critical eye.

Syllabus and Content Development

Syllabus development for this program was accomplished by the collaboration of a number of faculty from RWU as well as the faculty from ITU. To provide the aforementioned interdisciplinary perspective to the students who participate in this abroad program, faculty members from the departments of engineering, anthropology and sociology, communication, marine sciences, biology, construction management, and architecture worked closely in the development of the initial syllabus. To further develop the content, we three faculty members, from construction management (Çelik), communication studies (Scully), and marine sciences (Leavitt), worked together to optimize the syllabus under the main umbrella of Sustainability Studies in Turkey. We also had an opportunity to share the syllabi drafts and itinerary with our liaison, Aslihan Tavil, from the School of Architecture at ITU, who provided feedback on educational outcomes and the feasibility of the syllabus. In the end, with the understanding that the syllabus would continually evolve as a part of a quality improvement plan, we decided to develop this abroad program with a three-credit course that spanned a 14-day itinerary in Istanbul. In addition to the 14 days, students are required to attend three predeparture seminars titled as follows: Turkey: Society, Culture, and History; Dynamic Ecosystems in a Human-Dominated World; and Explaining Sustainability Using Media.

In light of the interdisciplinary approach that focuses on science, history, human behavior, literature, philosophy, and aesthetics, and our areas of expertise, we organized the program content in the following three areas:

sustainable architecture and construction, ecology, and communication. Each component is discussed next.

Sustainable Architecture and Construction

This section of the program explores the ethics and responsibilities of students in response to the evidence of global warming. It also outlines relevant regional and urban planning and architectural design principles for passive and active clean energy generation and for reducing energy use by increasing efficiency in the built environment. This section features lectures, guest speakers, and site visits that focus on the built environment of Istanbul with particular attention to the ongoing and future population increases in Istanbul and Turkey. Field trips led by faculty from RWU and ITU explore local green buildings designed and constructed as a response to sustainability goals of the federal and local Turkish government agencies.

Buildings and associated construction operations dominate the ecological footprints in most countries. Sustainability in the built environment must be addressed on a life-cycle basis from the origins of the building materials, through the construction process, ending with the eventual disposal of the building materials as the project is decommissioned. Topics in this section of the program include life-cycle costing, green technologies, sustainability as a value-engineering exercise, green site logistics, educating the sustainable workforce, sustainable construction and public relations, and the history and application of leadership in energy and environmental design. These issues are examined using local case studies, such as observation of local industrial or construction projects (historic and contemporary examples) and how these cases address and assess sustainability in the built environment (creation, operation, disposal), including successful as well as objectionable examples.

As part of this, Çelik takes the students to the newly constructed Zorlu Center, a high-end multiuse complex with shopping and living accommodations located in the Zincirlikuyu area of the European side of Istanbul. Built in 2013, the Zorlu Center features four towers that ring around a central courtyard, which some consider to be a model for sustainable architecture. The students observe the construction and architectural components of the center, and Çelik points out various materials and design elements used to meet sustainability standards. As students analyze and discuss difficult optimization problems in sustainability of the built urban environments, Çelik also describes local urban planners' and architects' reactions to the Zorlu project because of its exaggerated footprint.

Ecology

Humans interact with their environments in many complex and intimate ways, whereas ecosystems provide humans with a wide range of services that benefit human well-being. A major challenge for achieving a more sustainable biosphere is investigating how human sociocultural variables and anthropogenic environmental changes (e.g., urbanization, pollution, biodiversity loss) affect ecosystem services and then developing management and design approaches to mitigate negative outcomes and increase positive ones. In this section of the program, the unique socioecological systems of Turkey are examined as case studies for thinking about relationships among sociocultural and ecological variables. Topics include consumerism and resource use, water and waste management, biodiversity conservation, urban ecosystem services, and ecotourism. As we have indicated, a variety of case studies and locales in Istanbul allow in-depth observation and discussions on how the natural environment can coexist with the built environment, especially when compounded by a projected population of 14 million people in the near future. Touring the remediation of the Golden Horn, visiting the construction site of the controversial third bridge over the Bosphorus, walking the expanse of a new park and recreational area on the Asian side of the Bosphorous that was generated entirely by land reclamation, considering the ancient Roman aqueducts bringing freshwater to the city and the modern equivalent of those engineered systems, and engaging many other situations provide an unlimited opportunity for demonstrating old and new ways of dealing with the urban ecosystem.

Communication

Public awareness is a vital component of sustainability. To foster public awareness, students use social media and the key components of digital communication to explain complex sustainability initiatives for the mass media market. Specifically, they learn to create blogs; write for a digital audience; shoot and edit still photographs; and, at times, make videos. Finally, students apply these digital skills with an emphasis on public awareness of sustainability issues.

To better understand issues of public awareness, the students visit the Istanbul Metropolitan Planning and Urban Design Center to hear about urban development and sustainability issues. City officials explain that a key component necessary for their recycling efforts was a public service campaign designed to explain how and why citizens needed to sort their recyclables. Without these instructions, Istanbul citizens were unsure how to navigate the city's recycling program. On the issue of sustainability, during conversations with our students, Istanbul city officials noted that they needed help getting their message out explaining recycling procedures to city dwellers, a point that further established the value of communication as a tool for sustainability.

After every site visit, the students are required to write about their observations and experiences in a travel blog of their own design. The purpose is to get them thinking about how writing and photography can help build a visual narrative as they move through their studies in Istanbul. Along the way, we usually run into some technical problems, which only further enhance their understanding of global telephony issues.

Target Audience and Selection Process

When determining which students would be the best candidates to participate in this program, we considered a few criteria that we believe have a direct correlation with the successful completion of any structured study abroad program: students' major of study, academic class level and social maturity, interest in sustainability, and academic success.

Major of Study

We do not limit the applications for this program to a specific major of study. As we previously mentioned, the program was designed to be an interdisciplinary seminar, so our goal is to create a group from as many disciplines as possible. To accomplish this, we contact faculty members from various disciplines at RWU and ask them for their help to promote the program. Having students from diverse academic disciplines allows us to focus on the interdisciplinary nature of the topics.

Academic Class Level and Social Maturity

We focus on accepting students who are at least juniors. We prefer higher class levels because the program content is specifically designed to address a level of academic maturity with an interdisciplinary and global perspective.

One of the most important criterion in the selection of students for our program is their social maturity level. Regardless of the topic of discussion, any study abroad, short or long term, demands a certain level of social maturity for a student to be successful in demonstrating the learning outcomes. In addition to students' success with the course work, maturity helps students get along with their classmates, and in our situation, with their Turkish counterparts. This is critical to ensure a level of discipline in the program that ultimately increases the satisfaction level of the students and the faculty. The challenge is how to measure the level of maturity. Thus far, we have accomplished this by meeting face-to-face with all the applicants for our program. We believe that meeting in a group setting is even more revealing of a student's social maturity level. A group meeting such as an information session allows us to observe the interactions among the students and their level of respect for authority and peers.

We did have one incident worthy of note. One evening in Istanbul, many of the students went out for a late night in the city. The next morning, two of the students failed to turn up for our morning class session, and the faculty members agreed that we needed to take action immediately, so we sent a student back to the dorm room to retrieve the missing students. Upon finally arriving for class, the tardy students explained that they had been out until 6:00 a.m. and were exhausted. We told the students they needed to modify their behavior immediately or they would be sent home on the next flight. We also insisted that they spend the remainder of the day with the class and use their next free day to make up the site visit they missed. We recognized that if we allowed some students to indulge in such behavior, others might follow. We took measures early to establish a standard for our expectations.

Interest in Sustainability

It is advantageous for a student applicant to have an interest, or a minor, or at least have taken one course in the sustainability studies program. Although this is not a prerequisite, it is our preference. For students who seek to make their program application stronger, we frequently recommend that they first take an introductory sustainability course.

Academic Success

Condensing a full semester-long senior seminar into a 14-day study abroad program is a formidable undertaking for instructors and students. Even with preliminary meetings before departure and a time allowance for the completion of the final project on their return to the campus, the work load is heavy and time consuming. For these reasons we decided not to accept applications from those students whose grade point average was below 2.5 out of 4.0. Although the grade point average alone is not an indicator of students' academic success, it is one of the ways to ensure we did not place students who were already struggling into a rigorous academic situation abroad.

Program Learning Outcomes

We developed the program learning outcomes parallel with the content and the overall goals of the program. By the end of the program, we expected the students to be able to do the following:

1. Describe relationships between sociocultural and environmental variables with a focus on ecosystem services.
2. Recognize how personal decisions and activities have direct and indirect impacts on ecosystems, biodiversity, and ecosystem services on local and global scales.
3. Explore how actual clean energy sources can be integrated into buildings.
4. Identify technical design elements that could be incorporated into contemporary buildings on an international basis.
5. Define *life-cycle costing* and its application in sustainable building operations.
6. Discuss basic environmental toxicology and management principles to demonstrate the resiliency of the marine environment and the measures to correct environmental damages in transitional ecosystems.
7. Analyze and differentiate sustainability indicators, rating systems, codes, and standards.
8. Explain the purpose of digital media as a tool for communicating sustainability issues to a mass market.

Outcomes 1 through 5 are lower level outcomes requiring students to describe, recognize, explore, and explain a variety of issues in sustainability. We focused on higher level outcomes when designing outcomes 6, 7, and 8, which require students to be able to discuss, analyze, and differentiate a variety of sustainability topics. Having two levels of outcomes allows us to lift a diverse group of students to a fair level of knowledge while still offering challenges to others.

To attain the program learning outcomes, we designed an itinerary that includes predeparture seminars and on-site lectures and site visits.

Student Assessment of Program Learning Outcomes

Our program uses a number of direct and indirect assessment methodologies to determine the effectiveness of teaching quality and the overall program design. Each assessment focuses on a specific program learning outcome to make sure that every outcome has at least one direct and one indirect assessment.

Indirect assessment includes exit interviews with the group during which students are asked a number of questions regarding the course content and topics, site visits, length of the program, instruction quality, and how they evaluate themselves on attaining the learning outcomes.

We use a number of direct assessments, including group discussions, participation, daily blogs, and final program essays. For example, students are required to submit their daily blogs for our review at specific intervals, and they receive feedback from a different faculty member each time they submit their work. This allows students to reflect on what they learned, communicate their learning in a digital format, and receive feedback from faculty on a regular basis. Student reflections and feedback help us as instructors to grasp a daily understanding of student learning and to adjust future activities and discussions accordingly.

Unique Logistical Challenges

A study abroad program can be more challenging than a traditional on-site university course, not only because of its condensed schedule but also because of increased coordination requirements, along with cultural, logistical, and linguistic challenges.

Turkey is a country with a rich culture, and some of the norms may be unfamiliar to American students. It is critically important for instructors and students to develop an awareness of the cultural practices of the country to ensure appropriate respect for the local culture. Although we provide a predeparture discussion of cultural differences, it is important for instructors and students to be continuously aware of prevailing attitudes of local neighborhoods and adopt appropriate behaviors.

Istanbul is a cosmopolitan city with a significant percentage of Muslims, some of whom are conservative in their beliefs. We coach students on appropriate behaviors and cultural norms, particularly because we visit a number of significant religious sites. We are careful to describe the cultural behaviors that are expected, including removing shoes and dressing appropriately when visiting religious sites. We usually have a positive response to our group as we move through the Istanbul culture, with the exception of one small incident when without warning we came upon a street market in a conservative area of the city. Because we were not anticipating this visit, some of our students were not dressed appropriately, and an elderly citizen expressed her disapproval of the clothing one of our students was wearing. We were able to quietly and quickly depart from the area thereby defusing a potentially unpleasant situation.

When traveling in a foreign country with a group of students, an array of challenges and logistical problems have to be solved, not the least of which is the language barrier. Turkish is a difficult language to learn and use; therefore, it is essential for one of the instructors to be a native speaker. Navigating the city, finding restaurants, reconciling minor problems such as missing clothing, locating adequate medical attention, and a myriad of other issues that require someone proficient in the Turkish language continually arise. It is inconceivable that our travels in Istanbul and surrounding locations would be as successful without the assistance of the native Turkish-speaking faculty members (Çelik and our ITU liaison, Tavil). An alternative would be to hire a native guide proficient in English to stay with the group throughout the program. Although this is not as cost effective as having an on-staff translator, we do use this strategy for some aspects of the program.

Although it is relatively easy and inexpensive to contract with local private transportation for movement around Istanbul, the students would miss opportunities to integrate into the local culture if they were isolated from the normal activities in the city. We find that using regular mass transit venues adds an important dimension to the students' experiences in the city. Istanbul has a variety of public transportation vehicles, from taxis and small private buses to the funicular, trains, and ferries that cover the entire expanse of the city and its surrounding region. Whenever possible (and it is challenging at times to interpret transport patterns and schedules), we use public vehicles to move our students around the city. This is especially effective during the days spent discussing the restoration of the Haliç, where we use the ferry to tour the eight stops along the bounds of the urban estuary. Students not only get to hear and discuss details of the restoration process en route but also are able to view the estuary and the local citizens using the body of water firsthand.

The Takeaway

The best of all education experiences are those that have a lasting influence over the students. It took a few years, but one of the former construction management students wrote the following e-mail to Scully:

> Just wanted to say thank you for those photography tips during our Turkey trip. Even though I'm in construction, I find myself thinking about things like "break the picture into 3s with a top, middle and bottom." It allows me to use photos I take for job progress for marketing purposes as well.

The student is referring to the rule of thirds concept Scully discussed during the site visit to the Hagia Sophia. Photography—or even history, the arts, theology, or marine sciences—would not have been one of the subjects the construction management student would have found his way to naturally without the influences of an interdisciplinary curriculum.

Interdisciplinary study abroad provides excellent opportunities to expose students to content that is impossible to replicate in a traditional teaching and learning setting. Sustainability Studies in Turkey is able to offer students an opportunity to interact with a foreign culture and a variety of disciplines by using the global and interdisciplinary nature of a topic such as sustainability. As we cover each topic related to construction, ecology, and communication, we have the opportunity to observe students from two different countries because ITU undergraduates are invited to join our classes through our partnership with their institution and from a variety of disciplines and collaborate with one another as they move from one site to another. We watch our students observe, inquire, critique, discuss, convince, and compromise in an environment that is impossible to simulate at our university.

We learned valuable lessons along the way, which are discussed in this chapter. In a world that many consider to be less tolerant and more dangerous, it is critical to design and implement opportunities for our students to study abroad. Establishing the most appropriate site, well thought-out and relevant student learning outcomes, a clear set of admissions criteria, effective teaching events, authentic assessment, and a feedback loop are all important elements of a successful study abroad program.

References

Coleman, H. M., Kanat, G., & Turkdogan, F. I. A. (2009). Restoration of the Golden Horn Estuary (Halic). *Water Research, 43*, 4989–5003.

Düzgün, H., & Aladag, H. (2013). How sustainable are industrial buildings? A study in Golden Horn District. *International Journal of Architectural Research, 7*, 330–340.

UN Documents. (1987). *Our common future, Chapter 2: Towards sustainable development.* Retrieved from www.un-documents.net/ocf-02.htm

6

DESIGNING THE CURRICULUM FOR FIELD STUDY ABROAD

Marine Biology in Panama and Tropical Ecology in Belize

Paul Webb and Brian Wysor

A s seen throughout this volume, short-term study abroad programs provide unique opportunities for student learning and development, particularly for students who may not have the ability to participate in a semester-long program because of time, financial, or curricular constraints. Often, study abroad programs are framed in terms of experiencing a new culture, but in the natural sciences, exposure to ecosystems and biological processes that are not accessible near the home campus are of equal or greater value. Those unique habitats can be used in field-based programs, giving students the benefit of direct rather than remote exposure (Taraban, McKenney, Peffley, & Applegarth, 2004). Field experiences are not just limited to the natural sciences, however, as many disciplines such as anthropology, archaeology and geography are similarly enhanced by in situ experiences. Additionally, many cultures are intimately linked to their natural surroundings, making field study relevant to courses in almost any discipline.

Two Faculty-Led, Field-Intensive Study Abroad Programs

This chapter discusses the development and implementation of two field-intensive, short-term study abroad programs that fulfill a requirement for bachelor's degrees in biology and marine biology at Roger Williams University (RWU). Both programs include 300-level courses, each cotaught by two instructors, which explore evolutionary biology, tropical biodiversity, and Central American culture and history in disturbed and pristine environments of Panama and Belize. These faculty-led programs are intended for advanced biology and marine biology majors who have a foundation in biology but who may have little experience with tropical ecosystems.

Program 1: Neotropical Marine Biology in Panama

This field-based program, led by Brian Wysor, is offered in Panama and is designed around the emergence of the Isthmus of Panama as a significant geological event that shaped the evolution of diverse organismal groups observable from sites along Caribbean and Pacific Panama shorelines. At the Caribbean field site, students and instructors are immersed in an indigenous Guna Yala community, which provides a meaningful cultural landscape for exploring the social and ecological impacts of contemporary issues like global climate change. On the Pacific coast, access to Coiba National Park, a World Heritage Site, and the proximity to the nearshore continental shelf provide unparalleled opportunities to contextualize discussions of fisheries and marine conservation policy and practice. The program also takes advantage of the presence of the Panama Canal to explore the ramifications of human disturbances (i.e., biological invasions) to natural ecosystems.

Program 2: Tropical Ecology in Belize

This field-based program, led by Paul Webb and offered in Belize, serves as an introduction to tropical ecosystems and as a survey of tropical biodiversity and conservation, with roughly equal focus on rainforest ecology in western Belize and coral reef ecology along the coast. Belizean culture and history are integrated into the program, which includes visits to Mayan historical sites.

   The rationale for both of these faculty-led study abroad programs is to immerse students in the bountiful diversity of nature in the tropics to stimulate critical examination of basic patterns of evolution and ecology while reconciling that experience with other important social, cultural, and historical contexts. The combination of the immersive field experience in foreign habitats empowers students to be active learners who recognize themselves as members of a dynamic learning community (Boyle et al., 2007; Fuller, 2006).

Country Choices for Our Field Study Programs

In addition to choosing locations based on their ecological offerings, site selection is a function of several factors including prior research experience, ease of travel across multiple ecosystem landscapes in a short amount of time, access to appropriate facilities (e.g., laboratory space, boats) for accessing diverse ecosystems, cultural opportunities, student safety, and the strategic use of geography as a program theme.

Neotropical Marine Biology Program

The program was developed to take advantage of the unique geography that has so prominently influenced evolutionary theory. The well-resolved geologic and oceanographic histories of the region provide a backdrop for testing evolutionary theory in terrestrial and marine habitats. Furthermore, the region plays host to researchers and educators from all over the world who tap infrastructures for research and teaching through a variety of institutions, including the Smithsonian Tropical Research Institute, national universities, and private laboratories. The availability of infrastructural resources for teaching was essential to the development of this program, and this was facilitated by Wysor's decade-long experience working in Panama as well as a short, program-specific exploratory site visit before the first class was offered. As described next, established collaborations with professors at local institutes proved essential as well.

In addition to theoretical and infrastructural justifications, the short distance between highly contrasting yet comparable environments in the Pacific and the Caribbean offers a unique perspective to study biodiversity. For example, coral reef communities in the Caribbean consist primarily of reef-building corals, whereas Pacific reefs are rich with non-reef-building corals. Similarly, mangrove diversity and community composition differ by virtue of different tidal patterns along both coasts. Furthermore, unique climate conditions and ecological communities exist in each ocean, such as beds of calcified red algae in the Pacific and seagrass communities in the Caribbean. The significance of diverse landscapes becomes even more relevant following a visit to the Panama Canal, where threats to marine biodiversity are manifested in biofouled ships transiting an aquatic corridor that connects marine habitats otherwise separated for the past three million years. In total, the stark environmental differences, whether framed in Atlantic-Pacific comparisons or temperate-tropical comparisons, make for a compelling exploration of marine biodiversity, the evolutionary and ecological explanations for such high biodiversity, and the real and tangible threats to that biodiversity.

Although this marine biology program may be an integral component of some students' marine biology major, it is secondarily a program that emphasizes global values through exposure to Panamanian culture and history, which is accomplished in two ways. First, this program includes two students (out of 12 total) from the natural science programs at the University of Panama, and second, the Caribbean site is a small village in the autonomously governed Guna Yala region.

Panamanian students provide cultural ground truthing, local knowledge, and a reality check on language and communication skills for the RWU students who would otherwise tour a foreign country in an American bubble. When we polled the class about the inclusion of Panamanian participants, RWU students universally affirmed that the cultural experience would be diminished in their absence and, in fact, many RWU students remain in contact with their Panamanian colleagues to this day.

We work with colleagues at the University of Panama to identify Panamanian students with a genuine interest in marine biology. Panamanian participants are not required to be fluent in English; however, because they are commonly assigned primary literature in English as part of their science courses, they generally are well prepared for the demands of the program. In our experience, imperfect fluency actually facilitates a level of discomfort that can make unilingual U.S. students acutely aware of the value of multilingualism and the challenges that foreign students carry with them when they study at RWU. In several cases, Panamanian students who participated in this program also later participated in research-intensive training opportunities led by Wysor or his research collaborators at the Smithsonian Tropical Research Institute, and in one case, a Panamanian student later spent a semester conducting research with Wysor at RWU. Such collaborative opportunities can help U.S. faculty to meet broader impact goals for federally funded grants, such as those awarded by the National Science Foundation.

The other way that site selection is integral to the cultural awareness goals of this unique program is through the practice of integrating program participants in a local Guna Yala community of about 1,000 people. Participants stay in thatched-roof accommodations similar to the homes of the locals, and traditionally prepared meals are provided. Our students have been welcomed formally to the community during town meetings where they have the opportunity to speak briefly about their experiences in Panama, sometimes through trilingual translation (English to Spanish, Spanish to Guna). We have also had the very good fortune to be invited to a traditional coming-of-age ceremony and to use the local elementary school for delivering lectures. The local community is also invited to participate (with crude translation, as necessary) in evening program lectures that are facilitated by computer projection onto a bedsheet set up in the hotel's restaurant patio. Although accommodations with the Guna Yala are isolated to one end of the half-mile-long island, the small size of the island and welcoming atmosphere of the community offer program participants, including Panamanian students, vivid exposure to the Guna Yala people and culture.

Tropical Ecology Program

This program has run continuously since the 1980s, involving 18 students per offering. For the first two decades the program was conducted in Jamaica, at the Hofstra University Marine Laboratory, but in the early years of the twenty-first century, the program was relocated because of concerns for student safety and the declining quality of the Jamaican reefs. Belize was ultimately chosen for several reasons. First, the Belize Barrier Reef Reserve System is a World Heritage Site, and the good health of the reefs and numerous options for accommodations, from tourist resorts to research stations, provide easy access to reef communities. Second, Belize has significant rainforest cover, allowing us to examine tropical rainforest ecology. Third, significant historical, ethnic, and cultural diversity can be experienced by visiting western Belize, where people are largely of Mayan descent and where many Mayan archaeological sites are located, and the coastal town of Dangriga, which is the hub of the Garifuna culture.

Length of Program and Credits Earned

Both of our programs are offered in alternate years during our university's January break, allocating about 10 days abroad. The Tropical Ecology Program is offered as a 3-credit course, whereas students receive 4 credits for Neotropical Marine Biology, which is consistent with a lecture-plus-lab class. According to U.S. Department of Education (2011) guidelines, a 3-credit course requires 112.5 contact hours, and a 4-credit course requires 150 contact hours, including student engagement activities outside class (i.e., assigned reading, journaling, portfolio preparation). Tropical Ecology meets these hours primarily through the time spent in Belize, so other than a few predeparture organizational meetings, there is little additional program time on campus. In the Panama program, formal meetings over the 4 days preceding departure, coupled with several organizational meetings during the fall semester that include a swimming test, an invited guest lecture, and posttravel activities, and workshops designed to contextualize in-country experiences into a digital portfolio account for about 40% of program activities.

Student Selection Criteria

Both of our study abroad programs consist of upper-level biology classes that count as electives in the biology and marine biology majors and therefore target upper-level biology and marine biology students. There is a prerequisite of at least one completed biology course (or consent of the instructors) for both programs. Preference is given to senior students, followed by juniors, and then sophomores as space allows. Preference is also given to majors over students using the program to satisfy a minor or an elective credit in another major. Additionally, a student's academic record is considered, with roster spots often going to students with higher grade point averages and demonstrated academic ability. Once the tentative roster is created, the judicial record of each student is examined for offenses that could undermine the sanctity of the program, such as drug or alcohol abuse, violence, cheating, or indications of prejudice. The list of candidate participants is then circulated among departmental faculty to solicit recommendations or concerns before being finalized. The Panama program also requires a swimming proficiency test, administered by program instructors, in which students must demonstrate the ability to swim 200 meters without stopping and tread water for 10 minutes, which is the equivalent of the swim test for open-water scuba-diving certification.

The Belize program allows a maximum of 18 students accompanied by two instructors, although we have run the program with as few as 14 students. We arrived at this number through a combination of logistical and management limitations. Two faculty can supervise 18 students relatively easily for most terrestrial work, although additional supervision with local guides is used for in-water activities. Furthermore, 20 people are just enough to fit in a single boat for snorkeling or a small bus for transportation without the need for and expense of additional vehicles.

The Panama program allows a maximum of 10 RWU students in addition to 2 University of Panama undergraduates who are invited to participate in all in-country portions of the program. The 12-student cap for the Panama program was established to maximize in-water oversight by program instructors who are each responsible for 3 pairs of students in sometimes unpredictable and physically challenging conditions. Prior to our first offering, we thought we would be able to increase enrollment by 4 to 6 students to approach that of the Belize program, but given the intensity of fieldwork (4 to 6 hours a day in the water) we have instead prioritized in-water safety and always maintained a 12-student maximum.

Program Delivery

Predeparture

Advertising and orientation for both programs commences early in the fall semester or about four months prior to the winter session when the programs are offered. Advertising is primarily the responsibility of the program instructors who promote it in classes and through posters distributed on campus and at a study abroad fair that depicts the student experience. Orientation includes informational meetings, evaluation and selection of candidate participants (including a swim test), and a small reception and guest lecture (open to the university and public) given by a renowned anthropologist with extensive experience in Panama.

We hold a series of formal lectures to establish a conceptual framework for the Panama program before leaving the United States, including several practical sessions on cultural awareness, field safety, and underwater photography. To integrate the two Panamanian students into the social fabric of the program as soon as possible, we provide explicit recommendations to RWU participants to be inclusive, collaborative, and welcoming to their foreign hosts, such as by purchasing some RWU memorabilia to share with their foreign counterparts. We review basic greetings and useful phrases in Spanish, not as an exercise in language proficiency (neither instructor is fully fluent in Spanish), but as a reminder that even the smallest act of language compromise can show compassion, awareness, and sensitivity to local hosts while abroad. We complete a few simple translation exercises to help students realize that fellow students and phone-based online resources are available to help with problem-solving. Students are sometimes reluctant to take the initiative to resolve language problems, but when forced to, they can realize their own self-sufficiency. For example, three students approached Wysor during the stay in Guna Yala to get help opening a coconut, and when he outright refused to facilitate their simple request the students sought out one of our local hosts and proudly returned moments later, with straw-spouting coconuts in hand, quenched palates, and smirks of new confidence.

In addition to these everyday realities, we rehearse realistic scenarios to get students thinking about how to handle different situations. Scenarios that are concocted from prior experiences in this or other programs have proven very useful. In one instance, a Panamanian participant lost an underwater camera during a snorkeling foray. RWU students understood from the instructors beforehand that such occurrences are part of the costs of research, and that if loss or damage occurred to a camera while in their possession they should simply communicate that to the instructor. But when this happened to one of the Panamanian students, the loss was taken traumatically, despite the instructor's attempt to calm the student by minimizing any ties to the camera and sympathizing with the loss of image data. Ultimately, the RWU students shared their understanding of the policy with the Panamanian student, and that helped to ease the student's discomfort through some emotion-laden language barriers. Practicing this and other scenarios beforehand gave program participants the confidence to help quell potentially uncomfortable situations.

An essential element in preparing students for the in-water experience in Panama is a pool session during which we rehearse standard safety drills and give students, some of whom may have little or no snorkeling experience, an opportunity to try out new snorkeling or camera gear. All students are required to deploy the inflatable signaling device, and then we perform a series of relay races that are fun, and, more important, show the versatility of the signaling device as a buoyant support for a tired swimmer or as a towing sling. One component of the training is that swimmers remain in pairs, a rule that is strictly enforced when we are in the field.

Another strategic skill is getting into a boat from the water. We require students to climb out of the pool over the highest bulkhead to try to prepare them for climbing over the gunwale of a boat without a ladder, as is commonly encountered in Panama. At this time, students also learn how to safely assist swimmers over the bulkhead, a simulation that is as hilarious as it is useful for the inevitable occasion when a tired student needs assistance getting back into the boat. In addition to snorkeling practice (e.g., deep dives, clearing the snorkel, defogging the mask), instructors sink several toy animals throughout the pool for students to practice photographing subjects underwater. This is important because many digital cameras used in this class were gifts from the holiday season and so are getting wet during this session for the first time. It is far easier to deal with camera problems before or while en route to Panama than in the excitement and chaos of the first day of fieldwork. Figure 6.1 summarizes some of the important considerations in preparing students for a field experience.

In Country

In both programs a few formal lectures are given by faculty on general topics like tropical rainforest structure and the biology of coral reefs. In Belize these are supplemented by student presentations on more specific topics. The classes also come together for several sessions to discuss assigned readings. But most of the programs are delivered in the field with instructors and guides promoting discussion on points of interest as they are experienced or with students tasked with independent exploration of natural habitats. In the evenings some sort of debriefing is conducted to recap the day's activities, and some background information is delivered through faculty lectures or student presentations to put the following day's activities into context. In Panama this time is extended for portfolio drafting and writing in journals.

Figure 6.1. Student safety and logistical preparation for field-based study.

- Use predeparture meetings to establish expectations for conduct and attitudes throughout the program, including
  o enthusiasm, readiness, and timeliness for all meetings;
  o willingness to communicate concerns for personal or group safety, including cultural insensitivity; and
  o flexibility to changing weather conditions or travel rearrangements.
- Orient participants to clearly articulated course assignments that are carefully aligned with lecture and field activities to prevent idleness and guide student focus throughout the experience abroad.
- Ensure participant safety prior to departure. This includes
  o evaluating student competency for physical demands of the program (e.g., walking, hiking, swimming, lifting);
  o determining the need for health (e.g., CPR, basic first aid) or other certifications (e.g., SCUBA, administration of oxygen) that might be necessary to conduct routine or specialized fieldwork; and
  o requiring that students practice field readiness to ensure necessary equipment (e.g., snorkeling gear, timing device, safety equipment) has been assembled prior to travel and to ensure students are knowledgeable with its use.
- Establish a system of communication that facilitates group work in the field and promotes a positive group experience overall. This includes
  o setting time limits and rendezvous points when breaking into smaller groups;
  o practicing the deployment and use of specialized safety equipment;
  o establishing and practice a means by which to communicate distress; and
  o establishing opportunities to hear student concerns (e.g., journals, one-on-one consultations).
- Use role playing to
  o anticipate cultural practices of the host country and alert students to cultural insensitivities that might be amplified by (American) group dynamics;
  o facilitate the integration of local students and community representatives into the course group dynamic;
  o practice commonsense problem-solving in a foreign language,
  o simulate safety and rescue situations under simulated field condition; and
  o alert students to dangerous situations that could arise through normal fieldwork (e.g., organismal encounters in nature, human encounters with locals, anti-Americanism, within-group dynamics).

Outcomes-Based Student Assessment

At the end of either program students should be able to identify basic patterns of tropical biodiversity and conservation specific to the program destination and be able to compare and contrast these to the conditions at RWU while appreciating the sheer diversity of organisms and environments in tropical regions. Further, students should develop a deeper appreciation for the close marriage of the people of either destination to their physical landscapes, cultural practices, and history. These learning outcomes are consistent with those identified by the Department of Biology, Marine Biology, and Environmental Science at RWU. To facilitate quantitative and qualitative assessment of these outcomes, a variety of learning activities have been developed that draw on students' direct in-country experiences as well as the natural science underpinnings of each program (see Figure 6.2). Correspondingly, an important component of course evaluation for both programs is participation. Did the students participate in all program activities? Were they engaged with the activities? Were they punctual and prepared? Did they participate in class discussions and ask thoughtful questions?

Neotropical Marine Biology Assessment

In addition to one comprehensive predeparture exam (based on about 15 hours of traditional lecture content), other formative assessments include in-country organismal identification quizzes (often delivered using a projector with images derived from the current program) and analytical reading assignments with questions for discussion. Development of an electronic portfolio documenting some aspect of Panamanian marine biodiversity or conservation is the defining summative assignment. The goal of the biodiversity portfolio project is to motivate students to make observations in a very targeted way and to inspire their own sense of curiosity when snorkeling in novel habitats. When we first started teaching this class in 2010, digital cameras in underwater housings were shared throughout the class at a ratio of about one camera per two students. In subsequent years, however, nearly all students brought their own cameras, commonly including small video cameras from which still images could be extracted. Indeed, some of the most striking portfolio images have been collected in this way, but the practice certainly requires a higher demand on storage memory and very likely a longer time to review footage than still images alone. Students are encouraged to use video in the portfolio where it is appropriate to do so, such as when documenting organismal interactions like a fish defending its territory or a fish changing color to blend in with the environment. Because portfolios are submitted

Figure 6.2. Potential outcomes-based assessments for field programs abroad.

- Assessments to put the location in context:
  - Predeparture exams, quizzes, or assignments
    - Background information on the history, culture, or environment of the site
    - Formal exams or quizzes, or responses to assigned readings
  - Student presentations or discussion
    - In-country or predeparture
    - Each student presents on a different aspect of the site: history, culture, environment, politics, and so on
- Assessments to put the learning in context:
  - Discussion of assigned readings
    - Everyone reads the same paper(s) or jigsaw style where each student reads a different paper and the discussion synthesizes all the different readings
  - Research projects
    - Short-term projects carried out in the field
    - Assessed through student presentations or research report
  - Research paper
    - Traditional library research paper
  - Field surveys
    - Collect data on diversity, distribution, abundance, or opinions
  - Collections or portfolios
    - Students collect or catalog what they see and experience
    - Could be physical specimens, digital photos, video, or audio recordings
  - Exams and quizzes
    - Short quizzes identifying species, places, architecture, and so on.
    - Formal exams
  - Peer review of any of these
- Assessments to put the experience in context:
  - Keeping journals
    - Students document their thoughts and experiences while abroad
  - Reflection paper
    - Students reflect on what they learned, or how they were affected by the experience
  - Participation scores
    - Was the student engaged? Did he or she contribute to discussions and activities?

and reviewed electronically there is no practical limitation on the use of video versus still imagery.

The production of the portfolio commences in-country as soon as images or videos are downloaded from cameras each evening. Students are encouraged to feature an organism, an environment, a behavioral pattern, a conservation issue, or a comparison of any of these between Pacific and Atlantic habitats, and reconcile their documented observations with information from the primary literature. A set of observations and corresponding context constitutes a plate, and students work collaboratively in groups of two or three to produce a series of three to four plates.

One of the logistical challenges to the assignment is that plates are sometimes drafted from a collection of the best photographs, whether or not there is a compelling idea that links a series of images in a meaningful way. Thus, students are required to prepare a draft portfolio during the first part of the trip, which provides a forum for instructor and peer feedback and helps students identify targets for future image collection. Another useful activity to pair with photo editing is writing in a journal about the day's observations, so that as students prepare portfolio drafts they can use their mental download and their image record. Instructors help participants identify relevant portfolio ideas through journal reviews, evening discussions, and workshops; time for these activities is carefully allotted in the program design. The portfolio project is completed during the spring semester following study abroad when students can take advantage of library resources to elucidate the topic using primary literature. Draft portfolios undergo several group (i.e., the whole class) and individual (i.e., one-on-one with one or both instructors) review sessions, which ultimately culminate in the oral presentation of all portfolio plates to the class.

A potential drawback of the collection of image data necessary for the portfolio project is that students can develop a viewfinder vision of their entire experience. We try to remind students that efforts to frame every observation can result in a failure to experience chance or fleeting encounters. During one Panama program, for example, we had the exceptional experience of seeing a whale shark. One participant was so enthralled with having captured some footage that he retreated to the boat to safely stow his camera. What he failed to realize from his hypervigilance was that a second whale shark emerged from the depths and captivated program participants for the next 15 minutes. Thus, the constant focus on recording observations can, at times, lead to missing out on them entirely.

The portfolio project works exceedingly well for reconciling program content with the in-water, in-country experience. We continue to be impressed at the range of topics elucidated by each class. Although some topics tend to be repeated, there are always new projects and no limit to individual creativity. Although we have expected stories about marine biology, we have enjoyed, for example, learning about celestial-searching algorithms modified to verify whale shark individuals and puzzling over macrophotographs of garbage to describe dispersal and the design of marine protected areas. Ultimately, the value of this project can be measured as a tangible legacy to the international experience for instructors and students alike.

Tropical Ecology Assessment

Because access to laboratory facilities, libraries, or reliable Internet connections is limited, and because we are only in each location for a few days, it is difficult for students to carry out research projects or produce quality assignments while abroad. Thus, many of our major assignments are designed to be completed before or after the experience.

In-country student presentations have been a consistent feature of the program for several years. We provide students with topics, and each one creates a presentation before departure that will be delivered to the class while abroad (often by projecting it onto a bedsheet or a wall). These 15-minute talks are scheduled so the students will hear the presentation the night before a topic is addressed in the class (e.g., a presentation on Mayan history the night before we visit the Mayan sites). When we first started assigning these presentations, cultural topics included Belizean folklore, music of Belize, modern history of Belize, and so on, in addition to the more scientific presentations on Belizean wildlife and ecological issues. We eventually abandoned most of the cultural topics, particularly after one student presented her history of Belize only to be told that everything she mentioned happened in Honduras, not Belize (although in her possible defense, Belize used to be known as British Honduras). Now we limit presentations to ecological topics that focus on the natural history or conservation status of select species or on environmental topics such as sustainable timber harvesting or the design of marine protected areas. Students are required to include open-ended questions in their presentations to foster discussion. Mayan history and traditional rainforest medicine are two cultural topics that we still include; we assume that much of the cultural knowledge will come through their experiences rather than formal presentations. However, we are considering adding some more predeparture lectures on the basics of Belize as we have with the Panama program.

The other major assessment that we have used every year is a term paper that is completed after returning to campus. We experimented with a number of topics for the paper, instructor assigned and student selected, and have found that the best option lies somewhere in between. Lately, we have allowed students to pursue ecological topics of their own choosing but only after consultation with program instructors.

Another activity that fits well into a participation grade scheme is group discussion of assigned readings, which are generally drawn from the primary literature. We have used different discussion-promoting strategies including a common reading of a single article or the jigsaw approach in which each student reads a different article and contributes their newly acquired expertise to a group discussion. For example, to explore plant community ecology, we assigned papers on seed morphology, as well as wind-, insect-, or avian-mediated dispersal of seeds. In the discussion, each student presented the main point of the reading so the group could create a holistic view of the dispersal process. These readings and discussions provide a framework to help focus subsequent student observations in the field.

As a capstone to the program, students are required to write a reflective essay on their experiences abroad. The student must discuss two or three learning points acquired from the experience. At least one of the points must be about ecological issues, including scientific concepts and observations, human impacts, biodiversity conservation, environmental management, and so on. At least one point must be more personal or cultural in nature about what the students learned about themselves, Belizean culture or people, or the value of international travel. One of the most satisfying comments in one of these essays really points to the value of field-based experiences: "Dr. Webb told us that we would learn so much just by being here and experiencing everything, and I'm surprised how true that turned out to be."

Unique Logistical Challenges

Personal and Group Health and Safety

Although personal and group safety is a concern for all instructors, it is acutely important in a field-based program in which students spend most of the day in the water or dense rainforest where conditions can change rapidly and unpredictably. Fatigue, dehydration, shallow-water blackout, poisonous and venomous animals, predatory animals, getting lost, and being stranded are a few of the challenges to safety. The pool session described earlier serves to orient students to some of these in-water challenges and how to deal with them, but the variety of distractions in situ can undermine prior training. On one occasion, one of the most competent swimmers in the group became separated from his buddy and was effectively missing for 30 minutes. The student got caught in a current after veering away from the designated snorkeling region and had the wherewithal to climb out of the water onto an outcropping and rest while awaiting rescue. As a result of this experience, we learned that we needed

- a way for participants to communicate distress,
- a system to muster all students as soon as a problem was identified,
- signaling equipment and a call-response system of communication, and
- a timed snorkel plan in place.

We have addressed the first several concerns by requiring participants to wear safety whistles whenever they enter the water and by devising a series of whistle signals for in-water communication. In addition to these changes, we also establish specific time limits, generally 60 minutes, for each snorkeling foray with the condition that time limits can and often are extended after the initial time has expired. Violation of time limits results in a penalty toward the participation grade, and students who fail to equip themselves with a whistle, watch, safety sausage, and a buddy cannot enter the water. The implementation of these simple guidelines for safety has not impeded any facet of the in-water experience and has allowed instructors to build greater confidence with the group because all participants have clarity on their role in their own and others' safety.

These and other safety recommendations are communicated to students as a formal lecture in the predeparture orientations. In addition to emergency signaling, we also discuss the variety of common animal encounters that might cause problems from stings, spines, bites, and the challenges of dealing with surge and currents and getting into and out of a boat. It is important to note that we advise students not to collect organisms or disturb the benthic environment, and we remind them that any urge to interact with marine or terrestrial life should be dismissed for safety reasons (getting stung, bitten, walloped by an enormous fin, or lured off site) and because it only takes one careless interaction by one student to scare off the whale shark that everyone else had been watching for the past 15 minutes.

Field programs also raise logistical issues with student health ranging from bad cases of sunburn to serious tropical diseases to access to clean water. These can be exacerbated when remote locations limit quick access to medical facilities. Organizations such as the Centers for Disease Control and Prevention publish online health recommendations for travel to foreign countries, and students should be made aware of the recommended precautions. Although several students have regretted their decision to drink from a rainforest stream, we have otherwise been fortunate that while traveling through areas full of dangerous animals, steep climbs, and treacherous

Figure 6.3. Health and safety considerations in remote field locations.

- Fatigue, exhaustion, and dehydration (e.g., from strenuous physical activity such as hiking or swimming, poor diet, or gastrointestinal distress)
- Environmental overexposure to sun (e.g., sunburn, sun poisoning), heat (e.g., exhaustion, heat stress, heat stroke), rain, or cold (e.g., hypothermia)
- Encounters with dangerous organisms ranging from those with spines (e.g., cactus, sea urchins), to ambush predators (e.g., crocodiles, sharks, snakes), to poisonous or venomous plants and animals (e.g., stinging nettles, poison ivy, fire coral, stinging bees, biting ants)
- Insect-borne illnesses (e.g., Zika virus, malaria, Dengue fever, yellow fever)
- Separation from the group (e.g., related to changing ocean currents, poorly marked trails, fatigue, failed buddy system)
- Allergic response to food or medication, or general malaise or gastrointestinal distress from novel diet in host country
- Injuries associated with physical demands of the field site (e.g., ear barotrauma associated with snorkeling, falls associated with hiking)
- Group supervision when faculty accompanies student to health services center

currents; the only injury requiring a student to be sent home was a broken ankle as a result of a short fall from a cottage balcony. Some health and safety issues to consider while abroad are summarized in Figure 6.3.

Ecological Footprints

We would be remiss not to mention the irony or hypocrisy of developing programs designed to heighten awareness for biodiversity resources and their conservation while simultaneously expanding the carbon footprint for every program participant through carbon-intensive travel and the use of disposable and travel-ready products. A fellow tourist in Guna Yala pointed out that our conservation awareness was undermined by the substantial plastic waste we generated from drinking bottled water. To address this issue, we now travel with a gravity-based filtration unit that has proven reliable and convenient. The use of filtered water requires a source of local water, as well as the trust of program participants whose (paid) experiences could be compromised if the filter malfunctions. Thus, a spare filter should be available and the filter bags carefully packed to guard against damage that would be disastrous if no other source of drinking water were available as backup. The use of filtered water brings sustainability into sharp focus for all program participants, especially when they are charged with the responsibility of filtering sufficient water for daily needs. It also significantly reduces the burden of transporting water. We have not implemented other carbon-sensitive planning into these programs yet, but resources exist (summarized in Leggett, 2012) for instructors, such as ourselves, who lack specific training in this area.

Collecting and Harvesting

Students often feel the need to bring back souvenirs that are not available in the gift shops, including animal or plant specimens or cultural or archaeological artifacts. It is important for everyone to be aware of the laws regarding possession and transportation of these items. Without official permits, it is almost never permissible to transport living specimens internationally, including plant specimens. Common targets for students include shells and pieces of coral, and the regulations concerning these items can be tricky. For example, shells or products of shells of the queen conch are listed under the Convention on International Trade in Endangered Species of Wild Fauna and Flora and require an export permit to remove them from Belize, whereas other shells are not subject to these restrictions. It is also generally illegal and culturally inappropriate to take any archaeological artifacts, such as pieces of stone from a Mayan temple site.

Field Gear

The field-intensive nature of these programs requires bringing specialized equipment in the form of masks, fins, and snorkels, which add bulk to the usual luggage. Students are encouraged to transport this equipment in carry-on luggage to guard against loss, but it is also important for students to minimize luggage weight because they have to move it among several sites and because domestic flights may have a lower weight limit than the international flights. If more specialized equipment such as microscopes is necessary, program directors can take advantage of staying in locations that provide laboratory facilities, or they can carry or ship the equipment to the site, although this may incur considerable expense.

Budgeting

A challenge to field-oriented study abroad programs is that supervision of inexperienced students in remote, dynamic field conditions requires multiple faculty to reasonably ensure group safety. The combined expertise of two or more faculty members enhances the quality and breadth of field programs, but it simultaneously taxes program budgets with additional salary lines. At RWU solutions to run-away program fees have ranged from faculty splitting a single salary to university support that is separate from collection of program fees.

Another aspect of funding that can prove challenging is coordinating payments for services with local organizations. Our university preference is to issue payments before arrival or using a credit card, but not all organizations are set up to receive payments in these ways. Access to cash through local banks or ATMs may be limited in remote localities, and, in some cases, it may be strategically important to issue payment only after the service is provided. During the first visit to Guna Yala, and despite many conversations about payment, we found ourselves in the very awkward position of not being able to make a cash payment that was expected of us on arrival. We scrambled to secure funds via Western Union, which seriously affected the field experience because one instructor was tasked with securing the transfer at the closest bank, which was several islands away, on a slow boat from our field site. When the wire transfer failed because of typographical errors, our gracious hosts used personal funds that were paid back as soon as we returned to Panama City. Given that we have an established relationship with our hosts, we now pay in advance with a bank transfer, and we more carefully plan for cash payments.

Student Conduct

Both of our programs spend significant time in tropical beach settings, where the lure of colorful cocktails can promote a party atmosphere among the students. This is a difficult issue, as the students are generally of legal drinking age in the host country. Most problems are mitigated by clearly stating the expectations for student behavior in the program, supplemented by students signing a conduct form. Students are informed that they can drink if local laws allow it, but if their drinking impairs their ability to participate in class activities, it will have a negative impact on their course grade. Illegal drugs are a different issue, and we take a zero tolerance stance with their use or possession; any student caught with illegal drugs will fail the course and be sent home immediately at the student's expense. Students should be made aware that drug laws are very severe in some countries, and nothing can spoil a study abroad experience like a foreign jail term.

Provisions for Guided Critical Reflection on Cultural Experiences

Both programs provide opportunities for students to engage in new cultural experiences. Students in Belize visit at least one Mayan archaeological site, with an interpretive tour provided by trained tour guides. They also visit a Mayan museum where they learn about everyday Mayan life and participate in traditional dances and making tortillas. The Garifuna culture is explored through visits to a cultural museum and to the studios of local artists, craftspeople, and musicians. The class always ends with a musical and dance performance by a Garifuna cultural group, with plenty of audience participation. As important as these formalized cultural experiences are, we find that our students learn more about the social and political aspects of life in Belize through the daily interactions with the local guides and staff. At the end of the program, students write an essay reflecting on the cultural differences they experienced and how they have been affected by that cultural experience.

The cultural experience in Panama is facilitated by the inclusion of the University of Panama undergraduates and integration in an indigenous community in Caribbean Panama. The Guna Yala hosts have allowed access to their public school facilities for lectures, and students are invited to participate in evening lectures on the hotel restaurant patio, where a small generator runs a computer and an LCD projector. Despite the fact that no fewer than three languages are encountered, there are opportunities for everyone to contribute to the discussion. On one occasion, the issue of global climate change in the context of coral reef ecology and Guna Yala culture was addressed in an evening lecture. The intersection of local residents, Panamanian and U.S. student participants, and a few other international hotel guests made for a lively, authentic discussion. The discussion required translation among languages while maintaining sensitivity to the local culture where island resettlement strategies were actively being planned as a way to deal with increasing sea levels—a problem that has been kindled more by RWU students in their homeland than by the welcoming Guna Yala who bear witness to the approaching catastrophe. Students emerged from the discussion with a nuanced appreciation for the real impacts of sea-level inundation on a local community in a way that was completely different from the way they think about global climate change in their home states. In addition, a visit to the Miraflores Visitor Center at the Panama Canal offers students some perspectives on the rich history of Panama (and the United States), especially as it relates to the construction of the Panama Canal.

In both programs, we find the cultural experience to be transformational based not only on the fact that students often self-report their international field experience as life changing but also on our casual observations about the willingness of students, who subsequently take another of our courses, to engage at a higher level. Whether the enhanced engagement is a result of a longer history of experience together, the actual field experience itself, or the possibility that more highly engaged students may be drawn to international field programs, our qualitative observations are consistent with previous findings (Boyle et al., 2007; Fuller 2006; Walsh, Larsen & Parry, 2014) that underscore the role of field experiences to help students recognize themselves as members of a learning community and to empower them as active learners.

References

Boyle, A., Maguire, S., Martin, A., Milsom, C., Nash, R., Rawlinson, S., . . . Conchie, S. (2007). Fieldwork is good: The student perception and the affective domain. *Journal of Geography in Higher Education, 31*, 299–317.

Fuller, I. (2006). What is the value of fieldwork? Answers from New Zealand using two contrasting undergraduate physical geology field trips. *New Zealand Geographer, 62*, 215–220.

Leggett, K. (2012). Leaving light footprints. *International Educator, 21*(3), 40–52.

Taraban, R., McKenney, C., Peffley, E. & Applegarth, A. (2004). Live specimens more effective than World Wide Web for learning plant material. *Journal of Natural Resources and Life Science Education, 33*, 106–110.

U.S. Department of Education. (2011). *Guidance to institutions and accrediting agencies regarding a credit hour as defined in the final regulations published on October 29, 2010*. Retrieved from https://ifap.ed.gov/dpcletters/attachments/GEN1106.pdf

Walsh, C., Larsen, C. & Parry, D. (2014). Building a community of learning through early residential fieldwork. *Journal of Geography in Higher Education, 38*, 373–82.

7

DESIGNING THE CURRICULUM FOR GLOBAL SERVICE-LEARNING ABROAD

Power and Health in El Salvador

Autumn Quezada de Tavarez and Kerri Staroscik Warren

The rising popularity of international service-learning programs provides educators with an opportunity to create unique educational experiences rooted in new and innovative pedagogies. As universities embrace core values of experiential education and global learning, faculty find themselves at a complex nexus of interaction involving the institution, academics, global communities, and service-learning. The intent of this chapter is to examine how faculty at Roger Williams University (RWU) made the transition from a cocurricular club experience into an interdisciplinary, credit-bearing, service-learning, short-term study abroad program with pedagogy that was innovative, ethical, and rigorous.

Cocurricular Beginnings

In 2009, five RWU students founded a campus chapter of the global health, nongovernmental organization Foundation for International Medical Relief of Children (FIMRC). With the hope of performing international service, the RWU chapter of FIMRC asked Kerri Staroscik Warren to serve as club adviser and successfully applied to become an official RWU student club. In 2010 the students collected medical supply donations and travelled to El Salvador over spring break to volunteer at an FIMRC clinic site. By 2011 the club had grown in numbers, and Warren joined the students in spring break travel to El Salvador. The following year, there was a surge in student interest and a second club adviser, Autumn Quezada de Tavarez, was added as the club had become a popular outlet for non-credit-bearing, cocurricular service travel experiences. At this time we redefined the role of club adviser and responded to this growing phenomenon by working more closely with the students, examining all practical aspects of travel, engaging in professional development in experiential education and community engagement, cultivating a close and collaborative partnership with the leaders of FIMRC, and ultimately becoming immersed in intensely rewarding service experiences at FIMRC sites in El Salvador as well as small rural FIMRC communities throughout Latin America. There are presently about 200 FIMRC members in the RWU chapter, and they plan at least two service abroad programs a year.

We say we redefined the role of the club adviser because traditional campus club experiences tend to be student driven, and advisers are often instructed to assist at a distance. However, an international public health service club requires a different approach because of potential ethical dilemmas. Without oversight, students could feel overwhelmed in real-world health settings. Most important, students are not trained professionals and should never be placed in situations with unethical practices. Recognizing the potential ethical dilemmas of an international public health service club, we decided to take a different approach to club advising—guidance with active learning before, during, and after the service experience. In rejecting the directive to be hands off, we accepted the responsibility of teaching and learning alongside the students, modeling best practices on campus and on site. We became hands-on mentors, teaching tenets of cultural competency, empathy, active listening, and ethics in the practice of service.

Mentorship proved key to the success and growth of the RWU chapter of FIMRC. After adding faculty advisers, the club volunteer experience became an immersive learning experience based in content and context. From the start, we conducted predeparture orientations with information about the settings where students planned to work, relevant histories of the country and region, health and safety training, and public health information sessions. On the ground, we mentored students throughout the day with teaching moments and in the evening provided guided reflections. Officially, RWU FIMRC club travel was cocurricular; in reality, it had become a service-learning experience with knowledgeable faculty directing on-site education in collaboration with an active community partner.

Thus we began with our community experience and connection with FIMRC to create a global service-learning study abroad experience like no other at our university. Out of the cocurricular experience, we crafted what we term a *place-based collaborative learning experience* specific to our host site, Las Delicias, El Salvador. The service work became our vehicle to deliver relevant, real-world materials related to national history, social justice, economy, determinants of health, health systems, and public health education. Excitement grew among our students for this type of experiential education, and from that we developed a four-credit spring semester course that included a short-term study abroad session over spring break to work with our partners on site.

How is our study abroad program's story of origin different from that of others? First, we built a curriculum around an established international service program instead of inserting a service component into an existing study abroad program. Service insertion is often made possible through use of a commercial or an independent add-on volunteer option. Second, we designed the program on a foundation of best practices in community engagement (Butin, 2007; Head, 2007; Zuiches, 2008) and service-learning (Butin, 2003; Howard, 2001). Differences between service and service-learning seem to be not universally understood, yet despite this, many institutions urge faculty to jump into community engagement without guidance or training. Third, the disciplinary (history, public health) learning objectives, content, and assignments were constructed with a solid understanding of the on-site realities and potential. All three aspects of program development contributed to its success and allowed us to honor students, the institution, and professional and community needs.

Curriculum Foundations: Experiential Learning

Learning should be interactive and transformative. John Dewey (1997) defined *experiential education* as being rooted in a transformative experience through a variety of cooperative learning exchanges. In our case we imagined our program course work in a global living classroom. Before we took our experience into the realm of short-term study abroad, we reflected on how our philosophy of place-based collaborative learning originated through three high-impact practices: community engagement, service-learning, and global service-learning. See Figure 7.1, which illustrates the relationship among these high-impact practices.

Experiential Education Through Community Engagement

The foundation for our experiential learning experience grew from the relationship with FIMRC and the El Salvadoran community. Practitioners in the field of high-impact practices note important organizing principles in community engagement: collaboration, reciprocity, and diversity (Mintz & Hesser, 1996). Scholars advocate for shared ethical standards so that programs

Figure 7.1. Three high-impact practices.

can better navigate the nexus between academic institutions and communities for a more equitable experience (Hartman, Morris, & Blanche-Cohen, 2014). Administrators of academic programs should place an equitable interest in supporting community development from within, meaning that the community drives the development of academic goals. Academic learning can supplement local programming, which can serve two purposes: real-world learning for students and development potential for a community on its own terms through intercultural partnerships.

Service-Learning as Experiential Education

The service-learning component formed the base of our program and is critical to its success. *Service-learning* is defined here as

> a course-based, credit-bearing educational experience in which students (a) participate in an organized service activity that meets identified community needs, and (b) reflect on the service activity in such a way as to gain further understanding of course content, a broader appreciation of the discipline, and an enhanced sense of personal values and civic responsibility. (Bringle & Hatcher, 2009, p. 38)

It is important to recognize that service-learning is a curriculum-based endeavor, whereas volunteering is cocurricular. The difference is that volunteering typically resides in the realm of student affairs as a one-time event. Service-learning, stressing the learning component, is facilitated through sustained reflection with learning preparation and postactivity learning.

To begin, faculty must first assume a critical role connecting community partners with an intentional learning experience. Second, with service-learning, faculty select community service projects that deliver meaningful learning experiences and meet learning objectives. The partnership between faculty and community leaders should be reciprocal. Projects must be agreed on and mutually benefit all parties. Third, a service-learning course should link the community service to intentional student-based educational outcomes. Fourth, students should engage in critical reflection before, during, and especially after the service. Reflection helps to connect the service engagement to curricular learning. Students can participate in service, but if that experience is not prolonged (rooted in instruction and reflection over time), then it is simply an act of service, or just a volunteer experience. Meaningful reflection allows students to deepen their thinking to understand the importance and relevance of their service experience (Bringle, Hatcher, & Jones, 2011).

Scholars suggest that curriculum-based service-learning builds on a foundation of cognitive, affective, and connective learning (Parker & Dautoff, 2007). First, cognitive learning relates to the range of content rooting the experience into context. Students need to understand significant details about the community (or place) where they engage. This type of content learning helps students construct problem-solving and critical thinking skills. Second, affective learning helps students explore self-knowledge in relation to places and people they interact with. Building a curriculum that helps to facilitate interactions with diverse groups of people helps to build understanding and empathy in students. Third, connective learning helps give significance to experience for students. Building relationships through curriculum-based service-learning gives students a deeper sense of connection to a place, people, or issue (Parker & Dautoff, 2007). A feeling of connection is critical to personal change. A service experience without depth of understanding holds little hope for sustained behavioral changes.

Global Service-Learning: Pushing International Education Forward

International education continues to grow in all branches of higher education, and with that, new pedagogies evolve as practitioners critically examine their involvement as educators abroad. Traditionally, international education sought to shift students' understandings of civic involvement toward global citizenry. Which should we use as a label? International service-learning or global service-learning? This depends on the nature of the program. To begin with, international service-learning places a great emphasis on civic education, democratic action and engagement, and becoming global citizens. Bringle and Hatcher (2011) cite American Council of Education definitions:

International Service Learning—focusing on nations and their relation-ships. Global Service Learning—denoting systems and phenomenon that transcends national borders. Intercultural Service Learning—focusing on knowledge and skills to understand and navigate cultural differences. (p. 18)

A refined explanation of global service-learning from Alonso García and Longo (2013) delineates differences between international service-learning and global service-learning. International service-learning, they maintain, orients students to the nation–state, is usually location based, focuses on division (the other), and relies on linear learning. By contrast, global service-learning concerns deeper ties based on notions of globalization, thus a view of a more interconnected world (Alonso García & Longo, 2013). Global service-learning orients students toward networks of connections, ways of thinking, interconnectedness, and more holistic approaches to learning (Alonso García & Longo, 2013).

The age of globalization pushes the traditional confines of international service-learning, expanding our thinking; teaching; learning; and, most important, our engagement. International education no longer solely focuses on the amorphic notion of molding global citizens and instead places an emphasis on global: thinking globally and thinking about contexts and con-nections. It is no longer just about going over there but rather how to bring in global locally. Longo and Saltmarsh (2011) aptly sum up current thinking related to global service-learning.

an exploration of the multiple dimension of service learning is an interna-tional context which opens doors to new areas of literature, new questions about program design, and learning outcomes, and new perspectives on citizenship and intercultural understanding. (p. 71)

We now more than ever live in a global age. Information moves quickly, and people connect in ways unimaginable 20 years ago. Personal and pro-fessional relationships dictate a better command of global competencies, including the ability to engage with people from diverse cultures, to consider multiple perspectives, and to think critically about global challenges. Stu-dents must now know how to behave with a high level of comfort and confi-dence in their ability to relate to people from different cultural backgrounds. However, our global engagement in international education still has pitfalls. Now we turn to more current critiques of international education by ask-ing, To what extent can global service-learning experiences be too student centered?

Erasmus (2011), a South African scholar of international service-learning, questions the North American model of service as "self-serving" (p. 359). She writes, "Service learning in America is deeply elitist" (Erasmus, 2011, p. 351). Indeed, criticisms of international service-learning revolve around the notion of Americans acting on the world. Erasmus warns that institutions of higher learning are too student centered and that institutions (faculty members) need to wake from an elitist slumber. She cautions that higher education and international service-learning will be left "irrelevant" if we prioritize course goals and student learning over community needs and goals (Erasmus, 2011, p. 351). With this understanding, let us not forget that teaching service-learning in an international setting remains a privilege, which some may call an elitist exercise. Our program development centers on the critical awareness that our program only exists because the community exists.

High-Impact Practices of Experiential Education

Now we turn to a closer examination of high-impact practices in experiential education: service-learning, global service-learning, study abroad, and community engagement. Blending them requires attention to institutional relationships and ethics. Study abroad and service-learning were developed around two different philosophical models, which can make merging them challenging.

In a study abroad experience students tend to be the principal beneficiaries, not the host communities of study. By contrast, service-learning by nature exists as relational, an experience requiring engagement between an institution's partners and the community. With this in mind, the overarching principles of service-learning, global service-learning, community engagement, and short-term study abroad had an impact on and shaped the design, delivery, and outcomes of our program design. Our model of place-based collaborative learning allows us to envision a curricular structure within experiential learning in Las Delicias. The integration of the short-term study abroad objectives rooted in an encompassing framework of learning goals and teaching allowed us to use our model to transform our cocurricular experience into a transformative credit-bearing program. Figure 7.2 illustrates how we moved our program design through high-impact practices.

Place-Based Collaborative Learning: The El Salvador Program
Empowered by the knowledge that we already engaged in high-impact practices, we needed to formalize the experience into a credit-bearing, global service-learning program steeped in place-based collaborative learning. Constructing a program around an existing community-based immersive

Figure 7.2. Place-based collaborative learning.

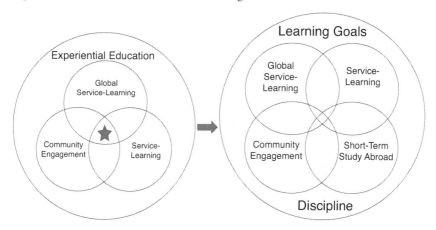

experience required scaffolding the guiding design principles. How do we effectively deliver course content, create intentional on-site exercises that match course content, and awaken student awareness to their learning? The intersections of community engagement and global service-learning offer us the vehicles for innovative teaching and learning.

Part of our design planning involved thinking about the prominent criticism of international volunteer projects. The public outcry against *voluntourism*, as service travel is sometimes called, has intensified of late, but even as early as 2009, the RWU club planned travel in an increasingly critical international service environment. Articles in the popular press with titles such as "As 'Voluntourism' Explodes In Popularity, Who's It Helping Most?" (Kahn, 2014) and "The Voluntourist's Dilemma" (Kushner, 2016) weigh the surge in popularity for volunteer experiences in impoverished regions of the world against the damage such work does to individuals and communities. Indeed, there is a definite level of privilege involved with service-learning in an international context. When you add the lens of global health, the ethical dimensions of our service-learning program expand to include consideration of medical ethics and the undergraduate volunteer (Crump & Sugarman, 2008; Pinto & Upshur, 2009). Aware of these challenges, we sought to find a balance of learning and ethics in the privilege of travel.

The strength of our connection to FIMRC global is central to the overall success of this course and our global service-learning experience. We have an open dialogue year-round with FIMRC leadership to ensure we are meeting each other's expectations and the expectations of the communities. Acutely aware of the potential for unintended consequences during global health volunteer experiences, on-site FIMRC staff members drive interactions between

volunteers and community members. Ensuring deep, meaningful partnerships, FIMRC staff work hard to educate and train volunteers, cultivate local
talent for staffing opportunities, and implement programs with community-
driven sustainability in mind. Even the decision to establish a FIMRC clinic
site is initiated through a community's invitation. Careful decision-making
and planning goes into establishing the site and staffing the clinic. Once up
and running smoothly enough to host volunteers, health promotion projects
originate with a thorough understanding of community needs. Activities are
tailored week by week to meet these community needs within the limits of
the expertise and licensing credentials of the individual volunteer. This last
aspect proves crucial to our partnership with FIMRC, as our students are not
medical professionals yet yearn to contribute.

FIMRC's primary structure is rooted in a community-based model of
improving the health outcomes of the community year-round. Its model of
volunteer support allows FIMRC to be on site 24 hours a day, 7 days a week.
In exchange, FIMRC provides an opportunity for students to participate,
grow, and learn in this transformative setting.

Getting Started: Proposing a Program

Establishing a global service-learning program can seem overwhelming.
Beginning a model of community engagement in a specific region requires
time, commitment, and connections but can prove to be the key to a successful program. We highly encourage faculty leaders to begin with a community
engagement experience and build the program around that core. The following should be considered before designing a program:

- Community needs
- Feasibility to fit learning into available and appropriate community
  work
- Regional and local safety
- Accessibility
- Seasonal issues (weather, health)
- Transportation
- Budget
- Language issues
- Travel logistics

A site visit prior to the implementation of the program is a must as it
provides the opportunity to test transportation, arrange housing, meet with
community leaders, and line up sites of cultural and historical curricular

interest. Some universities have funds to support site visits through curriculum development stipends, minigrants, or other resources.

Each institution calculates credit hours for non-classroom-based programs using an interpretation of academic engagement hours. At RWU, engagement hours include lecture periods, discussions, community activities, and time devoted to reflection and homework. In proposing our program, we needed to demonstrate a plan for meeting our university's threshold for one credit hour, which is 37.5 adjusted hours of academic engagement. Our plan surpassed that with 60 planned academic engagement hours. Most universities also have an application process for their short-term study abroad programs, likely involving a plan for travel logistics, budget, minimum student participation, and learning goals and outcomes. We advise requiring registered students to sign a personal conduct form. Short-term study abroad paired with global service-learning requires a certain degree of maturity and self-awareness.

Guiding Principles: Perspectives in Global Health: Health, Power, and Hope

Careful consideration went into which design elements to include in our credit-bearing curriculum, and we found a good match with the key international education principles proposed by Lutterman-Aguilar and Gingerich (2002), namely, problem-based content, process and personal integration, and critical analysis and reflection.

Group Problem-Based Learning

This type of learning uses what some call "liquid networks" of idea exchange (Johnson, 2010). Learning and innovative thinking is a collaborative exercise, and ideas bloom when we talk and interact with one another. Kaneshige (2014) suggests that complex questions stemming from real-world issues need to be discussed in liquid networks because ideas and answers do not happen in a vacuum. During service-learning experiences, group reflexive discussions help students realize the importance of working and thinking together rather than in isolation to solve problems.

Centering the Self

An intensive short-term study abroad program allows a focus on personal development and critical consciousness in the intentional design. Personal development and raising of consciousness (self-awareness) can lead to an important program outcome: globalmindedness (Kehl & Morris, 2008). RWU has a long history of providing problem-based learning in context and supports critical analysis in its core values. The institution challenges students to relate to their general education courses with the following questions: Who am I? What can I know? With that knowledge, what can I do? Centering the self in service-learning study abroad helps bring about an awakening of a critical consciousness of self, the other, and the world (Freire, 1974; Kumagai & Lypson, 2009).

Sustained Critical Analysis and Reflection
Learning begins before we leave the country. We emphasize the importance of context learning in relation to the particularities of place. We want the students to have a deep reading knowledge of where they are going, not just about the community where they will work and about our partner organization but the broader national context. Teaching focuses on historical learning and current situation learning with a knowledge of the country's public health. Blending these topics under an umbrella of social justice helps us teach themes of equity. These lenses help to make sense of why and how history and public health cross and inform the other. Teaching through an interdisciplinary approach helps students think holistically. All the world and issues are connected, interconnected.

As mentioned before, learning begins before the on-site visit and continues through engaged reflection based on preknowledge, on-site experience, and through continued learning on return to class throughout the spring semester. Short-term study abroad programs offer students a deep transformational experience yet pose a pitfall—students return to their normal world with ideas and emotions but with limited means for resolving thoughts and questions. Our model of the semester-long course allows deep reflection on return, which incorporates more instructional time and more learning for the group that experienced that transformational learning. The camaraderie in shared experience, questions, and frustrations enhances growth in knowledge.

Student Learning Outcomes

On this program design scaffold, we established the following broad student learning outcomes for our program:

- Cultivating intercultural competency
- Developing a critical consciousness
- Mastering a historical grounding and demonstration of public health knowledge
- Understanding the historical implications for present-day public health challenges

Our first broad learning outcome, intercultural competency, involves several dimensions, including cognitive, affective, and behavioral (Williams, 2009). Cognitive understanding relates to knowledge of cultural issues. We want students to have a grasp of two basic understandings, determinants of health relative to our specific site and historical-political and socioeconomic context of that site. Lectures follow a more formal structure but also heavily rely on the interpretation of what we have seen in real time. Second, we want students to develop the affective dimension; that is, to be motivated to act and behave in such a way that reflects open-mindedness and flexibility. Last, students should enter what Williams (2009) terms the *behavioral dimension*, which includes the development of critical thinking skills to act resourcefully in intercultural situations. The last two broad learning objectives pertain to our disciplinary foci for the program, understanding the history, including the present-day state, and the implications for public health learning.

Activities That Support Student Gains

We next developed activities to support student learning and achieve broad and specific learning goals. Tools we use to deliver outcomes include predeparture training and reflection, on-site experiential learning, lectures that help contextualize an understanding of current socioeconomic situations and health outcomes in local and national histories, and participation in FIMRC projects that reveal the complexities of global public health. Table 7.1 presents our specific program learning goals, learning activities, and program assessment tools planned to evaluate learning and the degree to which activities achieved outcomes.

As discussed earlier in this chapter, we dedicated the first half of the semester to preparing for the one-week on-site global service-learning experience. Class meetings focused on activities supporting disciplinary foundation building, travel logistics, and orientation to students' ethical and academic responsibilities. Carline Fleig, an RWU campus registered nurse practitioner, joined us in instruction on a range of medical specialties and expertise in treating conditions prevalent in Las Delicias such as diabetes and cardiovascular disease. Fleig provided essential information on travel safety and practical instruction on standard health promotion measures, and she offered a personal and professional ethical perspective to volunteering in resource-poor settings. In addition, she participated in classroom preparations, volunteered with the group in El Salvador, and proved to be a valuable partner in postbroad reflection.

Prearrival communications among faculty, FIMRC field operations managers, and local clinic staff allowed codeveloped and cosupervised activities that matched student learning outcomes. An initial orientation protocol shifted students into smaller groups allowing more manageable activities such as shadowing a pediatrician in the clinic as well as observing interactions

TABLE 7.1
Program Learning Goals and Activities

Learning Outcomes	Assessment Activities	Learning Activities
Demonstrate historical understanding of El Salvador, past and present, as a pluralistic country	1. Review student notes 2. Class discussion 3. Review student journal	1. Visit historical sites 2. Class lecture 3. Special guest lecturers
Engage in cultural experience, reflection, and writing	1. Review notes of case study development 2. Review student journal	1. Visit with locals 2. Accompany doctors on rounds to experience local health care 3. Cultural activities and ethnographic work 4. Case study preparation
Engage in cultural differences in the country and among students	1. Reflect in writing assignments on issues of ethnicity, class, and socioeconomic positions	1. Think about socioeconomics and social justice
Learn how to articulate the complicated social justice story in present-day El Salvador	1. Reflexive discussions of social justice and human rights issues in El Salvador in a feature-length-style article	1. Students meet with local health care professionals to discuss issues related to control and folk healing and modern medicine
Demonstrate an understanding of the lived experience in El Salvador	1. Incorporate this experience in travelogues	1. Students volunteer in the clinic, a school, and in a community project to interact with local community
Illustrate the interdisciplinary nature of global public health	1. Create a concept map of U.S. and El Salvadoran contributions from a range of disciplines and professions to improving health in El Salvador	1. Concept map workshop 2. Lecture 3. Video seminar on global public health

(Continues)

Table 7.1 (*Continued*)

Learning Outcomes	Assessment Activities	Learning Activities
Apply the public health approach (problem, cause, intervention, implementation) to a new public health problem	1. On return, students hand in papers and make presentations on student-identified topics: health conditions, associated risk factors, and key biological concepts required to address the issue in El Salvador	1. Lecture 2. Case studies practice 3. Volunteer experience with Las Delicias community members, discussions with FIMRC clinic staff and health educators
Explain how public health can use health information, communication to improve population health	1. Student photo exhibit on campus with photo narratives	1. Preventative health presentation experiences with Las Delicias community members and discussions with FIMRC clinic staff and health educators 2. Class material
Demonstrate the multidirectional links among health, social, and economic factors	1. Student photo exhibit on campus with photo narratives	1. Volunteer experience with Las Delicias community members and discussions with FIMRC clinic staff and health educators 2. Class material

between the Ministry of Health public health promoter and the community in house and school visits. Shadowing doctors allowed students to witness doctor-patient interactions, listen to discussions of diagnoses, and gain an understanding of common health issues in Las Delicias. An even more robust experience resulted when the public health promoter, responsible for a community of more than 7,000 people, incorporated students into her health education sessions in house-to-house visits and school public health talks. Students helped gather height and weight measurements of school-age children, analyzed the health data, and discussed with the health promoter common health issues affecting local youth. Faculty participated in these experiences as active learners alongside students during community visits.

We set no Spanish language prerequisite in the program application; however, we encouraged students to practice basic Spanish before and during the program. Immersion offered a unique language opportunity. On site, the FIMRC requested for students to create posters and deliver a health talk to school children in prescripted basic Spanish. Prior to traveling, students collected a large donation of toothbrushes and toothpaste, enabling students to craft a health campaign focused on dental health, a standing need identified by the FIMRC.

The model of engagement consisted of community service-learning from morning until after lunch on site alongside faculty. Late afternoons included historical visits and discussions of social justice issues related to wages, work, violence, globalization, and the legacy of civil war and its health and psychological impact on populations. Evenings included group reflection over a meal discussing events of the day and questions raised while students worked in different areas of the community. Each evening, students participated in a guided writing experience that allowed them to build toward critical consciousness and self-actualization by answering questions such as, Who were they in this experience? What were the cross points of cognizant dissonance? How do they begin to untangle those questions? Transformative thinking occurred in moments where students witnessed the connection between what they learned from reading or lectures with what they witnessed in person. Sometimes those moments created uncomfortable learning leaps, challenging students and their previous worldviews. Our week-long study abroad enriched learning as the six weeks of previous class time built a foundation of understanding that could help students make connections between theory—classroom learning—to praxis. Placing travel in the heart of the semester also provided protected time after the travel for reflection and synthesis.

On returning to campus, we had the opportunity to delve into new topics and expand on existing themes. Students were introduced early to the writings of Paul Farmer (2004), champion of global health equity, and conducted close examinations of his concept of structural violence. Postabroad, students could draw on relevant and important examples of structural violence in the community of Las Delicias, grasping the intimate intersections of health care and power. Students not only continued to study Farmer's works but also attended a talk by a global health doctor at Harvard University's School of Public Health.

A photo-essay assignment, which allowed students to creatively demonstrate their learning, was an important culminating exercise for students in the semester-long course. We asked students to select a photo from the experience and craft a narrative explaining the image. Displayed in the entryway of the campus library, the photo-essays allowed students to communicate to a wider audience, provide context to the captured moment, and share their experiences and perspectives. Students also composed a separate and more structured comprehensive essay on the program and its impact on their learning and outlook.

Transformative Change: Postprogram Perspectives

The combination of assessment activities we used during the semester gave us a satisfying snapshot of the level of knowledge immediately acquired and the extent to which students exhibited acute shifts in mind-set. It was clear the program had been an intense learning experience that continued to develop during the remainder of the semester. In addition to demonstrating solid disciplinary learning, students also showed personal growth, which was made apparent in discussions and reflection assignments. We wanted to know, however, if the transformations in evidence after this immersion would be sustained once time had passed.

Program Assessment

To systematically explore the long-term impact this program made on our students, we developed a survey modeled on the postprogram assessment of long-term learning gains described by McLaughlin and Johnson (2006). Sent to students three and a half years after their service-learning in El Salvador, the survey asked students to report on their retention of content-based knowledge, the degree to which the program affected their current level of performance of a range of skills, and the extent of program influence on global and conceptual learning. The survey also asked them to comment on the importance of service-learning and the study abroad component on their learning and offered an optional opportunity to comment on the experience.

We were able to contact eight of the nine students enrolled in the program and received feedback from seven of those eight students. We were very pleased with this 85% response rate, considering the now global distribution of the students. In response to the extent to which students felt the study abroad component and the service-learning component were essential to their overall learning, all students gave the highest rating of *strongly agree.* The overall program analysis question indicated that the sum total of program components—the global service-learning, service-learning, community engagement, and short-term study abroad—resulted in sustained learning and personal growth.

The following are anonymous student reactions to the program three years after completing it.

I'm glad we had the class to prepare us before we went down there [El Salvador] because it allowed me to think of everything in a new light. . . . It taught me about structural violence, something I had never heard of before this class. So when we were finally down there I was able to pick out all of the examples of structural violence at work.

I found one of the topics that had the largest impact on me through this course was the ethical implications/dimensions of service-learning. This is because I had never actually even considered this issue to exist. My mom is an avid community volunteer, so I had grown up volunteering/serving in various respects, but never thought about the effects of my "service" on those individuals and communities being served—I only thought about it in a self-fulfilling, good citizen sort of way, without considering whether my actions really had a sustainable, positive impact. I was missing the global perspective. But through the readings and discussions we had in class, I realized there is [*sic*] two sides to "service," and that "voluntourism" especially needs to be approached very critically.

Taking this course opened my eyes to how history and socioeconomic status can affect health outcomes. The course greatly influenced my post-course interest in public health. I was drawn to the interdisciplinary nature [of the course].

Our model of place-based collaborative learning incorporates high-impact practices of community engagement, service-learning, global service-learning, and short-term study abroad; and offers faculty a guide to an effective and challenging learning experience for students. The complexity of the moving parts in this model come together into a transformative experience that delivers far-reaching life learning.

References

Alonso García, N., & Longo, N.V. (2013). Going global: Re-framing service-learning in an interconnected world. *Journal of Higher Education Outreach and Engagement*, 17, 111–136.

Bringle, R. G., & Hatcher, J. A. (2009). Innovative practices in service-learning and curricular engagement. *New Directions for Higher Education*, 147, 37–46.

Bringle, R. G., & Hatcher, J. A. (2011). International service learning. In R. G. Bringle, J.A. Hatcher, & S. G. Jones (Eds.), *International service learning: Conceptual frameworks and research* (pp. 3–28). Sterling, VA: Stylus.

Bringle, R. G., Hatcher, J. A., & Jones, S. G. (Eds.). (2011). *International service learning: Conceptual frameworks and research*. Sterling, VA: Stylus.

Butin, D. W. (2003). Of what use is it? Multiple conceptualizations of service learning within education. *Teachers College Record*, 105, 1674–1692.

Butin, D. W. (2007). Focusing our aim: Strengthening faculty commitment to community engagement. *Change, 39*(6), 34–39.

Crump, J., A., & Sugarman, J. (2008). Ethical considerations for short-term experiences by trainees in global health. *JAMA, 300*, 1456–1458.

Dewey, J. (1997). *Experience and education.* New York, NY: Simon & Schuster.

Erasmus, M. (2011) A South African perspective on North American international service learning. In R. G. Bringle, J. A. Hatcher, & S. G. Jones (Eds.), *International service learning: Conceptual frameworks and research* (pp. 347–372). Sterling, VA: Stylus.

Farmer P., (2004). An anthropology of structural violence, *Current Anthropology, 45*, 305–325.

Freire, P. (1974). *Education for critical consciousness.* New York, NY: Continuum.

Hartman, E., Paris, C. M., & Blanche-Cohen, B. (2014). Fair trade learning: Ethical standards for community-engaged international volunteer tourism. *Tourism and Hospitality Research, 14*, 108–116.

Head, B. W. (2007). Community engagement: Participation on whose terms? *Australian Journal of Political Science, 42*, 441–454.

Howard, J. (2001). Principles of good practices for service-learning pedagogy. In J. Howard (Ed.), *Michigan Journal of Community Service Learning: Service learning course design workbook* (pp. 16–19). Ann Arbor: University of Michigan Press.

Johnson, S. (2010). Where good ideas come from. Retrieved from https://www.ted.com/talks/steven_johnson_where_good_ideas_come_from?language=en

Kahn, C. (2014). As "voluntourism" explodes in popularity, who's it helping most? Retrieved from http://www.npr.org/sections/goatsandsoda/2014/07/31/336600290/as-volunteerism-explodes-in-popularity-whos-it-helping-most

Kaneshige, T. (2014). How "liquid networks" can lead to the next great idea. Retrieved from http://www.cio.com/article/2376694/innovation/how--liquid-networks--can-lead-to-the-next-great-idea.html

Kehl, K., & Morris, J. (2008). Differences in global-mindedness between short-term and semester-long study abroad participants at selected private universities. *Frontiers, 15*, 67–79.

Kumagai, A. K., & Lypson, M. L. (2009). Beyond cultural competence: Critical consciousness, social justice, and multicultural education. *Academic Medicine, 84*, 782–787.

Kushner, J. (2016, March 22). The voluntourist's dilemma. *New York Times Magazine.* Retrieved from https://www.nytimes.com/2016/03/22/magazine/the-voluntourists-dilemma.html?_r=0

Longo, N. V., & Saltmarsh, J. (2011). New lines of inquiry in reframing international service learning. In R. G. Bringle, J. A. Hatcher, & S. G. Jones, (Eds.), *International service learning: Conceptual frameworks and research* (pp. 69–85). Sterling, VA: Stylus.

Lutterman-Aguilar, A., & Gingerich, O. (2002). Experiential pedagogy for study abroad: Educating for global citizenship. *Frontiers, 8*, 41–82.

McLaughlin, J. S., & Johnson, D. K. (2006). Assessing the field course experiential learning model: Transforming collegiate short-term study abroad experiences into rich learning environments. *Frontiers, 13,* 65–85.

Mintz, S., & Hesser, G. (1996). Principles of good practice of service-learning. In B. Jacoby & Associates, (Eds.), *Service-learning in higher education.* San Francisco, CA: Jossey-Bass.

Parker, B., & Dautoff, D. A. (2007). Service-learning and study abroad: Synergistic learning opportunities. *Michigan Journal of Community Service Learning, 13*(2), 40–53.

Pinto, A. D., & Upshur, R. E. G. (2009). Global health ethics for students. *Developing World Bioethics, 9*(1), 1–10.

Williams, T. R. (2009). The reflective model of intercultural competency: A multidimensional, qualitative approach to study abroad assessment. *Frontiers, 18,* 289–306.

Zuiches, J. J. (2008). Attaining Carnegie's Community Engagement Classification. *Change, 40*(1), 42–45.

8

DESIGNING THE CURRICULUM FOR INTERNSHIP IMMERSION ABROAD

Language and Praxis in Spain

Candelas Gala and Javier García Garrido

*L*anguage and *praxis* are two terms that best describe the Wake Forest University short-term internship program in Salamanca, Spain. Language is key because our program immerses students in the language and culture of Spain. By living with local families in a city filled with a variety of cultural activities, our students learn 24 hours a day. Praxis is equally important because students experience a hands-on approach to a wide range of local businesses and agencies where they work closely with personnel in each site's day-to-day activities. The large number of available internships covers a broad spectrum of professional fields, allowing students to accrue practical knowledge in their areas of interest. At the same time, they improve their language skills in one of the most spoken languages in today's global world. The pragmatic aspect of our program goes hand in hand with an academically sound approach and a very individualized implementation.

The idea for the program came about in 2005–2006 in response to the need for a type of learning experience that would extend instruction outside the classroom while preparing students to meet expectations in the professional world. Among foreign languages, the Spanish program was the first at Wake Forest University to explore the idea of internships because of the large number of students signing up for classes, mainly because of the language's practical application in most professional fields. Spanish majors and minors would benefit as well as any student who selected Spanish to meet the university foreign language requirement for graduation.

Although some departments at Wake Forest were developing internships locally, nothing had been done to establish them abroad. As director of the existing Wake Forest University semester and year program in Salamanca, I (Candelas Gala) realized early in the process that there was a need to offer an experience where students would have the opportunity to practice their language skills outside the classroom and in a professional context that would correspond to their career goals or simply to their personal interests. For that purpose, I thought Madrid would offer more options and opportunities than Salamanca because of the size of the city. Hence, in 2006 I took a trip to Madrid to explore available options. My contact was recommended because of his work with other universities in setting up connections with businesses and other professional agencies. At that time, little or nothing was happening in Spain in the field of internships, at least at the undergraduate level. I went prepared with the names of several companies and agencies, mainly in translation and interpretation, which were areas that seemed more in need of practical exposure at this early stage. To my surprise, the person who was supposed to open up the doors to professional companies did not know much more than what I had already compiled prior to my departure. He did take me to the companies I had already identified, but the rest of the process fell to me.

Choice of Host Country and City

The choice of Spain as the country to establish a summer internship program was largely determined by the previous existence of a semester and year program in the country. After considering how new the internship concept was in Madrid, and the long distances the students would have to cover to move around, I decided it was better to try Salamanca where sites would be more accessible, where connections with local businesses had the potential of being developed more significantly and personally, and where we already had the infrastructure with a semester and year program. Additionally, Salamanca is a much smaller, more manageable place; it is possible to walk everywhere; and it is a very safe city overall in comparison to other larger urban areas. It has a strong academic environment thanks to the University of Salamanca, host families and student residences are available, and Wake Forest University maintains a center there. Located in the heart of the city and barely five minutes by foot from the Plaza Mayor, the Wake Forest Center has classroom and office facilities, social and study spaces, a small kitchen, three bathrooms, and excellent Internet connectivity. The immersion approach to study abroad is the underlining philosophy of this center, which means that students are expected to speak only Spanish in all areas of the center and in all exchanges related to the program.

In 2007 the Wake Forest University Summer Internship Program was launched with the modest registration of two students. One student interned in a sports medicine clinic and the other in the translation program at the University of Salamanca.

Internship Selection and Expectations

It became clear from the start that the field of internships in Spain was very new and information scarce or nonexistent. With each of the companies I visited, I started the meeting by explaining, in general terms, the concept of an internship for undergraduate students. The challenge was to dispel the apprehension that the program might involve cost (to the companies) and to explain that the intern would provide assistance while gaining exposure to the functioning of the company or agency. Although the notion of someone in their midst without pay was received with surprise and disbelief, some more challenging questions were raised, such as how much training would the student need, how long would the student stay to make the training worthwhile, what was the student's knowledge or preparation in the field, and what sort of help or mentoring from the agency was expected? Some of these questions, such as length of training, had to be negotiated differently with each of the sites, as well as the duration of the internship because some places were not willing to take on the responsibility for a brief period of time. As for the help the student would provide, I made sure that menial tasks such as getting coffee and photocopying were not to be assigned to the student, unless there was a system in place whereby people took turns to carry them out. I also discussed at length the need to designate someone at the agency who would act as the supervisor and mentor for the student and maintain communication with the university's on-site internship coordinator. See Figure 8.1 for common questions staff of internship sites ask during the initial meeting.

Although the program has been functioning for the past nine years, similar questions are raised each time we set up a new site. When a student requests a site that is not on our list of offerings, Javier García Garrido, our on-site internship coordinator, checks the available options in the city, chooses the most suitable ones, and makes an appointment for a visit. If the facilities meet our expectations, he holds a meeting with the person in charge to discuss our proposal and the terms. Invariably, questions raised have to do

Figure 8.1. Common questions asked by staff at internship sites.

The following are some of the most frequently asked questions when staff of an internship site are approached for the first time.

1. What is the student's level in Spanish?
2. How many hours can the student devote to the internship?
3. How should the schedule be distributed during the internship period?
4. Does the student have medical insurance or, alternatively, has the student signed a document freeing the university and internship site of all liability?
5. How much pay should the student receive?
6. Where in the United States is the student from?
7. Should a computer be provided, or will the student bring his or her own?
8. What type of tasks may we ask the student to perform?
9. What is the student's previous experience in a similar position?
10. What is the student's career major?
11. Who is responsible for the student's transportation to the internship site?
12. Who is in charge of the student's lodging?

with the student's linguistic ability, preparation, length of stay, and knowledge. Thanks to the experience we have acquired during these past years, we are able to address them efficiently. However, there is always the job of convincing the site personnel that our proposal is a good one and that the agency will benefit from having a person who can speak English; who is knowledgeable of the culture and work style in the United States; and, because of his or her age, can connect well with young customers, patients, or other people frequenting the site. The intern's work is at no cost to the site, and in some cases, the site staff may find the student valuable enough to train him or her for a future position. See Figure 8.2 for our internship site selection criteria and site expectations.

In each agency or organization, internships are supervised by a person designated to assist and supervise the student's work. This person (site supervisor) is expected to contact the on-site internship coordinator (García Garrido in Salamanca) if any issues arise. In turn, the on-site internship coordinator maintains ongoing communication with the site supervisor and with the student. Once both sides reach a mutual understanding of what each is expected to provide, an agreement document that spells out the rights and responsibilities of the site and the student is signed, and the internship is established.

Figure 8.2. Internship site selection criteria and site expectations.

Site Selection Criteria

1. The student indicates a desire for a specific type of internship.
2. The internship site covers a field of expertise and knowledge that may not be requested by students but offers an innovative approach that we feel students should consider.
3. The location is geographically appropriate
4. The site administrator may be interested in hosting U.S. interns because of their English language ability.
5. The site handles a large enough workload to engage students.

Expectations Site

1. We expect the site to provide a site supervisor, that is, a person in charge of supervising and guiding student work.
2. We expect the student to be treated fairly.
3. We expect for someone at the site to engage the student in conversational Spanish.
4. We expect the site personnel to respect the agreement and not request the student to perform tasks that are not part of the agreed-on terms.
5. We expect the site staff to keep a record of student attendance.

Program Growth

From the humble beginnings of two students attending the first program, the Wake Forest Summer Internship Program continues to grow consistently but modestly. During two summer sessions, total enrollment might be 12 students, with 7 to 8 being a more usual number. The main reason for these figures is the high tuition students pay to their home institution. Other reasons are the wide range of other study and traveling options available to students at competitive prices, students' need to take other academic courses during the summer to meet requirements, their need to hold summer jobs, and the language proficiency required to perform well at the site.

The number of internship sites and courses has been growing to meet students' individual preferences and needs, which reflects the individualized character of the program. For example, the medical field was the first internship to be determined in response to student requests. Some of the clinics and hospitals were initially interested in having an intern for the language as they needed an English interpreter to help with English-speaking patients, which are a considerable number in a city like Salamanca where international students fill classrooms each summer. However, because of bureaucratic obstacles in the public health system, we have been able to establish a stable agreement with only one private clinic, as others have refused for legal reasons.

Presently, the program offers internships in a wide range of fields such as medical, business, education, translation, interpretation, sports, university offices, and veterinarian clinics, to name a few. Furthermore, courses have been added to complement the internship experience and to meet requirements for the major and minor in Spanish.

Timing and Duration of Program

The internship short-term study abroad program is five weeks in duration. In the earlier years, we offered only it during the first Wake Forest summer session. To provide more flexibility, as some students choose to sign up for the first summer school on the home campus, we added a second summer session program with dates corresponding to those of the home campus. However, the second session presents some on-site problems because it extends until August, a month when most agencies in Spain close for summer vacation.

Internship Companion Course Work

To participate in the summer abroad internship program, students must matriculate in a three-credit-hour internship course because it provides full immersion and a hands-on experience that regular academic courses do not always provide. The first of two internship courses is called Internship in Spanish Language, and is offered on a pass or fail basis for students from a broad variety of fields. The prerequisite is to pass a grammar and composition course or have permission of the instructor. It does not count toward the Spanish major or minor. The second course, Internship in Spanish for Business and the Professions, has the same prerequisite as the first course and is likewise offered on a pass or fail basis, but this course is geared to students interested or specializing in business. The Wake Forest University Business School accepts the credits as long as the student completes 200 internship hours.

It is strongly recommended for students to enroll in one other course in conversation or in literary and cultural subjects. For example, a companion language course, Language Study in the Context of an Internship, is intended to develop students' oral proficiency and writing skills. Reading, discussions, and writing assignments are based on texts relevant to matriculated students' internships. This course must be taken in conjunction with the internship course; however, a combination of this course and the internship course may count as a maximum of three hours toward the major or minor in Spanish.

Besides the conversation course, the program offers three more classes in Spanish literature and culture. Two of the literature courses are a survey type that are required for the major and the minor; the third course is a seminar that counts as an elective and has varying course content each summer.

To summarize, for this program, students typically enroll in a three-hour internship course and a conversation course for a total of six credits. Some students sign up for one of the literature classes besides the internship and with or without the conversation class. We believe students would apply for the internship plus enroll in one or two of the literature or culture classes if it were not for the high tuition cost.

Target Audience and Language Prerequisites

As indicated earlier, our program offers two internship courses: one that encompasses a broad range of internship sites and one that is geared to business students. Both courses appeal to a broad audience of students, not only Spanish majors and minors but also students in any field who wish to practice their Spanish language skills and acquire more fluency. The business internship targets students in the business school, but nonbusiness students who are interested in fields such as economics also often opt for that more specialized internship.

The better the fluency in the language, the better the student will perform at the internship site. Oral and written competence is the top requirement for internships. The prerequisite work for both courses is to have passed one course beyond the 200-level, which means that students may have had several years of Spanish in high school and place beyond the 200-level required course to graduate from Wake Forest. If they placed at the 200-level on entering Wake Forest, they will need to pass one more class to be eligible. The same rule applies for students who started Spanish when they came to Wake Forest or were placed at the intermediate level.

The Curriculum

In developing the internship curriculum, we were guided by students' academic needs and personal preferences. We also had to consider what could be accomplished during five weeks in the summer because internships have time requirements, and some sites require a minimum number of hours the student has to complete to be accepted as an intern. For the literature and culture courses, the curriculum also had to be adapted to meet the academic requirements of the home campus. Because a conversation class was already offered, the main goal when developing a syllabus for the internship conversation course was to adapt its relevance to internship sites. This meant including the immersion nature of the program, which is addressed through oral presentations and written assignments on geographical areas, local customs, climate, and traditions. Furthermore, students are required to give oral summaries including the main aspects of cultural sites they visit in the city.

The textbook *Curso de lectura, conversación y redacción* by José Siles Artés and Jesús Sánchez Maza (2007) was selected because it includes materials to facilitate learning grammar, provides exposure to different cultural and literary topics, and allows vocabulary acquisition. The textbook includes 23 units structured around a literary or cultural reading by well-known authors such as Wenceslao Fernández Florez, Julio Llamazares, and Carmen Laforet, among others. These selections are relevant because of their artistic quality, the authors' renown, and the relevancy of the topics. Cultural topics include sports, medicine, economics, media, and ecology, plus themes treated in each of the texts, which include film, rites of passage, diet, vocation, traveling, politics, and so on. Each reading selection is preceded by a brief biographical note about the author or, in the case of cultural topics, by some questions to promote an initial discussion about the topic. Texts are accompanied by a series of questions about content, vocabulary, sentence completion based on content, and grammar exercises teaching specific structures encountered in the text.

We have added a component on cultural differences to the syllabus in response to instances of culture shock that students frequently experience. Because of the immersive nature of the program, students are exposed to a very genuine cultural experience that places intercultural differences at the forefront. These open but formalized discussions on cultural differences give students the opportunity to voice their concerns, have their worries appeased, learn how to navigate in the culture, and avoid misunderstandings. For these intercultural conversations and exchanges, we use activities suggested by Paige and colleagues (2006).

Practically every summer, incidents pertaining to intercultural differences occur at different levels. Although reasons are varied and should be addressed in open discussion, expectations seem to be a major cause. As a case in point, a student who requested an internship in international relations was placed with an agency in charge of custom control with Portugal. The student did not think that this internship was international in nature because all transactions took place at the Transportation Center located in Salamanca.

The student was never in Portugal and failed to recognize that these activities involved communications between two different countries. Other cultural differences have also occurred with the Red Cross. Students sign up for an internship with that agency expecting it to be a hospital when the organization has a much broader social agenda than a strictly medical one.

Another cultural difference that comes up every summer deals with dress codes. Before departing for Spain, many students inquire about appropriate clothing. Dress codes for professional settings are much stricter in the United States than in Spain. There have been instances where the student showed up for the internship all dressed up when requirements at the site were much less formal.

Outcomes-Based Student and Program Assessments

Students signing up for an internship are interviewed by the Salamanca program director on the Wake Forest campus to determine their oral fluency levels. The outcome of the interview is conveyed to the on-site internship coordinator (García Garrido) to determine the most suitable site for each student according to his or her oral skills. If the students' choice of an internship site is not an appropriate match for their oral skills, students are advised to consider another site. Or when possible, students are informed that their initial placement at the site will be limited in contact with clients until their oral skills improve. Student progress in the internship and conversation classes is assessed throughout the five-week abroad period using a variety of tools. Internship students are required to

- give informal oral accounts of the internship experience in weekly meetings with the on-site internship coordinator as a way to reflect on their progress and formulate ideas for their final report;
- keep a weekly journal in Spanish that includes dates and work hours at the site, and a summary (about 7 to 10 sentences) of each day's activities and observations;
- compile a list of new words and expressions; and
- write in Spanish a reflective report or statement of about 800 to 900 words about the internship experience with an appendix containing a list of all new vocabulary words acquired during the internship.

Students in the conversation class related to the internship are required to

- speak on literary and cultural topics to improve oral skills, vocabulary acquisition, and grammar;

- develop comprehension skills by reading texts related to the internship and to Spanish culture and daily life; and
- write assignments that will also be shared with the class as oral presentations.

One point to be clarified has to do with the number of hours students are expected to complete at the internship site. The misunderstanding here is related to cultural differences. Conventionally, students consider their work at the internship site as being equal to completing the required number of hours to receive academic credit. The site, however, is concerned with students completing the number of hours that have been agreed on at the outset based on the site's needs for a specific project or task. In some cases, after counting the hours and thinking they have completed the necessary number, students simply did not return to the site and did not notify anyone.

At the end of the program, students are asked to fill out an evaluation form about all aspects of the program; these evaluations are reviewed by the Salamanca program director and the on-site internship coordinator to determine if adjustments or changes are needed.

Experiential Learning Events on Site

As part of the learning experience, students participate in an opening orientation consisting of a walking tour throughout the city of Salamanca, guided by the Wake Forest Salamanca program's cultural assistant, to familiarize them with main civic buildings (police headquarters, offices for foreign affairs, post office, etc.), medical centers (clinics and hospitals), and relevant social sites in the city. Students also take a walking tour of the historic sites and monuments with explanations about history, art, and culture.

Depending on availability at the time, the program also offers free tickets to cultural activities related to Spain, such as plays, films, or concerts. The on-site internship coordinator accompanies students to these events. In addition, the program offers

- two group meals with the on-site internship coordinator and a welcome and a farewell dinner;
- two one-day field excursions to surrounding areas, such as Ávila and El Escorial or Segovia (sometimes one of these excursions may be to Toledo);
- tutorials to help with language and grammar problems;
- assistance in setting up exchanges with Spanish students;
- advice and itineraries for students' own personal trips; and

- access to the Wake Forest Center, which, besides space facilities, offers free photocopying and printing services, a book and film library, free coffee and water, and connection to the Internet.

During the actual internship in Salamanca, the main course work delivery takes place in various academic and advisory meetings that are part of the internship course, in informal meetings at the Wake Forest Center, and during group meals and cultural events.

Postprogram Activities

Returning students can take a one-credit course, Cross Cultural Engagement and Re-Entry, which allows them to reflect on their experience abroad and the cultural learning that took place. Moving ahead, the Wake Forest Center for Global Programs and Studies is initiating several reentry events for students, such as a general event for students who have studied abroad in Spain. This event offers food (tapas of some sort), and students play reflection games in an effort to try to help them analyze their experience. The same office is working with the Office of Personal and Career Development to provide support for résumé writing for the returned study abroad students. See Figure 8.3 for an example of a reflection game.

Unique Logistical Challenges

One important logistical challenge that the program and its directors encounter each year is to convince sites to accept students as interns. The reluctance

Figure 8.3. Postabroad reflection game.

Prompts are written on slips of paper to be randomly chosen and answered by participating students in the group. The prompts encourage individual students to talk and also promote discussion and reflection among the group.

- What was your biggest challenge abroad?
- How can you apply your study abroad experience to your chosen career path?
- Name three things from abroad that you miss the least.
- What was your biggest cultural success?
- Describe an experience when you committed a cultural faux pas.
- What new insights do you have about today's global world after studying abroad?

to accept students is based on a number of factors, for example, apprehension that the interns may end up being more trouble than help because they require training and supervision, concern that the students' language skills will not be appropriate for the task, and a belief that the students' stay will be too short to make the training process a worthwhile one. To alleviate this challenge, the on-site internship coordinator meets with internship representatives to review the requirements that the student needs to meet to receive academic credit. During the meeting, he clarifies the supervision the student is under to make sure that all obligations with the site are met, he ensures that the student will have enough knowledge and interest in the specific area, and he confirms his own availability to address any concerns the site director may have during the internship period. Because a relationship based on trust and mutual support needs to be established from the outset and respected throughout, a review of these steps is very important. When these points have been discussed, and the experience proves to be positive, internship site staff are pleased to continue with the program and accept students each summer.

Considering these challenges, students need to be very aware of the importance of abiding by the rules listed in their student internship document regarding

- being on time according to the site's work schedule during the internship period;
- working diligently on the assigned tasks during the internship period;
- explaining any justified absence, and if because of illness, presenting official medical proof; and
- committing to attend weekly meetings of professional advancement taking place at the site.

The following illustrates some of the problems that may arise in this sensitive relationship. After an apparently positive experience, where the student seemed to be fully integrated with the site and had even developed personal relationships with some of the employees and socialized with them for coffee and tapas, the student left the site without saying good-bye at the end of the term. The site supervisor called the on-site internship coordinator to find out if anything had happened that would justify the student's behavior. She was surprised that after all the personal care and attention given to the student, the expected good-byes did not take place.

Another challenge that arises almost every summer has to do with students' inability to interact with people at the internship site. It is thus essential for the on-site internship coordinator to be in close contact with the site supervisor to be aware of the students' adaptation throughout the internship experience. There have been instances where the site supervisor has called to ask for advice about what to do to help the student integrate better. This challenge illustrates the fact that internships have to do with much more than academic skills. The student's personality is a major factor as well as the environment at the site and willingness of both parties to open up and help the integration process.

Stories From the Field

Comments students have shared with us after their internship experience confirm the importance of emphasizing many of the points we already include in our information sessions, personal interviews, and orientation periods. Students need to be well informed of what is expected of them at the site in terms of language proficiency; ability to connect socially with others; and being observant, proactive, and good listeners. They should also be guided in their selection of the site so that their placement fits their interests and expertise. It is important to avoid a selection based on mere curiosity or slight interest.

Several students who opted for an internship at a local elementary school benefited from clear advice on what to expect regarding interactions with young students, teaching methods that differ from the ones they know in the United States, and contacts with teachers. Right away one of the students faced the challenge of having to communicate with young children and adolescents. Without much previous experience, she observed the teachers closely and paid attention to the classroom environment. As the internship period progressed, she became so integrated with the school that at the end she confessed to missing "her children" very much. This student came to realize how teachers may become very attached to their students and how important those relationships may be for the child's education.

Comments regarding the relationship between teacher and student abound, as interns observe the impact they have on the children and how their connection with them grows as time passes: "They would yell my name as I entered the classroom and would fight to play with me!" says a student who confessed feeling quite lost when she first started her internship at the school. Another student, who also interned at the school, felt she was making a meaningful contribution when the English teacher asked her to pronounce words and sentences for the children's benefit. She learned about her own language by observing while the teacher taught English grammar to Spanish students.

In the field of translation, students talk about having their eyes opened to a world they knew very little about. If at first they thought it was easy to translate from Spanish to English, they soon realized the difficulties involved in the process and learned to value the expertise required for it. A student felt fulfilled after translating a whole Web page from Spanish into English. She expressed her enthusiasm for the internship experience at the University of Salamanca translation program in the following: "I would recommend everyone to sign up for an internship because what you learn in the classroom is very different from what you learn at work, where you have a hands-on approach." Through this internship the student learned how complex and exciting communication is.

At a medical site, another student confessed he learned something that went beyond new vocabulary and ways of dealing with patients. He learned to better appreciate the doctor's work and what is involved in this kind of profession, which he would like to do in the future. He also noted the difference between the United States, where health and illness are private matters, and Spain, where there is less of a taboo in discussing those issues. These cultural observations may be discussed in the classroom, but in a real setting, they become truly meaningful.

These examples accurately reflect some of the benefits students find in their internship experience such as a hands-on approach to a field of their interest, the importance of developing good social skills, the personal satisfaction in developing new relationships, appreciation of cultural differences, new perspectives for their future career choices, and learning to appreciate their own language and the complexities involved in communicating. These benefits are personal as well as professional and academic. They confirm the value that educational opportunities internships have to offer.

References

Paige, R. M., Cohen, A. D., Kappler, B., Chi, J. C., & Lassegard, J. P. (2006). *Maximizing study abroad: A program professionals' guide to strategies for language and culture learning and use.* Minneapolis: Center for Advance Research on Language Acquisition, University of Minnesota.

Siles Artés, J., & Sánchez Maza, J. (2007). *Curso de lectura: conversación y redacción.* Madrid, Spain: Sociedad General Española de Librería.

9

DESIGNING THE CURRICULUM FOR CULTURAL STUDIES ABROAD

Intercultural Learning in China

Min Zhou

At the age of 15, I was awarded a scholarship through the German Academic Exchange Service to spend a summer month in Germany with a group of students from several continents. It was my first time traveling outside my home in Wuhan in southern China. After studying German for three years, I was so eager to practice the language that I came out of my shell of shyness and spoke with everyone I met. Enthralled by the magic of language to connect people of different nationalities, I returned home less inhibited and even more interested in bettering my German so I could visit again.

The month in Germany helped me improve my German language skills significantly, especially in speaking and listening comprehension. Intercultural learning, however, was another story. What I witnessed in my host family and on tours through German cities and landmarks was overwhelmingly different from my home country of China. The two countries felt farther apart than the geographical distance between them, and I did not know what to think about the differences. The few incidents that did prompt me to pause and reflect only confirmed the preconceived notions about capitalism that I had learned at school. For the most part, tremendous waves of

I am grateful to Tyler Marvelli for giving me his journal about the China program and to Manveer Singh for reflecting on the program several years after participating in it. Both of them have helped me reconstruct many details for this chapter. I would like to thank Catherine Hawkes for commenting on and proofreading this chapter as well as many of my writings over the past 10 years.

adventure washed over me every minute without leaving many ripples within me, at least not at the time. At the end of the month, I packed up precious memories and went back to my real life.

My experience was not atypical. As Bennett (2012) points out, "Intercultural learning does not happen automatically during study abroad" (p. 90). To turn cross-cultural contact into intercultural learning, theoretical insights and research findings tell us that students need "cultural mentoring" (p. 129) and guided reflection on their experience to become aware of their habitual perspectives and to develop intercultural competence, which is the capacity to shift cultural perspectives and adapt behavior to cultural differences (Bennett, 2012). The importance of mentoring is vividly illustrated in the metaphors of a light with a motion sensor and a dimmer switch in the following:

> The appropriate emblem for learning abroad is not a yard light equipped with a motion sensor that is tripped when a student enters the yard, so that he or she is suddenly bathed in the light of new knowledge. Learning is more like a dimmer switch. As the student enters a dark room, he or she needs to find the switch and begin to experiment with the effects of moving it up or down. (Vande Berg, Paige, & Lou, 2012, p. 18)

During my first study abroad in Germany, I did not find the dimmer switch, as I had no one to share and reflect on my experience and go beyond the surface of the experience.

Designing a Faculty-Led Study Abroad Program

Now I am a professor at Roger Williams University (RWU), a small, private university in Rhode Island. In 2010 I designed and implemented my own faculty-led short-term study abroad program titled Introduction to Culture in Contemporary China. This program includes a three-credit course, which is conducted in English and requires no prior knowledge of the Chinese language. It is designed for RWU students to fulfill a requirement for a minor in Chinese and an elective requirement for those majoring in other disciplines. The duration of the program is three weeks, with one week of predeparture campus meetings during the spring semester and two weeks in Beijing and Xi'an during the summer session. I have successfully run this program twice since its inception.

My approach to teaching the program is to consciously guide students in their interactions with and reflections on China, a strategy that was drawn from my own experience of study abroad as a student and from study abroad research findings. Thus, while designing and teaching the study abroad program in China, I see my primary role as providing *cultural mentoring*, which Paige and Vande Berg (2012) define as "intentional and deliberate pedagogical approaches, activated throughout the study abroad cycle . . . that are designed to enhance students' intercultural competence" (pp. 29–30). Through my mentoring and student assignments, I ensure that students realize several learning outcomes.

Program Learning Outcomes

First, students are to demonstrate specific knowledge about Chinese history, religion, and culture; connect this knowledge with what they observe in China; and recognize cultural values and beliefs. Second, students are to develop an awareness of their own identities, cultures, and values. Third, with a growing capacity for self-awareness and an awareness of others, they are to apply the knowledge by analyzing and interpreting the behavior of people in the host culture. Ideally, as the fourth outcome, students cultivate strategies to interact more effectively and appropriately with the Chinese people, a goal that usually takes longer than two or three weeks to achieve. I hope that some students accomplish this fourth outcome, at least in specific contexts, during the abroad experience. Finally, for the fifth outcome, I ask students to design their own outcome, which is assessed by way of individual research paper projects.

How did I embed these program learning outcomes into my curriculum design? My plan was to develop and implement intercultural learning events and activities before, during, and after traveling abroad to China.

Program Learning Events

Predeparture

Predeparture preparation is designed to introduce students to the program outcomes and academic requirements; establish an understanding of study abroad as a learning experience; and cultivate a rapport among students and with me, their instructor. To accomplish this, I facilitate two activities. One involves readings and video screenings with subsequent discussions to help students acquire knowledge about China, which is the first of the program outcomes, and to familiarize students with intercultural concepts and skills in the program outcomes. The other activity requires students to identify their individual personal learning outcomes in an independent project in which they choose one aspect of their engagement with China, pay attention to the aspect while in China, and submit a paper on the aspect after the program is completed.

Four 3-hour meetings are scheduled for predeparture preparation. Needless to say, it is not easy to carve out time for these meetings during a semester when students are taking five or six regular courses. To have students complete assignments and come to the meetings prepared, I experimented with different genres and forms and was most successful with the documentary film *China: A Century of Revolution* (Williams, 1997) and Peter Hessler's book *River Town* (2001).

Parts two and three of Williams's (1997) film documents modern Chinese history from 1949 through 1997 with compelling footage and interviews with Chinese people. In contrast, Hessler (2001) chronicles a 27-year-old American's life of teaching English and American literature at a college in southern China and living in a small town there between 1996 and 1998. The book's astute observation of ordinary Chinese people and its insightful discussion of Chinese history, culture, politics, and intellectual tradition from an American perspective corroborate many views represented in Williams's (1997) documentary and add depth and complexity.

For the documentary, students work out an outline of events in recent Chinese history to gain factual knowledge about China. For the book, I ask specific questions to guide students in reading, reflecting on, and discussing the text in class. The questions draw students' attention to passages where the author-narrator explored cultural differences with acute sensitivity; to his poignant comments on his own culture of origin and identity; and to the moment when, after his first year in China, he shifted his perspective by adopting a friendly and unsophisticated Chinese persona, a new identity that contrasted with his American self (Hessler, 2001).

If students grasp from the learning outcomes what they are expected to achieve, then the book and discussions demonstrate how to approach these outcomes. Like the author-narrator, they too could train their observation skills, make meaning of encounters with China and Chinese people, cultivate the capacity for cultural and personal reflection of their own, and adjust their frame of reference to the Chinese way of thinking and behaving.

For their personal learning outcomes, students meet with me individually to discuss their projects. I make sure that the proposed projects are feasible, that is, neither too broad to lose focus nor too narrow to present difficulty gathering enough material. It is also important for students to draw on their own observations and experiences in China and not rely solely on books, journals, or online resources. Most students present projects that are connected with the disciplines of their studies and revise the projects while abroad.

Although predeparture activities improve students' cognition, they have little impact on students' affect because direct interpersonal experience with the Chinese culture is obviously missing in the U.S. classroom. However, reading about and discussing another person's view on China makes students aware of the important role of reflection in learning about another culture and helps them develop the habit of thinking about their experiences. Once in China, students are required to keep a journal for observations and reflections, and the journal, like the personal project, is to be turned in after students return to the United States. Both the journal and the personal project keep students focused and make them mindful learners during their intercultural experience in China.

In Country

Beijing and Xi'an, as metropolises of several dynasties such as Qin, Han, Tang, and Qing as well as contemporary China, document history and religion in their historical landmarks and exhibit clashes of tradition and modernity. They are therefore ideal sites for a program on contemporary Chinese culture with a focus on history and religion. At the same time, the difference between cosmopolitan Beijing and the so-called second tier city Xi'an also provides students with a more complex China to observe, interact with, and reflect on. I also chose Beijing because I had studied and lived there for 10 years and knew how to navigate the megacity and its people. However, it is challenging to embrace the complexities of Beijing and Xi'an within two weeks.

Because the students travel all the way from the United States to China, I want them to take full advantage of the location and to explore the seemingly unlimited urban space by actively engaging with their environments. As the instructor, I understand my role as mediator among the Chinese cities, people residing in the cities, and students from different cultural backgrounds. One of my key roles is to steer students through their cross-cultural encounters and their decoding (and, sometimes, misinterpretation) of these encounters and help them find the dimmer switch through guided reflection.

The city is our classroom. Discussions take place whenever opportunities present themselves: on shuttle buses, in waiting lounges, and almost always after dinner when the day is drawing to a close. Students are asked to describe and analyze their impressions and interactions. They listen to one another, ask questions, or offer thoughts to expand on one another's thinking.

In the following, I offer several examples of intercultural activities and guided discussions to demonstrate how the 2013 China program supported and aided the transformation of student attitudes toward various aspects of the local culture.

Tasting Authentic Chinese Food

When my program was first offered in 2010, I was dismayed that several students, frequent travelers actually, brought provisions from home so they did not have to sample the local food. Every meal eaten together felt like a struggle. At the time, I thought to myself that with such mind-sets, cultural exploration would be nearly impossible. When the program was offered again in 2013, during predeparture meetings I discussed how the cultural learning outcomes of the program translated into maintaining an open and nonjudgmental attitude as well as the willingness and curiosity to explore what the culture had to offer. In terms of meals, for instance, I strongly encouraged the students who did not have dietary restrictions to try everything, whether it was whole fish with the head and eyes, meat with embedded bones, or vegetables they had never seen before or did not previously enjoy. It was rewarding when a student who liked only beef enthusiastically enjoyed eating a plate of exotic Chinese vegetables or when a vegetarian ventured beyond fried rice with eggs and noodles.

Adapting to Commonplace Amenities

It is no exaggeration to say that the program in China annulled students' previous references and turned common routines into substantial efforts. In Beijing the dorm either had no warm water in the morning or had warm water that stopped in the middle of a shower. Window air conditioners were inefficient; Internet connections slow; toilets blocked every now and then; and because no dryer was available, students had to plan laundry well in advance. Additionally, there was a great deal of walking and stair climbing, despite a bus that took students to different sites. Unpleasantly surprised, students turned to me for explanations, and I in turn facilitated an inquiry activity.

For this activity, I asked students to walk through the campus where they were staying and take mental notes of what they saw. In contrast to the dorm for international students where our group stayed, dorms for Chinese students did not have air-conditioning window units. In the late afternoon, many Chinese students carried thermos bottles to a specific place to get hot water because no warm water was available in their dorms. An inconspicuous flat building advertised laundry service, which meant that, unlike our students, Chinese students did not even have access to washing machines in their buildings. No laundromat was found on campus or close by, yet laundry hanging outside dorm windows and in the rooms was visible from the streets on campus; it was not difficult to guess that Chinese students hand washed their clothes. Students also compared a shop in their dorm for international students and a shop on campus catering to Chinese students. Although the former had imported snacks for sale at a relatively high price, the latter carried much more affordable snacks produced in China. The university where students stayed, I reminded them, was one of the top Chinese universities, and education was regarded as an opportunity available to a few privileged people, as college students were called.

Having experienced the infrastructure at a college campus in China, students could imagine how living conditions might be for the majority of the Chinese population. Their observations, experiences, and discussions led them to grow more appreciative of campus life in the United States. Many of them realized that the strong economic growth of a nation did not necessarily translate into a good life for its citizens, at least not yet. They adjusted their expectations, complained less about air-conditioning and the Internet, and changed their daily routines by either getting up very early to take a shower before the warm water ran out or skipping a morning shower and taking a cold one in the evening instead.

Adapting to the Chinese Sense of Time
Students had to deal with the reality that daily plans were frequently changed without notice and that schedules for the next day were not available until the last minute. Why couldn't Chinese people be better organized and more efficient? Students were annoyed. I asked them to think about what they saw on the streets and at sites we visited in terms of what Chinese did with their time and whether they could recognize patterns. Students first talked about a familiarly hectic pace of life, as they saw in the Beijing subways; on streets during rush hour; and with their guide, who had to commute over an hour from one side of the city to the other to be with us every morning. Several students then mentioned their surprise at seeing on a weekday morning many people, young and old, doing Tai Qi, playing badminton, kicking shuttlecock, wielding a sword, or singing Beijing opera at sites like the Temple of Heaven. Because of the program's focus on contemporary China and its history and modernity, it did not take students long to realize that they were witnessing the coexistence of a traditional way of living with an accelerated modern lifestyle. Because of the influence of this slow living tradition, I told students that many Chinese are laid back and go with the flow. They do not carry a planner or schedule an appointment days or weeks in advance, and reasonable tardiness is believed to be polite and considerate in China, especially when one is invited as a guest, to give hosts more time to prepare.

Students learned through this experience that every culture has different customs and traditions and that it was ethnocentric to measure another culture against the standards of their own. If they wanted their way of doing things everywhere they went, why bother traveling? Wouldn't it be better to stay home? By the time students arrived in Xi'an, they were more relaxed and better at taking schedule changes in stride.

Understanding the Chinese Concept of Personal Space
When traveling from Beijing to Xi'an, we took an overnight train that gave students more opportunities to interact with and observe Chinese people,

many of whom came from humble backgrounds. In the hard berth carriage, students were irritated when Chinese passengers invited themselves to sit on their chosen lower berths. Instead of intervening on the students' behalf, I left it to them to resolve the situation, and several students tried to keep the space for themselves. In our debriefing after arrival, I reminded students that because of the higher density of the Chinese population, the scope of personal space was much narrower in China than in the United States. Chinese passengers would take lower berths as public spaces, just as Chinese would not say excuse me when they were in the way of other people. These behaviors resulted from Chinese people's living circumstances rather than from rudeness or disregard for privacy. On the train ride back to Beijing, even though students still felt uncomfortable when others sat on their lower berths, they withheld negative judgment and respected the social custom. The most valuable lesson for me was to be proactive about teaching the reasons behind traditional behaviors before students were in the position to experience them.

Adapting to Celebrity Status

Soon after their arrival in Beijing, students experienced being the center of attention as many Chinese stared at them or asked to have their pictures taken with them. After the initial excitement of feeling like celebrities, many of them became impatient and frustrated. When confronted with this phenomenon, students remembered our predeparture discussion about xenophobia (Hessler, 2001) and felt that the Chinese people asking for photos and staring were disrespectful acts.

To help students understand this behavior, I asked why this annoyance seldom took place on the Beijing college campus where they were residing. Students concurred that because many international students were studying on the same campus, they did not stand out as Westerners. As a preparation for a follow-up inquiry activity to address this standing-out phenomenon, I reviewed certain Chinese phrases such as, Do you live in Beijing? Where do you come from? Are you a tourist? and Have you been here before? After language coaching, I sent them out to Tiananmen Square to work in groups or pairs with at least one student who had taken Chinese classes to ask people these questions. Students came back with similar answers; nearly all the Chinese people they interviewed were tourists, many of whom were visiting Beijing for the first time. They in turn started to construct meaning from the interview responses by integrating previously gained knowledge from the predeparture reading and documentary screening. They came to understand tourism as a rather new phenomenon in China. With the recent economic boom, a result of Deng Xiaoping's reform and opening policy shown in Williams's (1997) documentary, ordinary Chinese had more disposable income for traveling. Students realized that as modern as Beijing appeared, it was not a typical Chinese city. Chinese people in most cities had seen Westerners only on TV or in films, never in person. Unlike children in the small town who repeatedly harassed Hessler's (2001) author-narrator, tourists in Beijing were eager to touch students' blond hair to confirm the hair was real; they wanted to have pictures taken as evidence of their very first encounters with people of a different race.

Understanding the Chinese Philosophy of the Middle Way
Visiting the Great Wall was the highlight of many of my students' study of China. Besides excitement, pride, and exhaustion, they were also confused about the ubiquitous graffiti. Despite reading and discussing Hessler's (2001) book during predeparture in regard to historical architectural sites and his comment that "there was a great deal of history in China and if you protected all the ancient sites the people would have nowhere to grow their crops" (p. 107), students were still shocked by the graffiti. After all, the Great Wall was not just any ancient site, and it did not affect people's livelihoods either. Students wondered why anyone would deface a monument that was more than 2,000 years old.

During discussions, I asked another seemingly unrelated question: Which of the sites we explored had only a few Chinese visitors and why? I reminded students of Williams's (1997) documentary that we had viewed and discussed predeparture. One of the campaigns during the Cultural Revolution was an attack on the Four Olds—old ideas, old culture, old customs, and old habits—as being feudal or bourgeois in an effort to pump the new Communist ideology into education, art, and literature (Ebrey, n.d.). The campaign, as students learned from the documentary, destroyed countless national and personal treasures. Its destructive force was still palpable in contemporary China, because, I suggested, most Chinese had not learned to appreciate their cultural and religious traditions or to protect archeological relics or sites. The lack of understanding of and respect for their cultural heritage led to Buddhist and Taoist temples and monasteries being bereft of many Chinese visitors. It led to graffiti on the Great Wall and to the destruction of many historical buildings to make a place for modern architecture.

In this context, I introduced to students the work of Chinese artist Ai Weiwei and told them about his projects, such as "Whitewash," in which he assembled more than 100 "Neolithic vases, each one a beautiful piece of art and a relic, but one-fourth of them completely covered or destroyed by white industrial paint" (Sigg, 2009, pp. 12–13). Students' immediate reaction to the project was that Ai symbolically broke with tradition and destroyed the past to create something entirely new: an avant-garde art. When I placed Ai's act against the background of how tradition was treated in China, students started to see Ai's art differently. Perhaps the artist intended to use the shock that audiences felt on seeing old vases destroyed to bring home the message that Chinese archeological and historical artifacts were being annihilated so frequently that it was high time for people to do something about it. Further, I divulged that the approach in Ai's project reflected a typical Chinese way of finding a happy medium. Contrary to a Western dualist approach according to whether a thing is either this or that, as shown in the Western avant-garde art, "in a Chinese mind, the same thing may well be this and that at the same time" (Sigg, 2009, pp. 12–13). In this sense, Ai's work represents a fusion of two contradictory paradigms: Although showing great respect for tradition, he treats "art creation as an evolving continuum drawing from the wealth of Chinese culture" (Sigg, 2009, pp. 12–13). For the remaining time during their program, students were asked to pay attention to behaviors they believed reflected this Chinese philosophy of the Middle Way.

Tolerating the Ambiguity of a Complex Society

One of the most prevalent advantages study abroad programs have over conventional home campus-based courses is the complexity that a host country presents to students, incorporating challenges that students often do not expect. If China was, and still is, associated with Communism in the U.S. media, then what students experienced in China was quite different.

Upon their arrival in Beijing, students were amazed by the presence of English on street signs, billboards, and building fronts and by the prominence of Western chain stores in the capital city. Some students had expected a Communist country to be void of Western-style consumerism. Many of them were also surprised by the sheer numbers of people waiting in a long line outside Chairman Mao Mausoleum to pay their respects to Mao. When setting foot in Tiananmen Square for the first time, students were mesmerized by the historical significance the place represented. Their guide was a woman in her forties who was talkative about her family and life in contemporary China and was critical of problems such as corruption, air pollution, city landscaping, and automobile regulation. When a student asked about Chinese students' demands for democratic reform in 1989, the guide pointed to a nearby building and started talking about it, as if she had not heard the student's question, even after another student repeated it. Back in their dorms, students searched online about Tiananmen Square but found nothing historically relevant. Later they met and talked to Chinese students who said they did not mind or even notice Internet regulation.

How does one reconcile Communism with Western consumerism, Chinese people's respect for Mao with his image in the West, the guide's critiques of China with her self-censoring silence, and an Internet firewall with Chinese students' indifference to it? Students were left with no definitive answers. These questions and their experiences, however, discouraged them from perpetuating the stereotypical black-and-white portrayals of China common in the Western media and instilled in them the curiosity and motivation to discover more of China while cultivating a greater tolerance for the ambiguities inherent in a complex society.

Reflecting on Speaking the Chinese Language

Visiting China without being able to speak Chinese is like living in a small midwestern town in the United States without a car. Even students who had taken Chinese classes for two years often felt helpless when they extended their communication with locals beyond greetings and basic phrases. The patience and enthusiasm that many Chinese showed after hearing students speak Chinese to them surprised, encouraged, and sometimes embarrassed students. Some of them developed greater empathy for the other. For example, a student remarked that she used to be irritated with the staff at a fast-food drive-through restaurant in her hometown because the staff lived and worked in the United States yet continued to speak Spanish. Now that she experienced the challenge of being an outsider and not knowing what others around her took for granted, she understood better the predicament of the restaurant staff and appreciated them in a different light.

Interacting With Locals

There were notable moments when several students were appropriate, effective, and professional in their interaction with Chinese people. After the initial discussion about their experiences of being stared at in Beijing, students traveled to Xi'an. Their visit to the city wall in Xi'an occurred on June 1, International Children's Day. Several of the students were surrounded by schoolchildren, pushed by their parents to have pictures taken or to practice English. Many of my students patiently posed for pictures and spoke in English or Chinese with the children. Instead of being annoyed, students graciously accommodated the local children and families. By the end of the day, despite the lost opportunity to appreciate the city wall and surrounding archaeological artifacts, students prided themselves on demonstrating polite and appropriate behavior toward the locals. In this instance, students chose cultural engagement over their more touristic impulses.

As Deardorff (2006) suggests in her process-based model of intercultural competence, it is possible for one to experience and demonstrate an "internal shift" (p. 256) in one's cultural competence through adaptability, flexibility, and empathy. To achieve this "internal outcome" (p. 256) is to embrace the different norms, customs, and traditions of another culture, and in the case of China versus the United States, the difference is immeasurable. We have seen in the preceding text a few cultural interactions in which my students were able to demonstrate a change in attitude (internal outcome) and, in some cases, a slight change in behavior that complemented the culture. Deardorff calls the latter change, "the external outcome," in which one begins to demonstrate "effective and appropriate communication and behaviors" (p. 256).

Together my students and I engaged in numerous field events focused on contemporary Chinese culture and its religious and historical contexts in Beijing and Xi'an. While learning facts about ancient sites, I encouraged students to use their senses to obtain a feel for the sites. Often, they discovered dissonances between old and new. These were moments when my cultural mentoring helped lead students to the dimmer switch, connecting the knowledge they had learned about China with their experiences there. By means of observation, interpretation, and analysis, students deepened their cultural knowledge and become more aware of their own culture and that of the Chinese people.

Unique Challenges to Implementing a Language and Culture Study Abroad Program

Language

As mentioned earlier, knowledge of the Chinese language was not required for this study abroad program. Because the Chinese language program at RWU was small, it would be difficult to recruit the minimum of 8 to 10 participants to run the study abroad program. More important, linguistic differences between Chinese and English, or Indo-European languages in general, made it challenging for students—after meeting three hours a week for one or two years on campus—to acquire a communicative level in Chinese that would enable them to improve their language significantly during a two-week visit to China. Moreover, as instructor and organizer of the program, I had neither the funds nor the connections to arrange activities such as homestays or conversation hours with native speakers. An opportunity for intensive practice with experienced native Chinese might have made a language requirement more practical.

This does not mean, however, that language was not a component of the program. On the contrary, as mentioned, students had many opportunities to use the language. They benefited from reading Chinese characters on billboards, posters, and restaurant menus; hearing spoken Chinese; and from speaking with locals, haggling, and helping order dishes and drinks in restaurants, all of which provided lively opportunities to learn about Chinese people and their culture, history, and religion.

Another activity is worth a specific mention here. While visiting the Stele Forest, a museum for steles and stone sculptures in Xi'an, students were assigned to go through the stone carvings, take pictures of characters they could recognize, and share the characters with the class. They reviewed characters, practiced reading them in different contexts, and were fascinated that they were able to read characters in texts written more than 1,000 years ago. Students saw in characters not only signs but also bridges between past and present. In the journal margins of some students who had not even taken Chinese classes, every now and then appeared characters they drew.

Transportation and Housing Logistics

In Beijing we stayed in the dorm for international students at a university campus, thanks to a connection from a former colleague from my campus. The Chinese university also provided us with a shuttle bus and a guide, and helped me make arrangements for our visits to Beijing and Xi'an. I highly recommend working out logistics with a reputable institution such as a university instead of working through travel agencies on one's own. The Chinese institution's long-standing relationships with travel agencies guaranteed the quality of service by our chauffeurs and guides, who could make or break the students' experience in China. Moreover, a common practice in the Chinese travel industry is tour guides taking visitors to specific shops for commissions or to maintain relationships between the shops and agencies. The staff at the university I worked with, however, made sure that students would not be dragged to shops, which saved valuable time and spared us unpleasant encounters.

Because sites were spread out across Beijing, and traffic was often congested, the shuttle bus not only saved us time and energy but also gave students the opportunity to observe the metropolis at street level (versus subway) while listening to the guide talk about history and contemporary life in China. Students did have opportunities to take a subway or taxi in their free time, although they were required to be in pairs or groups and always to have the university address in Chinese with them. It was fun and adventurous for many of them to figure out how to buy tickets, which subway to take, and how to communicate with taxi drivers about where to go. They learned basic phrases in Chinese and learned how to read various signs.

In Xi'an, we stayed on a campus in 2010 and in a downtown hotel in 2013. The latter worked out much better, as most sites in Xi'an were centralized in the downtown area, and hotels were also more affordable than in Beijing. Students walked everywhere to explore the city and interact with locals. They were motivated to learn Chinese so that they could haggle with shopkeepers and stand owners. Students learned that punching numbers on a calculator or speaking a few Chinese phrases would not necessarily get them better deals. Rather, it took sincere interest, humility, and communication to win over sellers.

Guides

My students' guides were all local, and their presentations of China's past and present added a personal touch the guidebooks could not provide. Their casual talks about family and friends gave students a glimpse into ordinary Chinese people's daily lives. More important, because of their interactions with people from all over the globe, the guides were often more open-minded and critical of what was going on in China (except for taboo topics such as the Tiananmen Square event in 1989) and provided perspectives that many Chinese students either did not have or did not feel comfortable sharing with our students. In 2010, I arranged conversation hours with students from the Beijing and Xi'an campuses for our students to ask questions about China and their personal projects. From students' journals, I learned that Chinese students typically gave standard answers, similar to what one would hear in the Chinese media, especially regarding such topics as Internet regulation or air pollution. Being out of touch with the larger society could be a reason for the Chinese students' lack of different perspectives. Being unfamiliar with our students could be another reason. In China, critical comments are often reserved for conversations among friends, whereas patriotism or saving face is more important when interacting with people from other cultures.

Meals

A challenge I did not expect but had to manage on a daily basis was eating meals together. It was not always easy for students who grew up eating their own individual portion of food to order and share Chinese dishes communally. It was a long process to finally agree on what to order to accommodate everyone at the table, and it also took quite some time for some students to learn to share dishes with others rather than keeping their favorite dishes to themselves. Staying on a college campus was beneficial because students could take advantage of the cafeteria on campus and choose from a variety of typical Chinese foods, especially for breakfast.

I had learned from organizing the program in 2010 that except for field trips to sites far away from the cities, it was best not to ask agencies to prearrange meals for us. As a result, in the subsequent program in 2013, the local guides and I decided where to eat. It was not necessarily cost-effective and almost always more work for the guide and me because menus, sometimes handwritten, had to be translated and orders negotiated among students.

However, students were offered opportunities to taste simple dishes at restaurants that Chinese people frequented instead of being shepherded to private rooms of luxurious-looking restaurants that specialized in entertaining international tourist groups.

The Daily Schedule

Because of the more relaxed atmosphere and the opportunities for students to discover the city on their own, Xi'an became many students' favorite city. Reflecting on their love for Xi'an, I think that a successful program is one that gives students time and space for individual experiences. Instead of packing their schedules with activities for every waking hour, it is more productive to give students the opportunity to see, hear, and feel a site on their own. Students could pursue their individual interests and visit a museum, a zoo, a shopping center, or a bar in the evening. They could interact with locals and other international students and tourists and discover the location from their personal perspectives in addition to enjoying the group activities their professor had organized for them.

Self-Preservation and Reflection

It is challenging to work with a group of students far away from home in a foreign culture. The division between class and out-of-class time is blurred. It is easy to get too involved in such things as group dynamics, which instructors are not usually a part of when teaching a conventional class on campus. It is easy to become too focused on giving students the best experience, overlooking that "a young adult's strongest developmental process [is in fact] experiencing, making mistakes, reflecting and learning from them" (Shallenberger, 2015, p. 262).

I am still learning to establish a boundary between work and personal time to be more present for students during explorations and discussions. I have also learned to let go of regret and frustration and to channel my energy into reflecting on and revising program activities. For instance, I did not anticipate students' questions about graffiti on the Great Wall when teaching the program the first time, nor did the program then include interviews with random Chinese people, even though students and I discussed why they were being stared at in China. I added these activities when the program was offered the second time. As when teaching any course, based on student feedback and my own reflections, I improve as I go.

See Table 9.1 for a summary of what I consider to be the most important elements of delivering a cultural program abroad.

TABLE 9.1

Important Elements of Delivering a Cultural Program Abroad

Instill in students ways they are expected to conduct themselves while abroad	• Approach the culture with an open mind and nonjudgmental attitude. • Be willing to explore and try new things. • Respect host behaviors, customs, and traditions. • Adapt to differences in facilities or common amenities. • Acclimate to the daily routine of host culture.
Provide cultural knowledge for students predeparture and in country	• Choose readings and films to add to students' cultural knowledge base (predeparture). • Encourage student observations in the context of field events. • Encourage students to analyze and interpret observations and experiences through cultural knowledge acquired in predeparture activities. • Design field inquiry activities to help students make sense of their observations and experiences. • Ask students to keep a journal to record observations, reflections, and revelations. • Compare host culture with students' own culture to discover similarities and differences.

The Return

Within 10 to 15 days after their return to the United States, students submitted electronically their journals and project papers covering a variety of topics, including infrastructure in Beijing, a study of architecture in Xi'an and Kyoto, the Beijing Zoo, disability, the Internet and media, and the school system in China.

When the new semester started, students and I went on with classes and our daily lives. Every once in a while, I saw a few of them volunteer at various campus events to share their experiences in China. The student who had to open his overweight luggage at the airport to take out a dozen bottles of water and rolls of toilet paper stopped by to tell me that his time in China had given him so much confidence in international travel that he signed up for a short-term program in Japan. Another student whose final project had been a comparative study of fast-food chain restaurants in China and the United States shared with me the good news that he had found a summer internship position in China. I also had a student who after this program spent a semester studying in China in his junior year, and after graduating, was offered an internship position in a company working with several Asian countries. Occasionally, when I bumped into students from the program, they would tell me how wonderful their time in China had been.

My own study abroad experience when I was 15 years old transformed my life. After my stay in Germany as a naïve high school student, I traveled to Germany many times later in my life. However, it was the very first experience of Germany that formed my "original impressions," a phrase that was coined presumably by the German writer Johann Wolfgang von Goethe to refer to the impression of a thing or an event that a young person encounters for the first time in his or her life (Seghers, 1948, p. 9). In my study of German and Chinese literature and culture, my original impressions of many episodes from that very first trip to Germany were repeatedly remembered, became more meaningful, and gave me insight into Germany and China alike. In many ways, it was that first visit to Germany that opened a door to the world for me, altered the course of my life, and made me the person I am today. It is my hope that later some of my students will also realize how much their first experience of China has affected their lives.

References

Bennett, M. J. (2012). Paradigmatic assumptions and a developmental approach to intercultural learning. In M. Vande Berg, R. M. Paige, & K. H. Lou (Eds.), *Student learning abroad: What our students are learning, what they're not, and what we can do about it* (pp. 90–114). Sterling, VA: Stylus.

Deardorff, D. K. (2006) Identification and assessment of intercultural competence as a student outcome of internationalization. *Journal of Studies in International Education, 10*(3), 241–266. doi:10.1177/1028315306287002

Ebrey, P. B. (n.d.). *Cultural revolution*. Retrieved from depts.washington.edu/china-civ/graph/9wenge.htm

Hessler, P. (2001). *River town: Two years on the Yangtze*. New York, NY: Harper-Collins.

Seghers, A. (1948). *Sowjetmenschen* [Soviet people]. Berlin, Germany: Verlag Kultur und Fortschritt.

Shallenberger, D. (2015). Learning from our mistakes: International educators reflect. *Frontiers, 26*, 248–263. Retrieved from frontiersjournal.org/wp-content/uploads/2015/11/SHALLENBERGER-FrontiersXXVI-LearningfromOurMistakesInternationalEducatorsReflect.pdf

Sigg, U. (2009). Confusionism. In E. O. Foster & H. U. Obrist (Eds.), *Ways beyond art: Ai Weiwei* (pp. 12–13). London, England: Ivory Press.

Vande Berg, M. & Paige, R. M. (2012). Why students are and are not learning abroad: A review of recent research. In M. Vande Berg, R. M., Paige, & K. H. Lou (Eds.), *Student learning abroad: What our students are learning, what they're not, and what we can do about it* (pp. 29–60). Sterling, VA: Stylus.

Vande Berg, M., Paige, R. M., & Lou, K. H. (2012). Student learning abroad: Paradigms and assumptions. In M. Vande Berg, R. M. Paige, & K. H. Lou (Eds.), *Student learning abroad: What our students are learning, what they're not, and what we can do about it* (pp. 3–28). Sterling, VA: Stylus.

Williams, S. (Director). (1997). *China: A century of revolution.* United States: Ambrica Productions.

PART THREE

IMPLEMENTING THE STUDY ABROAD PROGRAM

IO

MARKETING SHORT-TERM PROGRAMS

No Students, No Program

Michael J. Tyson

I have been the representative since 2010 for faculty-led short-term programs in Wake Forest University's Center for Global Programs and Studies. In any given year, I manage a portfolio of 15 to 20 short-term programs, which range from 1 to 6 weeks in length. The content and locations of our programs are diverse and include foci like intensive language immersion in Morocco, field studies in Peru, and internship opportunities in Spain.

A few years ago, a faculty member approached me about leading a four-week summer program in Nicaragua. The proposed program was to offer three hours of education credit, a major that has a strong reputation on campus but not a robust student population. The professor had substantial expertise in the location and was handling the logistics herself, which included placing students in a local elementary school where they would participate in diverse classroom experiences. She had also arranged for valuable excursions throughout the country that neatly tied together the academic and cultural goals of the program. Her program was meticulously planned and contained an ideal combination of student learning and cultural immersion opportunities. In March, two months before the program was supposed to run, we had only three students who had submitted deposits, and after beating the bushes for an additional two weeks, we reluctantly canceled the program because of the lack of participants.

What happened? On paper, this program had everything we wanted in a short-term program: It had high levels of cultural interaction with the local population, it was well-planned and logistically sound, and it was set in a nontraditional location. Unfortunately, the only thing that was not fully

183

considered was to whom the program would appeal. What caused the program to fail? Were there too few students who would benefit academically from the experience? Did the word not get out in an effective way? Was the program too expensive? In many cases like this, a combination of reasons explains why a program does not attract enough students. If faculty abroad leaders are aware of the marketing needs of their programs from the early design stages, they can successfully recruit the optimal number of students and ultimately ensure that their programs take place.

In this chapter I apply the classic marketing model of the four *P*s—product, place, promotion, and price—to marketing and recruitment required for faculty-led short-term study abroad programs (McCarthy & Perreault, 1987). This provides a blueprint for faculty leaders to develop marketing plans to ensure their programs are getting in front of the right students during the recruitment process. From the beginning of any new program design, if professors are not asking themselves to whom the program appeals and how students find out about it, they may find themselves scrambling to make their minimum program numbers. At the end of the day, a professor may have designed a program that is educationally rewarding and culturally rich, but if there are no students to populate the program, it is all for naught.

Marketing Basics: The Four Ps and Study Abroad

Since McCarthy and Perreault (1987) introduced the model, there have been numerous additions to and modern adaptations of the four Ps model, but for our purposes, a basic understanding of what the four Ps are provides a road map for subsequent recruitment efforts. The following is an overview of the four *P*s defined in the context of a faculty-led study abroad program.

- *Product*: This is the faculty-led study abroad program and about communicating the value of a program to the right audience.
- *Place*: This is concerned with where a student finds out about the study abroad program and defines where and how students learn about the program.
- *Promotion*: This refers to the methods used to get the word out about a program and is exactly what the word means, promote the program.
- *Price*: This ensures that a program has a competitive fee and how that fee is advertised; it is just as important as the other *P*s.

Why should a faculty leader care about all four Ps as opposed to zeroing in on just one component such as promotion? From my experience in administering short-term programs, the most effective strategy a professor can employ is to fully consider all four elements. A website or a flyer that incorporates all four Ps has the potential to deliver an attractive program. As McCarthy and Perreault (1987) suggest, all four Ps are connected and of equal importance, so considering them together when developing a marketing plan is the most effective way to get started.

Before discussing strategies and applications for marketing short-term programs, it is useful to know how past participants of short-term programs learned about them. Over the past six years, Wake Forest University has conducted postprogram student evaluations for faculty-led programs in the summer. The average student response rate during the six years was 55.6%. One of the more telling questions we asked students was how they heard about their programs. See Figure 10.1 for the results of this survey question.

As shown in Figure 10.1, students overwhelmingly heard about their programs from three main sources: the program application website, their peers, and the professors who led the program. Although this is a small sample, it is helpful to see where and how the majority of students found their programs.

Figure 10.1. How past summer program participants heard about their program.

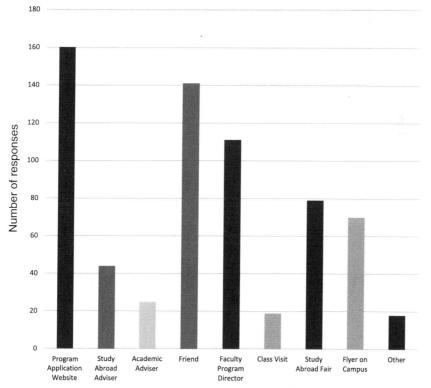

This does not mean a faculty leader should focus recruitment solely on these three areas, but the graph demonstrates that these are effective ways to promote a program. In the survey, when students replied they heard about programs from "Other," the responses included professors (not leading the program), parents, siblings, academic departmental e-mails, departmental open houses, and a pre-enrollment visit to campus.

The following are practical methods for applying the four Ps to marketing and recruitment of faculty-led short-term study abroad programs.

Product: The Program

Educators may cringe thinking of their study abroad programs as products, but regardless of the label, programs ultimately need customers (students). With internships, service-learning programs, research fellowships, and summer jobs, students have countless educational and experiential opportunities available to them. What makes a professor's short-term study abroad program stand out? What invaluable experience will this particular program provide to the student that alternatives will not? How will this benefit the student academically? Having clear answers to these questions is critical to a marketing strategy. As McCarthy and Perreault (1987) point out, "The most important thing is that your good—and/or service—should satisfy some customers' needs" (p. 38). The following are tips for showcasing the study-abroad program to fit students' needs.

Define the Value Offered

Program faculty leaders know the educational and cultural value of their programs. In addition to learning outcomes, it is important to identify and communicate tangible benefits an abroad program offers students. Detailing these benefits in promotional materials is key to attracting students to the program and may set a program apart from the competition. Benefits to communicate in promotional materials might include academic value (i.e., major or minor requirements), experiential growth (i.e., field research skills), intercultural communication (i.e., immersion through homestays), and personal growth (i.e., change in attitude).

Target the Right Student

Know the Student Pool

Once the value of a program has been defined, it is important to think about the type of student who would benefit from participation in the program. This is known as the student pool. An effective way for faculty leaders to market their study abroad programs is to strategically target the student pool when beginning recruitment efforts. In the example at the beginning of this chapter, the professor was offering a study abroad program that would appeal to a limited number of students. Once the recruitment of the department's majors and minors was exhausted, it was not clear to whom the program might also appeal. To get started, faculty leaders can make a list of the type of student who would benefit academically or who would find the course interesting. The list may include majors and minors within the field of study, those in different interdisciplinary programs, those in relevant on-campus student groups, and those involved in other academic departments. More about how to recruit these groups of students follows.

Know the Major and Minor

Knowing the answers to several questions about a major or minor while in the program development phase helps faculty leaders strategically build a program that already considers to whom the program will appeal. By identifying the demand for course work, faculty leaders create a built-in student pool for recruitment.

Questions to ask regarding recruiting majors and minors include, How many majors and minors are in the academic department of the course being taught abroad? Have these students studied abroad in the past? Is the major or minor curriculum rigid, requiring students to take classes in a sequential order? Is there flexibility about when courses can be taken? Are course substitutions allowed? Are there a number of prerequisites that act as gatekeepers to the deeper major courses? Do certain classes always have a waiting list of students? Do students have room to take elective courses in their major?

Knowing the pattern of how majors and minors take classes helps professors identify ways to strategically market the program and recruit students. When students have a rigid curriculum path (courses required in sequential order or during specific semesters), it is likely that they (along with their advisers) have mapped out every semester of course work. If this is the case, students often know where they have flexibility in their course work plan and where they can add or substitute a course. As a result, it is helpful to promote the program with suggestions like "An ideal experience for sophomores, juniors also accepted" or something that gives students a little more direction on the ideal time to consider the program.

Broaden the Program's Appeal

Cross-List the Course

To extend the pool of students, program leaders have a unique opportunity to approach chairpersons from other departments or schools to inquire if the study abroad program course work might be a valuable alternative to that department's required or elective course work. On my campus, this is particularly applicable to general education courses as well as to interdisciplinary majors or minors, such as international studies, humanities, and women's and gender studies. If chairs and faculty members of other departments are amenable to course work alternatives or substitutions, program leaders have the opportunity to cross-list the program courses with the appropriate match. This simple communication with other departments has the effect of broadening the initial pool of students interested in the abroad program.

Offer Two Levels of a Course

A few years ago, I worked with an art professor who was preparing a multicountry, five-week program in Europe where students would matriculate in introductory-level course work. This class fulfilled a general education requirement and was a good introduction to the major and minor but did not offer course credit that would benefit established art majors and minors. Because the program piqued the interest of many art history majors and minors, the professor opted to provide an additional independent study for the more advanced students, thus increasing the student pool.

I am aware this proposal might raise red flags with some readers who might ask, How can you ask me to teach two courses to the same group of students at the same time? This is true, but a professor may be able to make minor tweaks to an already established syllabus to open the program to a group of students who previously had no academic reason to participate. This is, of course, pending departmental and institutional approvals.

Place

Not to be confused with the location of a program, place is concerned with where students find out about a program. Did students learn about the program through the study abroad office website or at the study abroad fair? Did their academic advisers recommend the program? Place discussed in this section has strong potential for promotional collaboration. Being strategic about where a program is promoted and using established campus resources ensures that the program is getting in front of the right pool of students at the right time.

Program Application Website

Campus study abroad offices often have their own dedicated websites where students learn the details of a variety of study abroad programs and often where they will complete the application. Websites are commonly managed through the study abroad office or through an academic department and, in some cases, by the professor leading the program.

Faculty leaders should be thoughtful of the content they provide on an individual program's website. The following are a few suggestions.

1. Communicate the value of the program and how it benefits students.
2. Provide an overview of the location, detailing the historical or cultural significance of studying a specific subject in that particular location.
3. Include thoughtful pictures to tell the story of the program.
4. Include past students' testimonials about the program.
5. Provide a course overview and a list of abroad excursions and activities.
6. Advertise the price and include links to scholarships.
7. Emphasize the program dates and deadlines.
8. Describe housing accommodations in detail and include pictures if possible.

The program website is often one of the first places students go when they have heard about a program and want to learn more. Students also share these websites with their parents when trying to convince them that a program is a worthwhile addition to their academic experience. When designing the website, faculty leaders should also consider using a multiple audience appeal. Once the website is complete, it becomes a promotional tool by attaching the website's link to social media posts, targeted e-mails, electronic mailing lists, and any other Internet promotional platform. It is good to think of the program website as a virtual flyer that accommodates more information than a single sheet of paper.

Campus Locations

Academic Departments

Faculty leaders should not overlook their own academic departments when promoting study abroad programs. By providing program details to colleagues and administrative assistants in the department, professors create other channels that have direct contact with the target student pool. Academic departments often have their own promotional and marketing resources such as major and minor e-mails, electronic mailing lists, departmental websites, bulletin boards, and open houses for prospective students. If a faculty leader's own academic department cannot describe the merits of a program because members of that department lack information, then it is a lost opportunity in a place where the student pool is easily found.

Study Abroad Office

Many higher education institutions have an office dedicated to campus study abroad programs. These offices vary in size and the support they offer, but the staff members are usually strong advocates of short-term programs. In general, there are two types of study abroad offices: centralized and decentralized. If an institution has one office dedicated to all study abroad programming, it is often referred to as a centralized office. Centralized offices act as the one-stop shop for students to discuss options with study abroad advisers and acquire promotional materials.

With decentralized offices, different departments manage the study abroad opportunities that pertain to them. For example, the staff members of a political science department might manage their own separate portfolio of approved study abroad programs. In such cases, processes may vary as well as the support and resources available to faculty leaders.

One of the first steps faculty leaders should take while developing short-term programs is to meet with study abroad office support staff to learn about the resources they offer in marketing, promotion, and recruitment so that efforts are not duplicated. It is common for study abroad offices to have marketing events scheduled throughout the academic year including study abroad fairs, information sessions, and social media postings. In addition, study abroad advisers meet with interested students daily, so having detailed information about faculty-led programs and updated promotional material available for the office staff to distribute is essential.

Office of Academic Advising

In most cases, when beginning an undergraduate experience, students meet with academic advisers to plan their educational paths. Some universities assign this responsibility to faculty, while others have an established academic advisement office to mentor all students or just a targeted group, such as undeclared students. If faculty leaders have access to an established academic advising office, this is another place to advertise abroad programs. For example, if a faculty leader annually promotes a field studies program in Nepal for anthropology majors, he or she should contact the appropriate academic advisers and ask for their support. If advisers and students know early that social science majors might choose a field studies course in Nepal instead of taking a traditional on-campus course, they can plan a student's educational path accordingly.

It is probably unrealistic to expect academic advisers to share the intricate details of a particular short-term program abroad, but just making them aware of the program and leaving them a stack of flyers is a start. The bottom line is that many students visit the academic advising office early in their academic career, making it an ideal place to target.

Promotion

Just as it implies, promotion is getting the word out. What channels are best used for professors to communicate the value of their programs? What strategies help put their programs in front of the right students? These questions get to the heart of recruitment. The following are ideas for promoting faculty-led programs.

Student Word of Mouth

According to Wake Forest University's postparticipation student evaluations, one of the primary ways that students hear about programs is from each other. Word of mouth is one of the most effective ways to bring new students to abroad programs, especially programs that operate yearly.

A strong student advocate who spreads the word about a program significantly extends the recruitment reach. Gladwell (2002) identifies the types of people who affect the spread of ideas as *connectors*. Connectors seem to know everyone and are the students who are often deeply involved in campus life through clubs, social groups, athletics, and various activities. It is likely many professors know a few connectors who are more than willing to spread the word through established channels.

Faculty leaders might also want to invite past participants to informational sessions or share their students' perspectives on their programs on social media and the websites. In my experience faculty and administrators can tell students a program will be a fantastic, life-changing experience until they run out of breath, but if prospective students hear it from a peer, the message carries more weight.

The Faculty Leader

Professors leading the programs are their own best advocates. One of the first steps professors should take is to promote programs in their own classes and the classes of department colleagues. In three-minute classroom visits, faculty leaders have the opportunity to approach the very students for whom the subject matter is most relevant. If students express interest, professors should then invite them to the program informational session or for a private conference. The faculty leaders are the experts so any time spent face-to-face with prospective students is time well spent.

Online

Students spend a substantial amount of time on the Internet. Walking around campus, students with smartphones in their hands are nearly as ubiquitous as students with backpacks. Whether using social media, keeping up with current events, or doing research for papers, the Internet is the prime medium students use to obtain new information and to communicate with the world. Using the Internet in the right way is an effective strategy for recruiting students.

Social Media

Most faculty are familiar with the concept of social media and a few of its forms like Facebook or Twitter. Simply put, social media is used to connect and engage with others. From a marketing standpoint, social media is one of the best means to promote a faculty-led program.

If a program is new and just getting off the ground, faculty leaders should check with the study abroad office to see if they have already established social media accounts and if they would be willing to promote the program through them. Likewise, this strategy can be used with relevant student groups or other campus student life offices.

Whether a professor has an established or a new program, creating a Facebook group is an outstanding way to promote and maintain interest in the program. Some ideas for social media posts include inviting new participants through a link to the Facebook group on the program website, encouraging activity and frequent use by posting interesting articles or discussion points, and inviting past participants to post photos or memories about the abroad program.

In a similar way, blogs can be used to give prospective students a glimpse into the program. I have known some faculty who have students keep a blog as an assignment throughout the program and then showcase an exceptional one on their program's promotional website.

Other common social media platforms include Instagram and Snapchat (for photos), YouTube (for video) and Pinterest (an online bulletin board of ideas and photos). If faculty leaders do not have time to invest in maintaining these platforms, they can delegate the task to an administrative assistant or a student worker. For example, I once hired a marketing intern for a semester to manage all social media posts for Wake Forest short-term programs. As in all technologies, though, popularity and use of these forums change quickly, making it challenging to keep up with what students are using. If students are not on the platform, the promotion will not be effective. An entire chapter if not a book could be written on the applications of social media to promote study abroad programs. The thing to remember is that by not using them at all, professors are missing a medium that is heavily frequented by the student population.

Targeted E-Mails

Instead of sending blanket e-mails to students to promote a program, professors should be more strategic. Students in specific majors or minors are a good place to start. Academic departments often keep e-mail lists. Relevant student clubs are also a good option. If the course being offered abroad is International Finance, it would make sense to send an e-mail to the head of the finance club with the program's flyer attached. Professors can also contact the study abroad office to see if there is a list of students who are looking for a particular term or subject taught abroad. In this day and age when students' inboxes are bombarded daily by every imaginable solicitation, targeting students who have the most to gain from a program improves potential effectiveness.

Electronic Mailing Lists

Faculty leaders may choose to cast their program out to as many people as possible with the hope of receiving a few interested bites. Appropriate electronic mailing lists are good resources for this endeavor. Academic department, student campus group, and professional mailing lists in the field of the program are all good options. The study abroad field has a well-known electronic mailing list called SECUSS-L that is frequently used by administrators to promote a variety of study abroad programs. It is an excellent resource for administrators in the field, but unfortunately, students are generally not in the receiving community. Using this list requires having faith that the administrators reading a post will actually pass it along and further faith that the students will actually read that post.

Websites Focused on Study Abroad

A number of websites act as a clearinghouse for study abroad programs. This type of website often allows faculty leaders or administrators to create a program profile and then use their own marketing language to promote the program. Many of these websites offer a basic version of their platforms for free with additional advanced services available at tiered fees. Some examples of these types of websites include StudyAbroad.com, GoAbroad.com, or GoOverseas.com. Students visit these websites seeking a specific location abroad or type of program and then search through program databases free of charge. Students may often try these clearinghouse sites first when they do not know where else to start. Unfortunately, if a program is in a popular location like Spain, a program can get buried amid hundreds of other program profiles for the same location.

On Campus

Flyers

It is as old as paper itself, but a flyer is still an effective way for students to hear about programs. When creating flyers, faculty leaders should consider the goal. Is it to promote the program in general? Is it to invite students to an information session? The primary message of the flyer should be clear. When possible all four Ps should be used, as illustrated in the flyers in Figure 10.2 and Figure 10.3.

Figure 10.2. General program flyer distributed through the Wake Forest University Center for Global Programs and Studies.

Venice, Italy:
American Writers in Italy
WFU Summer Program

Courses: ENG 175/HON 258 (3hrs) (D)

Dates: Summer Session I, May 28 to June 24, 2017

Accommodations: Casa Artom

Cost: Program Fee (estimated) - $3,100
Tuition (3 hrs, estimated) - $2,700
Airfare (estimated) - $1,500
Personal Expenses (estimated) - $1,000
Estimated Total Program Cost - $8,300

Scholarships: Available through the GPS

Surrounded by water, Venice is an enchanting city built on 117 small islands. Its magnificent sights are best seen by walking along the narrow streets, crossing the many canals, and meandering through the busy piazzas. Wake students have the wonderful opportunity to live on the Grand Canal in Casa Artom, the WFU owned residence flanked by the Palazzo Venier dei Leoni, which houses the Peggy Guggenheim art collection, and the magnificent 15th century home Ca'Dario.

Students will take *ENG 175/HON 258 The End of Arcadia: American Writers in Italy* (3 hrs) (Div II). For American writers Italy has always been something of a shifting and elusive and imaginary place. Regardless of the era, Italy has always challenged American writers' sense of sexual, political, and religious identity, and caused them to wonder if it were indeed possible to discover in their traveling there a more perfect world and self--to find, in other words, Arcadia.

Spend the summer walking in the footsteps of American writers traveling in Italy. Students will read and discuss fiction, poetry, essays, and memoirs set in Italy by Ralph Waldo Emerson, Herman Melville, Nathanial Hawthorne, Mark Twain, William Dean Howells, Henry James, Edith Wharton, Henry Adams, Ernest Hemingway, Robert Lowell, and others. In addition to writing several essays about the literature that will be read, students will be asked to write their own brief memoir about being "An American in Italy."

To learn more, contact:	To apply:
Center for Global Programs and Studies	Go to studyabroad.wfu.edu
116 Reynolda Hall	and select Find a Program
336-758-5938	**Application Deadline:** February 15, 2017

WAKE FOREST
UNIVERSITY

Center for Global Programs and Studies

Extra care should be taken in regard to choosing the photos used in flyers because they are generally the first things that attract students. As stated by Sobieszek (1988), "Central to the image's purpose are communication and association. Before selling can occur, attention must be gained and a certain amount of understanding achieved" (p. 164). When students consider a program, they want to imagine themselves as participants. A photo helps

Figure 10.3. Interest meeting flyer for a short-term program.

Fez, Morocco Summer 2016

المملكة المغربية

Information Session
Wednesday, Feb. 9th
4:30pm
Wingate Hall, Rm. 202

- 6 hours of Arabic or Intermediate French taught at the Language Institute in Fez (ALIF)
- *REL 362 Islam in Morocco* (3hrs) taught by a Wake Forest University professor which counts toward the REL major/minor or the MESA minor
- Excursions include trips to Casablanca, Rabat, Marrakech, Volubilis, and an overnight desert excursion
- Scholarships available

For more information, contact
Center for Global Programs and Studies
336-758-5938

 WAKE FOREST
UNIVERSITY

or hinders that. Professors should be conscious of the messages they send through the photos they use in their flyers. A photo of four White females in front of the Eiffel Tower for a French language immersion program can send unintentional messages to those who see the flyer. It is a challenge, but whenever possible, it is best to avoid photos in which a particular racial or ethnic group is overrepresented or photos that promote the program as tourism.

Flyer placement location is also important. If a bulletin board already has 50 flyers, it is likely new ones will not be seen. The best locations are those with high student traffic, especially the target student population, and not oversaturated with additional advertisements. As previously mentioned, a professor should make sure flyers are also present in strategic offices around campus like the study abroad office, academic advising office, and the faculty leader's own academic department.

Information Sessions

Faculty leaders should hold information sessions to present their short-term program to many students at once. At these sessions, a professor typically gives an overview of the program, shows photographs of the location, and explains the program requirements. It is always best to allow time for students to ask program-related questions. Staff from Wake Forest's study abroad office often participate in our professors' information sessions, providing details about how to apply for the program and available scholarships. Professors should be mindful to offer information sessions during times when the majority of students do not have class, activities, or athletics. If professors wish to provide further incentive, food is always a strong student motivator.

Outside Applicants

If the institution allows, faculty leaders can recruit student applicants from other higher education institutions. For simplicity's sake, many professors prefer to recruit from their own institution, but in cases where one or two students could make or break a program, outside applications are welcome.

If faculty leaders are seeking applications outside the institution, the first place to start is with colleagues from other institutions who are in the same academic field. A colleague who knows the program leader and his or her reputation personally will likely be a strong advocate for the program. From my experience, cold calls have provided lukewarm responses at best, so using established contacts is key.

When recruiting from an outside institution, it is important to be mindful of that institution's makeup. Tuition fees at private and public schools can vary significantly. Approaching students from other institutions with similar pricing tiers is a good approach for improving the likelihood of an outside student participating in the program. Similarly, if a professor teaches at a state school, other state schools in the system are resources for recruiting additional students. If there is an established relationship among campuses for study abroad programs, professors should learn the specifics of study abroad and student eligibility in their own systems. If a professor teaches at the University of California, Los Angeles, and students on the Berkley campus are able to participate in the program and not worry about additional costs, institutional applications, or transferring credit, this creates an easier process to recruit students. The study abroad office staff should have an idea of any tuition and program agreements with other institutions.

For a summary of resources and ideas for program promotion and recruitment, see Figure 10.4.

Figure 10.4. Ideas for program promotion and recruitment.

On Campus

- Visit classes of targeted students.
- Attach flyers to bulletin boards in academic departments, university offices, and high-traffic student areas.
- Conduct information meetings for interested students.
- Use student word of mouth, connectors, and/or past program participants.
- Target promotion to relevant on-campus student groups.
- Advertise in on-campus student or institutional media such as the campus newspaper or other local, visual media.
- Provide information at academic department open houses and events.
- Set up an information table in strategic or high-traffic locations.

In Collaboration

- Participate in study abroad office events such as study abroad fairs and workshops.
- Notify appropriate academic advisers.
- Collaborate with other academic departments through interdisciplinary majors and minors, cross-listing courses, and so on.
- Join other campus events from residence life, multicultural office, and/or student life.
- Recruit outside the campus using colleagues from other institutions.

Online

- Engage students through social media such as Facebook, Twitter, YouTube, Pinterest, Snapchat, and Instagram.
- Send out targeted e-mails to prospective students.
- Use the program website as a promotional tool, placelink in other online recruitment promotions.
- Create a program page on websites focused on study abroad promotion.
- Spread the word through electronic mailing lists focused on study abroad, academic fields, your department, student oriented, and so on.

Price

Most universities require faculty leaders to include the total cost of the program in promotional materials. Even if this revelation results in a few students immediately dismissing the program, experience has taught us that, as with any product, consumers need to know the total cost up front.

Competitive Pricing

The key to pricing is making sure a faculty-led program is competitive relative to other similar programs. A faculty leader should research programs that are similar in structure and time frame to become familiar with what other programs charge. A program that travels for five weeks in Europe and visits multiple cities is going to have a much different pricing tier than a two-week program in Costa Rica where students live in homestays. If a program's fee is not in line with other programs' fees, professors risk losing student interest if the cost exceeds institutional norms.

Advertising the Price

When I started my position at Wake Forest, I remember a group of excited students telling me that they planned to study abroad in Italy over the summer and it would cost only $2,500. I remember thinking that this price seemed very low. When I asked where they heard this, they responded that the professor leading the abroad program had told them. I unfortunately had to break it to these students that this was just the program fee, and it did not include their flights nor the tuition fee, and if they wanted to eat, they needed to have money for that too. These types of exchanges prompted a change in policy in how we advertise the fees of short-term study abroad programs. We began listing on websites and general program flyers all estimated fees and expenses students would incur if they were to participate in a particular program. This included the program fee (housing, excursions, faculty expenses, etc.), tuition fee, estimated flight cost, and estimated amount for personal expenses. See Figure 10.5 for a total cost advertisement. Also see Chapter 1 in this volume for Cole's approach to building a budget.

We knew that when students saw these figures together, they would most likely experience sticker shock, but we also knew that it was more important to be up front about the actual costs of a program. That way, students are able to make a realistic decision about whether they are able to participate and not drop out at the last minute when they realize what the actual costs are.

Figure 10.5. Summary of program costs as advertised online by Wake Forest University.

The total cost of summer study abroad can be broken down into four categories:

1. Program fee—usually covers room, excursions, and other costs associated with the program
2. Tuition—students on Wake Forest University summer programs pay summer school tuition per credit hour. The 2017 summer rate is $900/per credit hour.
3. Airfare (estimated)—varies per location; students are responsible for their own airfare unless otherwise noted.
4. Personal expenses (estimated)—these vary depending on the students' spending habits and the cost of living in the destination country and may also include visa fees, vaccinations, academic supplies and books, most meals, and other miscellaneous daily expenses

Program fee: $3,100
Tuition (3 hours): $2,700
Airfare (estimated): $1,700
Personal expenses (estimated): $1,500
Estimated total cost: $9,000

Scholarships

Faculty leaders should familiarize themselves with any available aid for short-term programs. Scholarships and additional funding can often be the catalyst that make short-term study abroad a reality for students. Knowing what is available and then advertising the awards in the promotional materials is a good way to generate further interest. This is especially true with student groups that may have considered short-term programs too expensive for them to afford.

Timelines

Once the four Ps of marketing are determined, when should faculty leaders implement their marketing plans? In most cases faculty leaders should allow a full academic year to market and promote their programs.

If programs are expected to run in the summer, the very latest that marketing and recruitment should start is the beginning of the fall semester. If a professor is looking at a nonsummer time frame, possibly over spring break or after an academic term ends in May or January, it is useful to start advertising a full year in advance. Students plan their summer and academic breaks well in advance, so starting later in the semester will immediately put the program at a disadvantage. If professors can get their programs out in front of students before they start looking for internships, summer jobs, or someone else's international program, the better off they will be.

Why is starting early so important? At the beginning of the semester, students are at their freshest. They have not yet overextended themselves in social groups and clubs. Projects and papers usually have yet to come due. The beginning of the semester is when students are still forming the plans of what their year will look like. They are open to new ideas. They are less likely to use the excuse that they don't have the time, which I hear far too often. If they approach their study abroad experience as something that is a necessity in their academic planning, they will fit other commitments around it. The bottom line is that students' schedules, social and academic, fill up very quickly, so professors should grab students' attention early.

Conclusion

At first glance, it seems easy: Design a course with an international focus, build in a few excursions and guest speakers that tie the academics and the location together, and book some housing and some flights. Learn, explore, experience, go home. The reality is that for a short-term study abroad program to actually happen, it requires students. At the end of the day, nobody wants to put in more than a year of work for something that does not happen.

My best advice is, whenever possible, do not reinvent the wheel. Talk to other professors who have led short-term programs abroad. Seek their advice and learn from their successes and mistakes. Meet with the staff at the study abroad office at the nascent stages of planning to learn about the marketing resources they have in place. Use the four Ps and build a marketing plan. A strategic approach to marketing will put you in a position to fill your program with the eager and committed students all professors seek.

References

Gladwell, M. (2002). *The tipping point.* New York, NY: Back Bay Books.

McCarthy, E. J., & Perreault, W. D., Jr. (1987). *Basic marketing* (9th ed.). Homewood, IL: Irwin.

Sobieszek, R. A. (1988). *The art of persuasion: A history of advertising photography.* New York, NY: Harry N. Abrams.

II

LAYING THE GROUNDWORK

Faculty Preparation for Teaching Abroad

Susan Lee Pasquarelli

More than a decade ago, I traveled to Sicily on a presite visit to investigate if the old town of Ortygia with its Greek origins and temples was a suitable site for my first faculty-led program focused on Greek and Roman mythology. After two days of meandering through the ancient streets, exploring the archaeological treasures, and wandering through museums, crowded with distinctive orange and black pottery depicting mythological stories, I knew it was the right place to situate my program. While continuing to investigate nearby World Heritage Sites, my Sicilian colleagues and I began working on the logistical details: faculty and student residences, classroom space, land transport, guest professors, and English language translators for the part of the program that would be delivered in the Italian language. I also charted the walking classrooms associated with my developing curriculum and attempted to predict what was needed upon arrival with students. One week later I returned home with maps, museum ephemera, costs for various venues, applications for students to volunteer in local schools, Italian contracts, and stacks of business cards to prepare the university proposal that would bring me one step closer to teaching in Sicily the following summer.

After 10 months of ongoing work and a 12-hour return flight to Sicily, I quickly learned what I *should have* prepared and accomplished before arriving in a remote location with 15 American college students in tow.

I would like to recognize two Rome colleagues: Cristina Cavalieri, coordinator of student life at St. John's University in Rome, and Michael Beazley, dean of student life at Loyola University, John Felice Rome Center. Both were generous to share student orientation concepts as I gathered information for this chapter. I also thank my colleague Kate Mele for her permission to impart details of our jointly designed Rome program in these pages and the Roger Williams University Foundation for Scholarship and Teaching, which funded travel to conduct research for this book.

Prior to going abroad, students need extensive preparation and orientation; however, as others in this volume have advocated, predeparture orientation is just the beginning. Cristina Cavalieri, coordinator of student life at St. John's University in Rome, suggests that a predeparture orientation is the prologue of what she calls continuous orientation (personal communication, October 25, 2016). Her work with American college students who study in Rome for a semester has taught her that student academic assistance, personal support, and cultural orientation are continuous from the minute students are accepted into the program until long after they return home. This model of pre-, during, and postorientation and reflection is more difficult to actualize in a short-term program but is a worthy standard if we strive to maximize student learning outcomes.

This chapter focuses on necessary faculty groundwork before going abroad to prepare for all three phases of a faculty led program, including student preparations for the abroad experience (pre-), student experiences while abroad (during), and student affirmation on return (post-).

Organizing Student Preparation (Predeparture)

As Cole suggests in Chapter 1, predeparture preparations for faculty are complex and time consuming. Between the time the university faculty-led proposal is accepted to boarding the flight, program logistics and student orientations have to be organized for all phases of the program. I begin this conversation by reviewing predeparture student learning events in the following categories: content-knowledge preparation, language orientation, cultural orientation, guided reflection on the learning process, and safety and well-being orientation.

Delivering Predeparture Student Learning Events

Student Content Knowledge Preparation

Much like preparing to deliver a traditional syllabus, we must decide how to deliver an abroad syllabus. One substantial difference is that we will not be introducing the syllabus on the first day of the semester in the familiar comforts of our technology-ready classrooms. In Chapter 2 of this volume, I emphasize that one of my often quoted adages to encourage students to study material before going abroad is, The more you know, the more you see (Huxley, 1942). To prepare for the study abroad experience, we must ask ourselves, What content specific knowledge do students need before arrival at our destination to understand what they are seeing or learning abroad? For example, when designing a three-week program in Rome (see Chapter 2),

I determined that students needed an understanding of pagan mythology before they stepped foot into the museums where they would view and interpret mythological art and artifacts. To accommodate this prerequisite, I designed the program to include a predeparture content knowledge segment in which students agreed to participate in 16 hours of instruction including reading and discussing a significant amount of material in designated Greek and Roman mythology texts.

It is my experience that teaching events for the predeparture content knowledge portion of a study abroad program is dependent on three variables: the identified student learning outcomes, the depth and breadth of the written curriculum, and the length of the program abroad. Some programs may require a significant amount of predeparture content knowledge preparation before going abroad. Some may have time to deliver the content knowledge goals on site. Faculty must decide what types of predeparture seminars are needed to ensure that students realize the content knowledge learning outcomes by the end of the abroad program.

Student Language Preparation
Another area of predeparture learning is directly related to the language of the abroad sites. This is an additional consideration only if language proficiency is not included as a learning outcome. When preparing students for their abroad experiences if they have no knowledge of the language of the site, it is sensible to teach introductory around-the-town vocabulary. Free language programs are available on the Internet to learn polite greetings, use of local currency, and other functional phrases. As part of my Italian programs, in predeparture orientation seminars I teach students fundamental phrases and ask them to practice through a preselected online program. I find that students feel more secure if they know how to meet and greet, order in a restaurant, and buy basic items in a grocery store.

Student Cultural Preparation
Intercultural learning is continuous and ongoing throughout the program and beyond. To lessen culture shock and potential student embarrassment, certain customs should be addressed before departure. Again, decisions about what to introduce prior to arrival is within the purview of faculty leaders. The following are a few cultural customs I find important to address.

Appropriate dress and packing. The ways students dress while abroad have repercussions in the ways they are perceived by their hosts (see Chapter 12 for a longer discussion). Packing for study abroad depends on the location, the purpose of the program, and the religious or cultural traditions of the site. For example, if the abroad program is designed for students to work in the field, they will pack differently than if they were traversing a major metropolitan city. If students are visiting world religious sites, they must have suitable clothing to even be admitted. It is inevitable that students ask faculty leaders what to pack, and it is important that we are prepared to answer.

A Roman orientation leader once told my students that

> Americans are very practical. When it is hot, Americans are comfortable wearing beach or athletic clothes both by the sea and in the city. Italians, however, dress for the occasion. They wear city clothes in the city, beach clothes only at the beach, and sports clothes only at the gym.

Determining what students should pack for locations where inappropriate dress has embarrassing or serious consequences is a necessity. Perhaps it is appropriate for women to pack shawls, head scarves, and less revealing clothing, and for men to pack jackets and ties and religious head coverings. To make things easier for students, I provide a packing guide that includes everything from dressing head to toe for our various walking classrooms as well as what to pack in regard to electronic converters and plugs, laptops, tablets, cell phones, health and beauty aids, and other necessities. See Figure 11.1 for a sample page from my Rome Packing Guide.

Cultural daily life practices. One of the reasons for studying abroad is to experience a different culture. Students have possibilities to learn about cultural beliefs, ideologies, moralities, ethics, values, and other attitudes while on site. These experiences help students shape perspectives about this new and different culture in which they are living for a few weeks. Cultural daily life practices are worth teaching prior to arrival as they will make students more comfortable living in their new location. To help my students acclimate to the day-to-day Italian culture, I created an Around-the-Town Guide that I distribute and review during our predeparture orientation sessions. The guide includes information about etiquette in various situations, shopping information, ordering and paying the bill in a café or restaurant, and how to use the euro. Day-to-day life topics worthy of inclusion in the guide are dependent on the site. A list of common topics to include are shown in Figure 11.2.

Other cultural considerations. Depending on the type of program, it is the faculty leader's responsibility to determine the contents of students' cultural orientation. Perhaps an ethical conversation about photographing indigenous populations is needed or a learning event on how to greet patients in a hospital or young students in a school. Sometimes it is not possible to determine all topics one must address in the predeparture orientations. Very often, sensitive cultural issues arise during the abroad program in which further teaching or community problem-solving becomes a necessity.

Figure 11.1. Packing guide excerpt.

Weather

The temperature for Rome in May-June is 74-90 degrees. Pack for high humidity as well as for rain. Layers work well.

Clothing

Romans are elegantly dressed at all times. We, as study abroad travelers, as opposed to tourists, make a point of assimilating into the local culture. To that end, we expect you to pack clothing that is appropriate for a metropolitan city.

- We visit numerous churches as part of the art walking classrooms. Religious customs in Rome and Vatican City require shoulders and knees covered.

- For our family dinners, excursion to Florence museums, and your nights on the town, pack a couple of dressier outfits. Male students should pack at least one nice collared shirt and one tie.

- We walk every day – many kilometers. Pack a couple of pairs of comfortable sandals. We discovered that no matter what we wear, we all get blisters, so it's good to have a few pairs of shoes that are different enough to rotate the band-aids.

- Travel Tip: Make sure your new shoes are well broken in to prevent developing blisters the first day.

A Roman Perspective :

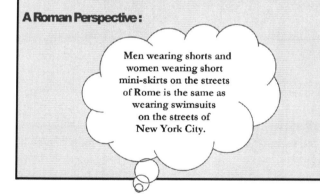

Men wearing shorts and women wearing short mini-skirts on the streets of Rome is the same as wearing swimsuits on the streets of New York City.

Student-Guided Reflection

An important component of the St. John's orientation program in Rome is a prompt that asks students to set goals for their study abroad program (C. Cavalieri, personal communication, October 25, 2016). This goal-setting

Figure 11.2. Topics to include in the Around-the-Town Guide.

Around-the-Town Guide Topics

❖ Appropriate greetings of townspeople and teachers
❖ Photograph etiquette
❖ Comportment in various situations, including religious if
   appropriate
❖ Touching and personal space
❖ Concept of time and being on time
❖ Protocols for public transportation
❖ Shopping protocols, including bargaining customs
❖ Siesta times and customs
❖ Protocols for timing; ordering; using utensils appropriately; and
   paying in a restaurant, café, or bar
❖ Currency conversion
❖ 12-hour versus 24-hour clock usage
❖ Metric conversion for weather and weight

measure is a vital element of guided reflection as it becomes the gauge for students to reflect on their growth before, during, and at the end of their programs. In many chapters of this book, faculty leaders suggest having students keep travel journals as part of their course requirements. Journal writing predeparture is an ideal time to develop the habit and mind-set of reflecting throughout the study abroad program. Why not ask students to use journals to set personal goals for their study abroad? This simple exercise allows students opportunities to think about why they are participating in the upcoming experience as well as to determine personal learning outcomes, well beyond those included in the syllabus.

As Savicki and Price suggest in Chapter 3 of this volume, guided reflection and student journal writing is effective if faculty leaders ask the right questions. In Figure 3.2, they recommend that students begin their study abroad reflective practice by predicting their reaction to being in the host culture: "Describe what you think your host culture will be like and how you see yourself interacting with your host culture. Are you excited, apprehensive, uncertain? Why?" Having students begin the practice of reflection before departing has positive effects on students' metacognitive awareness of their growth during and after the abroad program. In chapters 5 through 9 of this volume, faculty leaders provide suggestions for predeparture guided reflection. The important message is that guided reflection begins at the very first meeting of participating students and continues during and postprogram.

Student Safety and Well-Being

Most universities require faculty leaders to review safety regulations with their students prior to departure. Student safety regulations vary by type of program as well as by university. Faculty leaders should also be attuned to what they feel are appropriate safety guidelines for the location. For my own programs, I include a list of nonnegotiable student regulations in orientation materials. Prior to departing and immediately upon arrival at the abroad site, I review the regulations and ask students for compliance. A sample of safety and well-being regulations is included in Figure 11.3.

A few safety and well-being topics are worthy of deeper discussion, namely, situational awareness, alcohol consumption, field and lab safety, and site-specific health precautions.

Situational awareness. *Situational awareness* is simply defined as paying attention to what is happening around you. Many university study abroad programs provide situational awareness training for students headed abroad. During my abroad programs, I have observed students sprinting by a 2,000-year-old temple with their heads buried in their cell phones or chatting excitedly to each another instead of appreciating the architectural wonder in front of them. Providing students with a few tips on situational awareness goes a long way toward maintaining students' academic focus as well as keeping them safe from traffic, pickpockets, or other potential hazards.

Alcohol consumption. Most abroad leaders initiate an alcohol dialogue with their students before and during the program. As we know, excessive alcohol consumption impairs judgment and compromises student safety abroad. It can inhibit students' active participation in program events, and public intoxication has the potential to make students a vulnerable target for known and unknown perils in various locations.

Having an up-front dialogue about expectations regarding alcohol consumption offers another opportunity for cultural immersion. A segue into the topic might include asking students to conduct an on-site observation of local drinking customs, followed by confirmation of their observations through reading or seeking affirmation from locals. To wrap up the alcohol forum, students might brainstorm and write down a list of ways they plan to respect the local drinking conventions during their time abroad.

Some years I find that conducting a culturally based alcohol forum is enough to keep students safe and in top form for their study abroad, but there are some years when a more persuasive approach is necessary. If I find that

Figure 11.3. Sample university and faculty safety rules and regulations.

Responsibilities of Participants
(Created by Roger Williams University Global Programs)

In study abroad, as in other settings, participants can have a major impact on their own health and safety through the decisions they make before and during their program and by their day-to-day choices and behaviors.

Participants should:

- Read and carefully consider all materials issued by the sponsor that relate to safety, health, legal, environmental, political, cultural, and religious conditions in the host country(ies).
- Inform parents/guardians/families and any others who may need to know about their participation in the study abroad program, provide them with emergency contact information, and keep them informed of daily whereabouts and activities.
- Understand and comply with the terms of participation, codes of conduct, and emergency procedures of the program.
- Be aware of local conditions and customs that may present health or safety risks when making daily choices and decisions. Promptly express any health or safety concerns to the program staff or other appropriate individuals before and/or during the program.
- Accept responsibility for your own decisions and actions.
- Obey host country laws.
- Behave in a manner that is respectful of the rights and well-being of others, and encourage others to behave in a similar manner.
- Avoid illegal drugs and excessive or irresponsible consumption of alcohol.
- Follow the program policies for keeping program staff informed of their whereabouts and well-being.

Course Safety Requirements
(Created by program faculty leaders)

- While abroad, no student may go out without another member of the program group. Students must travel in minimum groups of two at ALL times.
- Students are not allowed to invite anyone to our apartments.
- Students are not allowed to travel in cars or Vespas without permission of instructors.
- While abroad, students must report to faculty when feeling ill so we can make appropriate medical arrangements.
- At all times, students must carry the ID card made for the purposes of this study abroad program. This card contains essential information: the address and phone number of the residence/hotel and faculty cell phone numbers.
- While abroad, students must remember that they are representing their university. When out on the town, students are expected to be polite and be respectful of the local culture. This includes appropriate dress.

alcohol consumption negatively affects an individual student's participation, I reiterate, in private, the purpose of the travel—to study—and suggest that it may be in the student's best interest if she or he returns home early. In most cases this gentle reminder is enough to prevent further incidents.

Field and lab safety. Depending on the type of program, well-designed safety and well-being protocols ensure students are prepared to work in unfamiliar environments using unfamiliar tools. This may include programs where students work with viruses in science laboratories, sharp knives in culinary kitchens, treacherous terrain on archaeological sites, soldering irons in art studios, needle sticks in field hospitals, or poisonous flora and fauna in the wild. Faculty leaders must take the lead on designing protocols for safety training in their own settings. In Chapter 6, Webb and Wysor describe two marine biology field study abroad programs. Because their students are scuba diving at their abroad site, their predeparture orientations include a swimming test and pool sessions where students rehearse standard safety drills and try out unfamiliar gear. Similarly, Quezada de Tavarez and Warren in Chapter 7 describe service-learning programs in which students need significant preorientation work to learn how to comport themselves in medical situations.

Site-specific health precautions. Faculty may also have to address additional risks that certain destinations pose, such as contaminated water, sun poisoning, dehydration, mosquito-borne diseases, and other health-related issues. The U.S. Department of State in conjunction with the Centers for Disease Control and Prevention help faculty leaders determine health-related precautions as well as required and recommended vaccinations for worldwide locations. Finally, faculty leaders may wish to inquire if a university staff member or safety consultant is available to attend predeparture orientation meetings to further legitimize important health and safety precautions abroad.

Identifying a Model of Delivery for Predeparture Student Events

Credit-Bearing Course Work
A unique way to provide predeparture content knowledge and abroad orientation is offering it as credit-bearing course work. A few of our university's summer short-term abroad programs offer one- or two-credit courses that are required for participating students. A one-credit course is roughly the equivalent of 15 hours of instruction and is easily delivered over two Saturdays. There are multiple benefits to this model. The course is usually covered under the students' tuition plan at no additional cost if offered during the standard terms, the students take the course seriously as credits and grades are attached, the readings essential to the program are assigned in the course structure, students have a chance to bond among themselves and with the

faculty abroad leaders, and students have opportunities to create a project or assignment that further prepares them for the abroad experience.

Seminar and Orientation Models
For faculty leaders who do not wish to formalize their predeparture sessions, there is the option of conducting face-to-face seminars, online forums, and informal gatherings. Whatever the venue, students need to know about and agree to take part in these additional learning events before they commit to participate in the abroad program. Because the abroad phase of the program usually carries credits, it is only fair for all students to have equal opportunity to participate in the predeparture learning events.

See Table 11.1 for questions to help negotiate the types of student learning events needed predeparture.

Accommodating Students and Parents or Guardians

Create Student Identification Cards
On one of my most memorable walks through Ortygia, Sicily, during that first study abroad program, I was accompanied by 15 jet-lagged, starving students who had just arrived for a three-week program. My plan was to orient the students to the town by treating them to Siracusan flat-bread pizza; introducing them to ATM machines; and pointing out the pharmacy, the restaurants, grocery stores, and other necessity shops. At the end of my two-hour town orientation, it was my intention to turn the students loose to explore on their own. In the middle of Piazza Duomo, I queried: "Who can point in the general direction of our residence?" The resulting gesticulations displayed an image similar to the cardinal points of a compass: arms lifted to the North, to the South, to the West, to the East. "Hmm," I murmured, "I can see you are turned around. What is our address?" The response: All shoulders raised in a shrug.

Even though our resident address was printed on just about everything I handed out in our orientation sessions, it did not occur to me to make something for the students to refer to on site. That day, in the middle of a busy piazza, we paused while I letter-for-letter dictated the unfamiliar multisyllabic Italian address. Wiser now, at our predeparture orientation meetings I hand out laminated identification cards, which serve two purposes. One is for students to have the resident address as needed. The other is for emergency personnel in case the student is incapacitated. For both purposes, the card is written in the Italian language with an added decorative icon from the site. These cards happen to become students' favorite ephemera from the program. See Figure 11.4 for information to include in an identification card.

TABLE 11.1

Negotiating Predeparture Student Learning Events

Predeparture Learning Events	Questions to Ask Yourself
Content knowledge	• What site knowledge is critical for students to learn before departure? • Given the length of the study abroad program, is it too short for students to realize the content goals within the time frame?
Language and cultural practices	• Given students' language abilities, what words and phrases should they learn? Is there a free online program for practice? • If the food abroad is very different, is there a way to familiarize students before departure? • Dress: What is appropriate for packing? • Cultural customs: Which important customs and behaviors are necessary to review before students depart?
Guided reflection	• How will students begin their program with a mind-set of deep reflection on the abroad experience? • Is this the time to introduce the reflective journal?
Student safety and well-being	• Which safety measures must be taught or reviewed before departure? Does my university have set rules and regulations? • What health considerations must be reviewed or attended to before departure? • What logistical materials (health, ID cards, safety guidelines) need to be prepared and distributed to students before departure?
Predeparture Delivery Models	Questions to Ask Yourself
For credit	• Is it possible to include this predeparture course on the schedule as a special topics course? If so, how many credits? • Is this a course I can open to other students not attending the abroad program?
Online	• Do my predeparture learning events lend themselves to an online forum? Which platform?
Face-to-face seminars	• Are participating students willing to attend non-credit-bearing seminars to prepare for study abroad? • When should the seminars occur? Evenings? Weekends? • How far in advance should the seminars begin and end? • If students cannot attend because of prior commitments, how can they make up the seminars?

Figure 11.4. Student identification card.

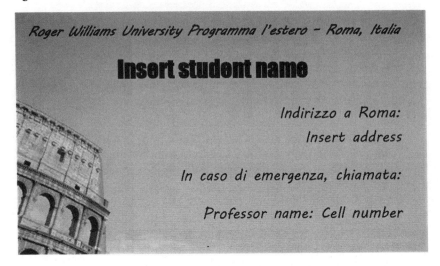

Roger Williams University Programma l'estero - Roma, Italia

Insert student name

Indirizzo a Roma:
Insert address

In caso di emergenza, chiamata:

Professor name: Cell number

Send Parents or Guardians Emergency Information Cards
Even in these days of instant messaging, FaceTime, and Snapchat, I learned that it is important to assuage parental concerns predeparture. Instead of answering the many e-mails I received long ago, I am now proactive. Six weeks before departure, I send home a parent or guardian letter that introduces the faculty in the program, outlines our safety guidelines, and has two enclosures. The first is a copy of our abroad daily schedule and the second is a refrigerator magnet with our address abroad and emergency contact information. I find this uncomplicated gesture reassures parents and guardians about sending their children abroad with two unknown faculty members. See Figure 11.5 for information included on the refrigerator magnets.

Attending to Program Logistics

While providing students with predeparture course work and orientation, we faculty leaders are also occupied with the numerous logistical details Cole discusses in Chapter 1. Because I have eliminated the cost of an agency to manage my site-specific logistics, the following is my predeparture task list:

1. Make faculty and student resident apartment reservations and wire funds.
2. Coordinate faculty and student airline transportation through a travel agent and communicate the flight arrangements to students.

Figure 11.5. Parent or guardian refrigerator magnet.

Roger Williams University
School of Education Rome Study Abroad Program

May 14-June 4, 2017

Study Abroad Residence in Rome

Insert address

RWU faculty cell phones:

Faculty name:
Cell phone number with prefix to call from USA

Faculty name:
Cell phone number with prefix to call from USA

3. Orchestrate all abroad land transportation, including airport transfer, buses, and trains.
4. Make reservations and payments for local attractions, museum visits, and other venues where advanced reservations are required.
5. Communicate with abroad personnel (translators and adjunct faculty) and plan for payment or honoraria.
6. Coordinate through the university to have access to cash and credit for on-site expenses.
7. Prepare the university bookkeeping system for expense reports.
8. Ask students to provide two copies of the first two pages of their passports. One class set is for the local resident hosts as required in most locations. The other set is retained in case of emergency.
9. Make a contact list that includes two emergency contacts and phone numbers for each student and faculty.
10. Attend to the details required for students to register for the course work abroad.
11. Give students identification cards that include faculty cell phone numbers.
12. Send parents a letter with program details, event schedule, and emergency contact information (refrigerator magnet).

Organizing the Student Experience Abroad

With predeparture orientation complete, there is still much to do in the coming weeks prior to leaving for the abroad location. I divide this section into preparing for curriculum delivery and orienting students to the site.

Preparing to Deliver the Curriculum

Create an Online Platform

Depending on the abroad location, availability of the Internet is something all faculty leaders need to consider before arriving at the site. Faculty leaders fortunate to have reliable Internet can use their university's learning management system or any other online learning platform to provide curriculum support. These systems provide the means for faculty to post items such as the syllabus and schedule of events, teaching documents and other resources, student readings, podcasts, journal tasks, tests and quizzes, and portfolio-related development tools. There is also the capacity for participants to engage in a chat room, e-mail everyone in the program, and submit documents for grading. These platforms simplify program delivery in locations with reliable Internet access. Conversely, if programs are in secluded locations without reliable Internet access, it means returning to the past by creating paper packets of important course documents. When I embarked on my first study abroad program in 2005, I carried multiple copies of materials in extra luggage. Moving forward, I prepare materials well in advance to distribute to students to carry on their own.

Create an On-Site Guide

Even with an online platform, students may need certain materials when engaged in walking classrooms or in the field abroad. For example, in Sicily, we attend a Greek tragedy in the ruins of an ancient amphitheater. Because the drama is performed in Italian, I bind the English translation to enable students to follow word-for-word as they listen and watch. In addition, I find it useful to have hard copies of the daily schedule and other information that students need while participating in walking classrooms. For these items, I create a spiral-bound on-site guide that is small enough to fit in a student's day bag, the first two pages of which display the daily schedule, including meeting places and times.

Our on-site guide for the Rome program contains the daily schedule, the syllabus with learning outcomes, and journal prompts that students must respond to while participating in walking classrooms. Such a guide is also an advantageous tool for programs based in remote areas with spotty or no Internet access, such as field study or service-learning programs. The

Figure 11.6. Rome on-site guide sample page.

Walking Classroom: Musei Capitolini

Journal Tasks

Journal Task 1:
Go to the *Hall of the She Wolf* and view the Capitoline wolf suckling Romulus and Remus. Pause and remember the myth about the BIRTH OF ROME. Think about when you first read the origin story, how did you picture the she wolf nursing the twins? Has this sculpture changed your mind about the origin story?

Journal Task 2:
Go to the painting gallery on the third floor and view Peter Paul Rubens' famous painting of Romulus and Remus (Romolo e Remo). Try to identify the other characters and symbols in the painting and think about why they are depicted. Compare the she wolf sculpture from the 1st floor with this painting. Is there a variation in ways the two artists portrayed the she wolf and Romulus and Remus? Which better matches your interpretation of the story: the sculpture or the painting?

Journal Task 3:
This museum has quite a significant pagan collection. You will see representations of your assigned god/goddesses or depictions of the myth stories you studied. There are surprises at every turn. Choose two works of art and complete the following tasks for both:

While you view: Think about your interpretation of the myth or characteristics of the gods/goddesses. Ponder these works of art and think about the artist's interpretation of the pagan stories.

After you view: Compare your interpretation of the stories before and after you viewed the artwork. What else do you now bring to your interpretations and why?

information in the guide will vary from program to program. See Figure 11.6 for a sample journal task page from our Rome on-site guide.

Pack Desk Materials

The first time I went abroad with students, it did not occur to me to pack basic tools for teaching and maintaining the daily expense account. Now I always pack self-sticking easel charts to capture students' collective comments or to itemize main points; large sticky notes to leave messages for students on their residence doors; standard office items such as a calculator, paper clips, stapler, tape, writing implements, envelopes for program receipts; and a stack of blank university stationary to write thank-you notes to our hosts.

Preparing for On-Site Student Orientation

There is nothing like attempting to teach a well-planned curriculum to disoriented, jet-lagged students, but every book written on study abroad suggests starting the program immediately upon arrival. For that reason, my faculty colleagues and I prefer to arrive two to three days ahead of the students. Arriving ahead of students offers us a reprieve to settle in, prepare our teaching materials and mind-set, make final logistical arrangements, and recover from jet lag ahead of the students.

The minute students arrive, we begin the narrative that makes up the ground-level orientation. After settling the students into their residences, we often meet for our first formal orientation, not forgetting that orientation to the site and to the culture is continuous and ongoing.

The Site

Michael Beazley, dean of student life at Loyola University Chicago, John Felice Rome Center, has created an orientation program for Loyola's semester-long college students, which is easily adaptable to short-term programs. He suggests a model of *radiating orientation* (M. Beazley, personal communication, November 3, 2016). When students arrive, he and his student life assistants acclimate the students to their campus and campus protocols, followed by orientation of the neighborhood or *rione* in which they are situated in Rome. Over the next few days, they orient students to increasingly distant hills and neighborhoods and then begin their exploration of other regions within the country. Beazley's plan is an ideal way to provide orientation to the site during a short-term program. First, we orient students to the protocols in their residence apartments, hotels, homestays, or youth hostels. This may include how to operate unfamiliar stoves, complex recycling programs, and idiosyncratic hot water. Second, we move on to the neighborhood and orient students directionally and teach them how to locate needed items such as groceries, pharmacies, and so forth. Third, as the program length and subject matter allow, we orient students to the larger town; village or city; and finally, the country at large.

Review Student Safety and Well-Being Protocols

Although student safety regulations are highlighted in the predeparture seminars, it is judicious to review them again at the beginning of the abroad phase of the program. I find students are more apt to pay attention once they are immersed in an unfamiliar environment.

Figure 11.7. Community-designed standards: The emergency protocol.

In Case of Emergency

ROME PROGRAM 2016
COMMUNITY STANDARDS

1. Set up an emergency group text thread that faculty and staff can access from American cell phones. This thread can ONLY be used in case of a city-wide emergency.
2. Keep USA cell phone charged fully at all times.
3. Carry USA cell phone and ID card (with apartment address) at all times.
4. In case of emergency, turn on cellular data and send location through the group text.
5. Head back to the apartments immediately.
6. If a group cannot get back to the apartments, seek safe haven, and send new location to group text.
7. If no cell service is available and you are not able to move through the streets, seek safe haven, and follow the directions of city or national emergency service personnel. As soon as possible, contact faculty and your family.

Arrival at the destination is an opportune time to hold community engagement forums to develop additional safety protocols. This past year in Rome, my colleague Mele and I used a community engagement forum for our students to collaboratively design safety protocols. These protocols ranged in topic from what to do when roommates do not return to the residence as expected to what to do in case of a citywide emergency (i.e., terrorism, earthquake). See Figure 11.7 for our collaboratively designed protocol for citywide emergencies.

Prepare for Ongoing Intercultural Learning
With the exception of language and culture programs, the emphasis of many short-term programs is delivering a content-specific syllabus. This focus often takes precedence over providing opportunities for students to engage in intercultural learning. Time set aside for intercultural learning is well invested and is easily embedded into any abroad program. The following are a few strategies to encourage intercultural learning:

1. Leave time in the schedule for cultural self-study and reflection. This includes daily time for students to interact with locals in shops, bars, restaurants, and areas of interest. Self-discovery is enriched by professors

suggesting areas where students might engage with local populations as opposed to with tourists or other student travelers.

2. Organize participation in public cultural activities. I often research the local events calendars of my location to find social events such as religious ceremonies, political gatherings or demonstrations, art exhibits, or sports competitions to add to the cultural aspects of the program.

3. Build time and money into the program to organize a cultural class that is outside the periphery of the intended course work. For example, as food is a considerable part of any culture, one might arrange for students to learn how to prepare a local delicacy. One year I arranged a gelato-making class with a local cooking school. The director of the school not only filled a delightful afternoon with gelato making and tasting but also taught students the history and cultural significance of the national treat. Alternatively, another year I arranged a walking classroom to artisan studios where my students learned about the livelihood of various artists and their craft.

4. Organize forums for your students to meet students from local universities. Cavalieri from St. John's in Rome, has designed what she calls Chit Chats, which are forums for American college students to interact socially with local Italian college students (C. Cavalieri, personal communication, October 25, 2016). Cavalieri is convinced there is no better way for students to learn about a culture than from someone their own age. She also organizes short-term service-learning opportunities for her students, such as working alongside locals in soup kitchens or participating in citywide service events. Following her lead, if our programs are connected to local universities or agencies, organizing a Chit Chat is an exceptional way to introduce our students to peers from another culture.

Preparing for Ongoing Guided Reflection

Once again I discuss the importance of guided reflection but this time during the abroad experience. Being on-site and working with students 12 to 14 hours a day presents unanticipated occasions for professors to encourage students to reflect not only on their course content knowledge but also on their intercultural experiences and personal growth. If we faculty develop a habit of mind to prompt students to think, write in their journals, reflect and talk with others, we encourage the reflection emphasized throughout this volume.

The term *reflection* is first and foremost grounded in the reflector's level of metacognitive awareness in a given area. Therefore, assigning a metacognitive essay is an exceptional tool for guided reflection on subject matter knowledge gains. A metacognitive essay requires students to tell what they know after several learning events. The essay can be designed to have students tell what they know about a process they learned, such as a writing or engineering skill; describe content knowledge they learned, such as the configuration of a Corinthian column; or describe a change in perception they may have had. Our Rome program requires students to read ancient mythology before we depart, view and interpret fine art depicting mythological stories while in Rome, and finally write a travel narrative about this experience. The additional reflective task we assign for inclusion in the writing portfolio is a metacognitive essay in which students discuss the trajectory of their learning from reading mythology to viewing and interpreting art in museums or churches to writing a travel narrative about these experiences. The metacognitive essay tells us what students learned and how they learned it, and the act of writing itself aids students' confirmation of knowledge gained. Several methods communicated by Savicki and Price in Chapter 3 of this volume are helpful for the preparation of students' intercultural guided reflections as well as in Deardorff's Chapter 4.

Organizing the Student Return (Poststudy Abroad)

Various contributors to this volume suggest that the poststudy abroad component is the most ignored practice in short-term study abroad programs. This important component is sometimes difficult to implement when programs are in the summer and students do not return to campus until fall or students graduate from the university and obviously are not available for postprogram work. The international research is clear that it is important to consider reunion events to engage students in final reflections as well as program evaluation.

Reunion Events

In my experience, albeit difficult, I have managed to meet with students at least one time postprogram. Because I have a penchant for cooking, and my programs take place in Italy, I enjoy having a culinary focus to the reunion event. For my Rome and Sicily programs, I have conducted a gnocchi cooking class at my home followed by a dinner in which we eat mountains of homemade pasta and reflect on program learning outcomes as well as our own growth. See Figure 11.8 for the prompts I created for one of these events. I found that even though students had discussed similar questions at the end of the program, their answers were more thoughtful and elaborate a few months later.

Other types of events do not have to mess up faculty kitchens or even take up large amounts of time in preparation or duration. Holding short seminars at the university or meeting at a local restaurant are just as effective. As Savicki and Price maintain in Chapter 3, faculty must *create* occasions to stimulate reflection.

Figure 11.8. Final intercultural reflection prompts.

Critical Reflections of Roman Culture

After experiencing the Roman culture, consider these questions:

1. Think of ways in which ancient Rome has an influence on or presence in culture today, either in Rome or in the United States.
2. How does Vatican City affect the culture of Rome?
3. What did you find the most interesting in your research about mythology and its role in shaping ancient and current Roman or global thinking?
4. Why would you want to live in Rome?
5. Think about how and why the food is such an important part of the culture of Rome.
6. What is your view of the current day Romans as a people? How would you describe them and their society?
7. Speculate as to why Rome is considered one of the greatest cities on earth.
8. How did your knowledge, skills, and/or attitudes change as a result of this study abroad program?

Program Evaluation

The popularity of short-term, faculty-led programs in the past 10 years has produced a growing body of literature about postprogram evaluation. In these articles and essays, international educators suggest collecting anecdotal evidence and conducting action research or qualitative and quantitative research designed to provide evidence of program efficacy as well as areas of program improvement. In Chapter 4, Deardorff suggests using students' outcomes assessment for program improvement by "quantifying the qualitative" (p. 90)

For my first program 11 years ago, I prepared a simple program evaluation, designed to gather qualitative answers to the following questions:

1. What knowledge did you gain in your program abroad?
2. What skills did you learn in your program abroad?
3. What attitudes did you develop in your program abroad?

After receiving less than satisfactory results from these broad open-ended questions, moving forward, I refined the questions and designed the survey shown in Figure 11.9. Still open-ended, this qualitative survey has the potential to capture worthwhile feedback from students.

Figure 11.9. Student study abroad program evaluation.

1. What were the most important things you learned during your time abroad?
2. Did you learn a problem-solving skill while abroad that you use now? Example.
3. How did the study abroad program help to improve your ability to accommodate, understand, and respect ideas of others?
4. List three specific ways you learned about the local culture.
5. How did the study abroad program help shape your personal values?
6. Think back to your abroad experience and identify behaviors that are different from yours, but beneficial for the environment.
7. How did the knowledge or skills you gained abroad affect your life or career now?
8. Do you have any general suggestions for the faculty leaders before they implement this program again?
9. If you were the faculty of this study-abroad program, what would you change about the curriculum (i.e., readings, predeparture orientations, walking classrooms, etc.)?
10. Do you have any suggestions for the faculty leaders about logistics (i.e., living accommodations, travel arrangements, health and safety concerns, etc.)?

Final Note

This chapter opened with a vignette about preparations for my first faculty-led study abroad program. Over the years, my programs have changed significantly. Much as I summon Huxley's insight to enrich my students' learning, I also summon it to enrich my own learning. Since that first time abroad, I consider each successive program an opportunity to enhance program preparation and delivery. To support my own program review and reflection, I invite students to make recommendations, and I find that they are more than eager to assist. I hope this chapter provides practical guidance to all readers planning to design and deliver faculty-led study abroad programs. In the following chapter, O'Connell reiterates some of this information from the unique perspective of the other side: faculty and staff who live abroad and work in programs that minister to American college students.

Reference

Huxley, A. (1942). *The art of seeing.* New York, NY: Harper & Brothers.

12

SPEAKING FROM ABROAD

Roxanne M. O'Connell

"**W**ill ya look at yez! Yez are all like the Japanese with your Nikon cameras!"—a shocking comment on how we must have looked wandering about as a group, cameras draped around our necks, through a labyrinth of backstreets, shops, and tenement blocks in working-class Dublin. While the greengrocer standing in his shop's doorway was clearly pulling on common stereotypes, his comment gave us a rare moment to see ourselves as others see us. He alerted us to the reciprocity of the "tourist gaze" and "being gazed at." Setting aside, for now, the essentializing and stereotypical nature of his remark regarding both my students and the Japanese as picture-taking tourists, this observation gave us something to realize about ourselves: Our cultural inclination to rely on stereotypes to know and order the world. It is our first filter and the one most hidden from us. What is more important, we needed to know and understand that *we* were the other in this place we were visiting. We were being seen through the stereotypical filters of *their perception* of every other American who has ever gone abroad.

This chapter is about two things. The first concerns how we are perceived—as Americans, as students, as spectators, as strangers, or as some combination of all these things. The second is how we—and those native to places we visit—address, process, and perhaps ameliorate those perceptions. These two things are examined through the voices of those who interact with our students in short-term studies abroad, whether for a few weeks or a few months. Some are teachers, some are program staff and administrators.

The colleagues canvassed in the writing of this chapter are cited according to their preference for full, partial, or anonymous attribution. I would like to thank them for providing their stories and advice: Stefano Baldassarri, Günter Haika, Kristin Hickey, Lucia Pistritto, Roberta from Italy, Javier from Spain, and those who wished to remain anonymous. All have the same motivations—to have our students experience growth by being exposed to new peoples, places, and cultures; to have them return home with a new appreciation for the diversity of our world; and to show students what is most precious in their host communities in a way that demonstrates honor and respect and brings more understanding into the world.

But first, a word about why I feel I can write about these things. I have been bringing students to Ireland for more than 10 years now. It is a place I know well. Although I am not a native of Ireland, it is where my married life began, where I have worked, and where two of my children were born. It is also the locus of my research in media and cultural identity, and the one place I travel to most in the course of any given year, making me intimately aware of being a "stranger in a strange land" and "being of that place." The anecdotes and words of wisdom from my experiences and those of my colleagues reflect the universalities and the particularities of our specific experiences with students and knowledge of the visited place. If any of what follows repeats or reinforces what has come before in the preceding chapters, it is likely because these are universal observations shared by all involved in study abroad programs.

Foucault (1994), in *The Order of Things*, argues that how we know and order our world is constructed through language and culture—what is the Same and what is Other within and between cultural contexts. Nowhere do we see this more dramatically illustrated than in short-term study abroad programs. The on-the-surface Other, as illustrated in dress codes, food, and architecture, is easily identified and perhaps even processed on an equally surface level; it is what we expect based on what we have absorbed in the media and in our own upbringing. Not so easily recognized, let alone processed, are the differences in how a culture deals with space, time, relationships, behavior, and practices of hospitality. It is my intention to bring to the reader a view from the Other side—thoughts from people who are of the place being visited about how to best experience and absorb both the surface and the underlying cultural differences and similarities in a reflective and, it is hoped, transformative way. After all, if some level of personal growth is not the goal of travel and study abroad, what is?

Seeking the Culturally Immersive Experience

McLuhan was fond of saying "We don't know who it was discovered water, but we're pretty sure it wasn't a fish" (Gossage, 1996, p. 37). Our own culture is our "water." We only recognize its existence when we are a "fish out of water"—a phrase we often use when we refer to being on the outside of something, different, alone, perhaps alienated. To avoid being on the outside, American students on study abroad often coalesce into groups of the same, seeking and staying within groups of other American students. On a very short-term program with an established cohort, this practice becomes the first hurdle those leading the program have to address. On the one hand, we want students to be open to where they are and dare to let go of their fixed ideas by engaging with the people they are visiting. On the other hand, we often encourage our students to do this with necessarily cautionary instructions to "stay together," "do not wander off," and "take care of each other." After all, we have a responsibility to make sure they stay safe.

It is a dilemma.

In introducing my students to the challenge of being a fish out of water, of being the stranger, of getting outside the cocoon of one's peer group in order to experience a culture, I tell them there are really only two kinds of stories: a person leaves their village or a stranger comes to town (an idea attributed to several writers). But not all traveling students feel like strangers. Some have traveled beyond their national borders with their families or on their own. Many students have root connections that may play a role in their expectations and preconceived ideas about the place they are visiting. These ideas also contribute to the mythologizing that occurs when the land of one's forebearers is viewed from afar. The nature and personal histories of study abroad students are not homogenous, and these subtle differences can profoundly affect a student's experience.

Time and Space

Time and space are so much a part of our lives that we do not notice how we use them. They are the water we swim in. It takes a while for students to notice that others may not be using time and space in the same way. In the beginning of their stay, students behave as if they are in their own space. Lucia Pistritto, a school principal in Siracusa, Sicily, observed that young people "tend to be too self-confident, they go out on their own and sometimes bring all their documents and money with them. They sometimes lose them or get pickpocketed." She has noticed that "they sometimes do not ask for proper information [or permission]" behaving as if "their own culture is the *only possible* culture" heedless of local habits and traditions (personal communication, September 21, 2016)

Hangen and Sen (2016) wrote, "The cultural project of study abroad lends itself to a complex relationship between the native space and the foreign student where experiences in the moment and within the space are the privileged form of learning about other cultures" (p. 62). Although their research focused on concerns regarding privileging the purely experiential over other forms of cultural learning, the authors draw attention to the fact that an important and essential quality of the study abroad experience is that it is in a time and space that is not always familiar to the student—that time and space are intricately connected and convey meaning if one chooses to pay attention.

Doerr (2016) also wrote about time and space in the following:

> The encounter with the cultural Other in study abroad occurs in a specific "abroad" space, the host society, in a demarcated block of time. Given that the time with the cultural Other will eventually end, study-abroad students' time is imagined, arranged, and managed in particular ways, especially through the discourse of immersion. This time is mapped in space, which creates and articulates notions of "abroad" and cultural Otherness in specific ways. (p. 80)

Behaviors concerning being on time or being relaxed about time (Hall, 1983; Gell, 1996; Levine, 1997) that may cause little comment at home, can irritate people one interacts with abroad. Being late for meetings or for departing motor coaches can be interpreted as rudeness or wasting other people's time. It gets more complicated when this happens in a country that might have a reputation for being easygoing. What the student does not always consider is that attitudes about time and timeliness are contextual and not standard across all situations.

Günter Haika, the resident director for an Austrian program, recalled two incidents where students experienced disconnects regarding time and space. In a shop where people were queueing up to pay for groceries before heading home to cook the evening meal, a student was "yelled at" because she didn't pack her purchases quickly enough (personal communication, September 21, 2016). In the United States, we are accustomed to the clerk at the end of the counter bagging our groceries. In many countries abroad, bagging groceries is done by the customers who bring their own shopping bags. Part of this is due to a rising eco-consciousness and laws regarding sustainable containers but much of it is cultural and deeply rooted in places where shopping in open markets and small shops has been the practice for millennia.

One of Haika's male students recounted a tense situation while he was waiting for a train. He was called an arrogant American by an older man for having his feet on the chair across from him, perhaps taking up more space than is customary. This seemed to trigger a bigger reaction than the student's carelessness appeared to warrant. "The old man went on to tell him that rather than pointing out misdoings and 'telling everyone what to do,' Americans should remember their own faults past and present, such as their genocide of Native Americans." When asked if they argued over that, "The student said, 'No,' because, although he thought the older guy's views were rather extreme, he realized for the first time that there was a different perspective of the United States from outside he had never considered." The result was that the student had a "thought provoking conversation" with the older man, and they parted on friendly terms, perhaps both coming away with a deeper knowledge of the other (G. Haika, personal communication, September 21, 2016).

Often students develop a notion that time in another culture is more relaxed. While traveling in India, Hangen and Sen (2016) observed that students came to view "Indian time" as indicators of the everyday challenges of "frequent delays, last minute schedule changes and events that take far longer than anticipated" (p. 68). In Ireland students would refer to being on "Irish time" as a reason for being less than punctual about nearly everything. "The idea that multiple forms of time exist within India [or Ireland] is not readily apparent to students because it contradicts dominant models of cultural difference that presume homogeneity within the 'other culture'" (p. 68). And this is exacerbated when locals, especially those in the hospitality industry accustomed to dealing with tourists, tell students, "Relax, you're on your holidays!" while we are telling them that they are *not* tourists and *not* on their holidays—they are here to study and learn. To help students see that they are perceived as vacationing tourists and how this is a misperception is necessary, as it becomes an opening for important discussion of how a culture can have multiple constructions of, and relationships to, time.

Although it might seem unnecessary to tell students to have a cultural respect about time and their spatial environment, a lot of time and space practices may be noticed and absorbed only by observing others. How do the locals deal with recycling, energy use, or technology usage like talking on mobile phones? How does one get a bus to stop in the middle of a big city? Are road signs in miles or kilometers? Even in a small island country like Ireland, unless you pay attention, you may not notice, as you cross what is currently an almost invisible border from the South into Northern Ireland, that speed limits are now in miles per hour. It affects one's judgment about distance and time and might lead to a speeding ticket.

Kristin Hickey, a program manager in Spain reminds her students that "studying abroad will change your daily routine" (personal communication, October 5, 2016). For the best way to deal with these changes, Hickey and others suggest avoiding burning the candle at both ends or getting worn out the first few days. Getting over jet lag is important, especially on a very short program of only a few weeks. The recovery rule of thumb is one day for every hour time difference. This is challenging for students visiting countries on the other side of the world. One of the best ways to speed up recovery is to give the body messages by eating meals, sleeping, and maintaining exercise regimens in the new time as if one were at home. Javier recommends that students "buy an agenda (diary or calendar) and give yourself extra time to get to meetings," because being in an unfamiliar place or building makes finding one's way challenging and can cause delays. However one achieves these adjustments, it is important, as Javier reminds students, "to be very positive and optimistic accepting and enjoying the new culture's way of life" (personal communication, September 27, 2016).

Cultural Collisions

In addition to time and space, local practices regarding everyday things like dress, drink, and food—even when and how to eat—more than identifies the stranger; these can cause an inadvertent insult or miscommunication. An Italian program director wrote, "One of the main ways to recognise a foreigner before he or she even opens his or her mouth and speaks is indeed the very small details in their [*sic*] behaviour!" Although he does not suggest that students pretend to be Italian, he lists a series of small things that lessen cultural collision: no shorts for men at restaurants in the evening, no sleeveless tops or shorts when entering churches, no cappuccino after meals (only for breakfast), bread is not served with olive oil, and water is almost never from the tap. He also points out that when paying the bill at restaurants one should ask for the check. After all, "It would be extremely rude for the waiter to bring it without you asking, as it would mean they're trying to 'kick you out'—which is very rare, unless it's a very busy night and, in any case, they'd tell you in advance, otherwise your table is yours for the night" (personal communication, September 22, 2016). This one cultural observation is profound—it speaks to more than mere commerce. It tells us something about the hospitality practices of a culture, the value placed on the act of eating out and hosting the meal. This is a "silent language," the everyday unspoken give and take of human communication that exists in a shared culture (Hall, 1959). It is difficult enough to observe, let alone understand, when one is an outsider.

American society, Hall (1983) observed, emphasizes speed; Americans tend to be in a hurry, trying to multitask and be productive. This is not always seen as a virtue in other cultures. Although this may be changing, one rarely sees to-go cups for coffee in France, Italy, or Ireland. Drinking coffee or tea is something one does to slow down, take a break, relax, be with a friend, or get focused. In fact, until very recently, tea in Ireland and England was purchased by the pot and, once steeped to the desired strength, poured into a porcelain cup or mug. How can you do that if you are walking and talking?

The consumption of alcoholic beverages is often another indicator of disconnected cultures. In countries where the legal drinking age is relatively young compared to the United States, practices of drinking alcohol are very different. Even young people under the drinking age in France will get watered-down wine at family meals. Consuming alcohol in Ireland is not done at home, unless it is a big occasion like a birthday party or a wake. The locus of drinking is generally the hotel bar or local pub. It is part of the social activity of being with friends and is not considered an end in itself. To be sure, there are people who abuse alcohol just about anywhere that alcohol is consumed. However, these people tend to be the exception rather than the rule. Imagine, then, the American student on his or her first trip to Ireland, who learned much about what it means to be Irish through St. Patrick's Day celebrations in college back home where rivers are dyed green and people are openly intoxicated at the roadside of the annual parade. Such was the case with my student, Michael.

From the beginning, Michael, whose distant roots were Irish but who had never before been out of the United States, thought he knew all about Ireland. As we waited to be seated for dinner in a small country hotel, Michael immediately went to the bar, perched himself on a stool, and proceeded to order a very expensive single malt—on the rocks—which he downed in one gulp before ordering another. I was about to intervene when the elderly gentleman sitting next to him gently put his hand on Michael's drinking arm and said quietly but firmly, "Man, you have to respect the whiskey!" Michael had clearly telegraphed that (a) he didn't know much about drinking, and (b) what was worse in this context, he didn't know much about drinking expensive, crafted whiskey. I truly appreciated the grace with which the more experienced native got this across.

Amy Choi (2014) wrote, "Food feeds the soul. To the extent that we all eat food, and we all have souls, food is the single great unifier across cultures" (para. 1). It is identity, survival, status, pleasure, and community. And it is more than just food. Think about all the things about culture that are communicated through the places where we eat food and the rituals and behaviors associated with eating. Our colleagues suggest trying out local specialties at restaurants, trying every new food dish even if it looks strange. Learn the restaurant vocabulary and how to alert wait staff about allergies or other risky food issues. Ask about these politely with a smile.

We once had a student who was allergic to corn and all corn by-products. This was inconvenient, but it was probably a bigger challenge back home in the United States where corn oil, starch, and syrup are ubiquitous. Understandably, it was a serious concern for her. We worked out a polite way to ask how the foods she was eating were prepared, and when necessary or even possible, we asked to see a product label of ingredients. It worked, but there was a range of reactions. For example, at one restaurant, the student asked the server if she could see the package that contained the mashed potatoes used in her shepherd's pie. The server went into the kitchen and came back with the chef. The student asked again, and the chef replied without skipping a beat, "They came in a truck, but that was yesterday and it's long gone." In Ireland, people do not make mashed potatoes from a package.

Just as students should be sensitive to cultural time and space norms, they should also observe cultural mannerisms and behaviors, and learn which they should adopt so they "leave a small footprint" and promote mutual intercultural understanding. They should ask the locals whenever they are not sure how they should behave in a certain situation. "Is it expected for us to tip here? How much?" "Is this a grocery store where locals would shop?" "Can one talk in a church when it's a tour?" A general rule is to avoid talking loudly even in public places. Watch how locals talk, and emulate that volume level. A common question is, "How do I order and pay for this?"

I remember stopping at a service island on a main highway in northern Italy to get an espresso macchiato and a pastry. It was a very busy morning, and the place was full of people eager to take a break from driving, anxious to get something sustaining for their journey. After a few minutes of confusion about where to start, I watched a local truck driver and followed his actions: First, the order to the attendant at the first station; second, pick up the pastry at the second station; third, pick up the espresso at the third station; and fourth, pay at the exit. To an American accustomed to driving up to the Starbucks window, this seemed a little crazy, but after some consideration, I realized that each customer got what he or she wanted without a great deal of waiting, and each part of the service team had to deal with only one activity without a lot of needless walking around. It appeared to be very economical and surprisingly efficient, but only once I learned the ropes.

We have already covered tipping, bill paying, and quickly bagging purchases at the supermarket, but table manners are also important. In India, Africa, and the Middle East, where hand-to-mouth eating (no utensils) is common, it is considered rude to eat with one's left hand. In some countries, one does not pass the salt from hand to hand—one places the salt on the table in front of the person who asked for it. Some consider it a superstition, others just consider it bad manners. The fact is that many of the things we consider bad manners are rooted in culture, their origins shrouded in the mists of time. That does not mean anyone should ignore customs or consider them silly. However, it might lead to an interesting cultural exchange of ideas to ask why something is done a certain way in a particular culture.

Being a Stranger in a Strange Land

Going to a new and different place means learning ahead of departure about cultural norms; relationship structures; embedded gender roles; the way those in the visited culture use time, space, hierarchy, social, and political contexts; and, depending on the place and the context, any prohibitions regarding photography and social media. Given the current state of the world where there may be refugee populations in the host country, being mindful of how images of those people might be perceived, or worse, spread virally through social media, should make people reflect deeply on issues of privacy and the consequences of irresponsible blog or Instagram posting. Documenting one's own behavior abroad also requires judgment. The scandal concerning gap-year student tourists who posed naked at the top of a sacred mountain in Borneo is not the kind of story anyone wants careening through social media or that parents should see.

Students also need to develop a level of tolerance concerning sociopolitical contexts that may be what they consider to be sexist, racist, elitist, oppressive, and bigoted. Particularly if homestays are part of the experience, respecting indigenous family structures and gender roles is important. Of equal importance is accepting that professors in other countries conduct their classrooms in a very different way from their American counterparts. As one colleague advised, "Remember that it's temporary and you came here to experience personal growth and learn from the local culture." Hickey suggests teaching students to be "flexible and patient because they may experience cultural differences that they have never encountered before." She has observed that "some students may feel frustrated or distressed that it's not 'like home' but we always try to encourage them to adapt to the local culture in order to facilitate the most enriching experience possible" (personal communication, October 5, 2016).

Just about everyone contributing to this chapter cautioned that students should try to avoid places full of tourists. Tourist traps, unlike places of genuine cultural significance, tend to contribute to the Disneyfication of a culture. They are often constructed and shaped to attract tourists' attention and consumption and provide little of the experiential cultural learning for which most study abroad programs are designed. Being able to tell the wheat from the chaff is sometimes difficult, but guidance is always there in the staff and faculty involved in the program.

Mobile phone use in public or with friends is becoming an interesting area for the study of cultural behavior. I have noticed Irish people at a pub might take their phone out and leave it on the table face side up so they will see it light up if someone is texting them, but the phone is always on silent, and they would never interrupt the conversation by picking up the phone and texting or talking on it. They wait until the topic of conversation changes and then say, "I need to check on this—I'll be right back." The attitude is to be with your friends where you are. Javier reinforces this and asks that students not "be connected all the time with . . . family and friends back home" (personal communication, September 27, 2016).

What Are You "Saying"?

Intercultural communication has many forms: verbal, nonverbal, written, and oral. It begins with "Hello" and ends with "Good-bye" no matter where one is in the world. Learning a few phrases in the language of the country is essential. Pay close attention to the nonverbal gestures people use along with their greetings, questions, apologies, and compliments. Roberta makes the point that

> Italians use and tend to read body language a lot, are sensitive to the tone of people's voices, and generally know at least some English. So they will appreciate one's attempt to relate to them and partake in the construction of a conversation. (personal communication, September 26, 2016)

And this is not unique to Italians. Even the quieter gestures, or the total absence of gestures, convey meaning.

For verbal communication, Pistritto suggests, "Learn a few key words in the local language and always bring a vocabulary/translator with you in case you need to communicate with local people" (personal communication, September 21, 2016). Roberta advises, "When it gets too hard, simply switch to 'friendly English'" (personal communication, September 26, 2016). She sees this as a "gesture of openness" that people appreciate. Javier warns that "some students believe that being in a new country will help them increase their language level just by breathing in. They need to have an active role in switching to the language and every effort will be important" (personal communication, September 27, 2016). At the same time, students should not overestimate their knowledge. Knowing just a few words and nonverbal codes is only a start. Students should be mindful of their limits and have a little humility. They should learn to say, "Thank you. You are so kind." The extra bit is guaranteed to bring a smile— a universally understood nonverbal communication. However, they should also understand when and where smiling at strangers is appropriate. It may not be interpreted in the way one thinks, especially by random people on public transportation. The guideline is that if you wouldn't do it on the subway in New York, don't do it elsewhere. One should also be aware of the unspoken verbal communication embedded in clothing, especially clothes with logos, phrases, and imagery.

In summary, when it comes to manners and behaviors, "Be curious about the things that you do not seem to understand and even those which you don't seem to like, and don't miss the chance of reflecting and of talking about these things" (Roberta, personal communication, September 26, 2016). After all, this is one of the reasons a student undertakes a study abroad. Understanding a different culture often requires the realization that we do not need to share the same values and frames of mind to enjoy being together.

Whose Rules?

People from the host countries who work with study abroad students often mention how young Americans tend to think of themselves as being exempt from the rules, regulations, and laws of the places they are visiting. These can be the rules of the host institution; the hostel or guest accommodations; or local noise, public drinking, or littering ordinances. Many communities visited by our students also rely heavily on general tourism and spend a great deal of public and private money making sure their communities look their best. Those who live in these communities know all too well that first impressions are lasting memories, and they are justifiably upset when an evening of binge drinking on Saturday night leaves their Sunday morning streets full of cans, bottles, and sometimes much worse. It is not as much an issue of sobriety as it is a requirement for judgment. "You can drink a beer in the street," writes a colleague from northern Italy, "but please be discreet and don't make too much noise or garbage" (personal communication, September 21, 2016).

Another London colleague warns, "Our rules are very fixed and ignorance is not an excuse so the consequences can be large" (personal communication, September 27, 2016).

Stefano Baldassarri, director of the International Studies Institute in Florence, Italy, reports the most serious issues that have important health, legal, and disciplinary consequences are related to excessive alcohol consumption, trying to hide a "mistake" hoping not to get caught, and being overly self-confident (personal communication, September 22, 2016).

I tell my students they should leave their preconceived notions at home but not their brains or their good manners. I also warn them that they will be meeting people I know, people with whom I have had long-standing relationships and share a high regard. I let them know that if they embarrass me in any way while they are with me, they will be on the next plane home at their parents' expense. Although there have been some close calls (a damaged hostel bunk bed comes to mind), I have not yet had to make good on my threat. Apparently the bunk bed incident was the result of a small wager on how high one of them could jump into bed. The guilty student paid for the damage without being asked.

While telling students, "If you wouldn't do it in the United States, don't do it here either" is an obvious caution, but it is only the beginning. Students have to be aware that local laws and ordinances may affect them if they are not aware, and ignorance is no excuse. For instance, there is a 100 euro fine in Italy for not stamping your ticket the minute you board the bus. Drinking and driving laws in Ireland and Australia are incredibly strict. Littering and recycling laws and regulations are getting increasingly more stringent in all parts of the world.

Safety First!

Everyone I interviewed for this chapter emphasized safety, from "Watch out for crazy bikes!" to "Review your insurance policy and acquaint yourself with the local health care system before you need it." The list of dos and don'ts was extensive and, frankly, intimidating. However, it is useful to point out to students that all we are asking for is the same level of street smarts we hope they exhibit even when they are travelling in an unfamiliar city or town at home. It is never a good idea to take all one's cash and credit cards along or to be out alone late at night, and passports should be kept in a safe place. It is even more foolhardy to hand an expensive camera or smartphone to a complete stranger to take one's picture. It is hard to believe, but I have seen it happen. And explaining how that camera or phone got stolen to the local police can be pretty embarrassing.

Simple things like having the e-mail and phone number of the local contact person and the group's leader or having a fully charged cell phone cannot be overemphasized. One of my students was delayed at immigration in the airport for more than an hour because he could not remember anything but my name. He had not printed out or brought with him any of the preprogram information we had provided, including where he would be staying, the schedule, tips and guidelines for getting transportation from the airport to the hostel where he would be staying, or my Irish mobile number. It was another student, arriving on a later flight, that got him out of his difficulties. (See Chapter 11 for creating wallet-size identification cards.)

Reflect, Reflect, Reflect

Baldassarri tells students "that traveling will help them to better understand who they are, what they want from life and learn how to ask for it" (personal communication, September 22, 2016). One of the ways we help students become more aware of what is going on around them, and how this might lead them to better understand themselves and their experiences, is the practice of reflection as described in Chapter 3. In my program we provide ongoing guided reflection by writing morning reflections. Each morning starts with students writing three free-style handwritten pages in their journals reflecting on whatever comes to mind. We then mine these for "aha!" moments and instances that show us what we are learning. We then work around the table asking the following questions:

- How do we know?
- How can we learn more?
- What does that mean?
- Does this change me? In what way? Why? Why not?

For some students, this practice of morning reflections continues long after they have gone back home.

As Doerr (2016) and Hangen and Sen (2016) remind us, recognizing that the host society is full of contextual richness and variety is not something that merely experiencing the culture will uncover. Reflection is essential in creating the inner dialogue that helps untangle and process perceptions and the feelings they raise. "Don't avoid moments of solitude: They are precious in offering the chance of exploring sides of yourself that you may not know, or not enough," advises one colleague. When reflections are shared with other students, everyone gets to see how there are common themes and individual situations. Being in a strange place amidst people one does not know is stressful. The turning point for many students is being able to reflect and share and move to a new awareness that even among strangers one is not really alone.

Voices From Abroad: Top 10

To summarize the most common and important reflections of our colleagues from abroad, I have collected and merged them in a top 10 words of wisdom list for students.

1. Research the culture before you arrive.
2. Once you arrive, get to know some of the locals.
3. Pay attention to *time* and *space* cues and codes.
4. Get to know the culture through its food.
5. Pay attention to mannerisms and behaviors, yours *and* theirs.

6. Pay attention to how you communicate verbally and nonverbally.
7. Dress appropriately.
8. Be safety smart about yourself, your passport, your money, where you go and with whom.
9. Know the laws, ordinances, and rules.
10. Reflect, reflect, reflect.

Bringing students abroad to encounter new people and cultures is a very special part of my teaching. I love making Ireland my classroom and sharing my students and their interests with my colleagues and friends there. I know from the hugs and tears that are shed when students leave to go home that we have created special memories. What I believe and sincerely hope is true is that it was, for them, more than a surface experience, more than a holiday—it was an encounter with themselves through the eyes of the people they met there. And I believe that is the desire of all my colleagues engaged in the cultural adventure of study abroad.

References

Choi, A. S. (2014). What Americans can learn from other food cultures [Web post]. Retrieved from ideas.ted.com/what-americans-can-learn-from-other-food-cultures

Doerr, N. M. (2016). Chronotopes of study abroad: The cultural other, immersion, and compartmentalized space–time. *Journal of Cultural Geography, 33*(1), 80–99. doi:10.1080/08873631.2015.1065030

Foucault, M. (1994). *The order of things: An archeology of the human sciences.* New York, NY: Vintage Books.

Gell, A. (1996). *The anthropology of time: Cultural constructions of temporal maps and images.* Oxford, England: Berg.

Gossage, H. (1966). Understanding Marshall McLuhan. *Ramparts, 4*(12), 37.

Hall, E. T. (1983). *The dance of life: The other dimension of time.* New York, NY: Anchor Books.

Hall, E. T. (1959). *The silent language.* New York, NY: Doubleday.

Hangen, S., & Sen. R. (2016). Negotiating time and space on a study abroad program in south India. *Journal of Cultural Geography, 33*(1), 62–79. doi:10.1080/08873631.2015.1084114

Levine, R. (1997). *A geography of time: The temporal misadventures of a social psychologist.* New York, NY: Basic Books.

CONTRIBUTORS

Bilge Gökhan Çelik is a professor of construction management at Roger Williams University. He earned his PhD in design, construction, and planning from the University of Florida and his MS and BS degrees in architecture from Anadolu University in Turkey. He has taught construction management, architecture, and sustainability courses at graduate and undergraduate levels in American and Turkish universities. Çelik also designed and led a number of successful short-term study abroad programs and initiatives in Turkey. His research and publications focus on green buildings, construction education, and project management and scheduling and have been presented and published at a variety of national and international conferences and journals. Çelik is also currently serving as the program coordinator of the construction management program at Roger Williams University.

Robert A. Cole oversees global and international programs on his campus. He has been a conference program reviewer for groups such as NAFSA: Association of International Educators and the American Association of Colleges & Universities, and he has made presentations at conferences on topics such as the Arab Spring and the role of liberal education in emerging democracies, estranging undergraduate ethnographers through fieldwork abroad, international internships, and situating general education abroad. Cole was a participant on a U.S. Department of Education Fulbright-Hays grant for an immersion, capacity-building, and curriculum development project related to Egypt and the Middle East North Africa region and was a contributor to a U.S. Department of Education (Title VI) Undergraduate International Studies and Foreign Language Programs grant. He has also developed short-term, faculty-led curricula for students' cultural immersion in The Netherlands, Belgium, and northern Germany. Cole holds a PhD in communication.

Darla K. Deardorff is executive director of the Association of International Education Administrators, hosted at Duke University, where she holds affiliated faculty positions in education and in international comparative studies. In addition, she holds numerous faculty appointments at universities in the United States and abroad, including Harvard University's Global Education Think Tank and the Intercultural Communication Institute. Regularly invited to speak and consult around the world, she has published widely on intercultural and international education topics, and has six books including as lead editor of *The SAGE Handbook of International Higher Education* (Sage, 2012), author of *Demystifying Outcomes Assessment for International Educators* (Stylus, 2015), and coeditor of *Intercultural Competence in Higher Education* (Routledge, 2017). Founder of ICC Global, she holds a master's and doctorate from North Carolina State University.

Candelas Gala earned her PhD from the University of Pittsburgh and is Charles E. Taylor Professor of Romance Languages and Literatures at Wake Forest University. The focus of her research is twentieth-century Spanish literature, particularly Federico García Lorca and poetry written by women. For more than 30 years she has been general director of the Wake Forest study abroad program in Salamanca, Spain, where she earned her BA degree at the University of Salamanca. Also in Salamanca, she initiated the Internship Summer Program and has been the on-site academic director of the semester and year program several times. She has published books on García Lorca; creative cognition; interdisciplinary exchanges among poetry, physics, and painting; and numerous essays on various literary topics in national and international academic journals.

Javier García Garrido earned his master's degree in Spanish as a foreign language from the University of Salamanca, Spain, in 2001. As part of his degree, he developed one of the first Spanish websites for autonomous online learning. He has been an instructor of Spanish at Cursos Internacionales of the University of Salamanca and resident director for International Studies Abroad. In 2005 he became the on-site administrative director for the Wake Forest University study abroad program in Salamanca, his hometown. Since then he has been instrumental in further developing the program, coordinating and supervising summer internships, and overseeing all on-site aspects of the Wake Forest full immersion program in Salamanca.

Dale Leavitt grew up as a clam digger from Scarborough, Maine, before going to the University of Maine at Orono (PhD in animal nutrition, 1986). During his graduate work, he moved to Woods Hole Oceanographic Institution to finish his degree and continued working there as a research associate for the next 20 years, eventually managing the Woods Hole Sea Grant Marine Extension Program in collaboration with Cape Cod Cooperative Extension. He took a faculty position at Roger Williams University in 2003, where he is professor of marine biology and an aquaculture extension specialist. Leavitt splits his time between teaching marine-related courses and providing outreach and research services to the marine aquaculture and resource management communities, focusing primarily on shellfish. He has published numerous peer-reviewed articles as well as a number of technical bulletins and outreach materials for public consumption, mostly associated with clam, oyster, and scallop culture and management.

Roxanne M. O'Connell, PhD, is professor of communication, specializing in visual communication and media ecology. She is also a singer, photographer, and designer. Her professional life "dances at the crossroads" between visual media, media ecology, ethnography, and music. She is the editor of the two volume series *Teaching with Multimedia: Pedagogy in the Websphere* (Hampton Press, 2010, 2012) and the author of *Visualizing Culture: Analyzing the Cultural Aesthetics of the Web* (Peter Lang, 2015). Recent CD publications of her work include an interview with Seamus Connolly on "Fieldwork" (ICTM-Ireland, 2013, track 23) and backup vocals ("Pretty Saro") on a tribute album *Dear Jean* to legendary folk artist Jean Ritchie (Lane, M., Pilzer. C. & Schaltz D., 2014, Disc 2, track 6). She spends most of her time between Ireland and the United States, teaching, doing research, or designing and leading student study abroad programs.

Susan Lee Pasquarelli earned her doctoral degree in language, literacy, and cultural studies from Boston University in 1996 and is professor of literacy teacher education at Roger Williams University. Integrating multicultural literature across the K–12 curriculum is the focus of her research and teaching. For the past 10 years, she led successful short-term study abroad programs in Rome and Sicily and served on the university's study abroad advisory board to enhance the proposal process for faculty-led programs. Pasquarelli has published and presented research and best practices at regional, national, and international conferences on improvement of K–12 literacy instruction and faculty-led short-term study abroad programs.

Michele V. Price earned her master of arts degree from Western Oregon State College in 1994 and is emeritus director of Study Abroad and International Exchanges at Western Oregon University. At Western Oregon University she participated in many international site visits and evaluations; implemented photo blogging and digital storytelling projects for the required study abroad capstone course, which she taught; and, with Victor Savicki, established an ongoing research and assessment project of student reflective writing. Following her retirement, she and Savicki have continued their research and assessment project with a Portland-based study abroad provider. They have published their work in several journals. Price strives to help other education abroad professionals find solutions to improve programs and to enhance student learning.

Autumn Quezada de Tavarez, PhD, is associate professor of history and program coordinator for the Latin American and Latino studies minor. As coadviser for Roger Williams University's chapter of the Foundation for the Medical Relief of Children, she leads service-learning trips throughout Latin America, linking intersections of social justice, history, and public health for undergraduate students. In addition to her global service-learning work, she has published articles on Mexican ethnohistory focused on Mayan history in the state of Chiapas. Quezada de Tavarez is also coeditor of *Decentering Discussion on Religion and State: Emerging Narratives, Challenging Perspectives* (Lexington Press 2015).

Victor Savicki, professor of psychology, emeritus, at Western Oregon University, has taught university students eight times in Austria, Germany, Greece, Argentina, and the United Kingdom. Twenty-eight of his peer-reviewed publications emphasize some aspect of culture, including the research-based book *Burnout Across Thirteen Cultures* (Praeger, 2002), the edited book *Developing Intercultural Competence and Transformation* (Stylus, 2008), and the coedited book *Assessing Study Abroad* (Stylus, 2015). His entry in the *Encyclopedia of Intercultural Competence* (Sage, 2015) "Stress, Coping and Adjustment in Intercultural Competence" synthesizes his views on study abroad student development. His current research interest is the influence of study abroad on student identity and the role reflection plays from a constructivist viewpoint.

Michael Scully is associate professor of journalism in the communication department at Roger Williams University where he has been teaching since 2007. He has an MS in journalism from Columbia University and hopes to complete a PhD in humanities at Salve Regina University in 2018. His dissertation research is on digital publishing.

Michael J. Tyson is assistant director for study abroad in Wake Forest University's Center for Global Programs and Studies, where he has served as the dedicated representative for all summer abroad programming since 2010. His responsibilities include managing up to 20 short-term, faculty-led programs annually; assisting faculty in their program development from inception to completion; and administering program details like marketing, the budgetary process, and student registration. He also advises all students interested in summer study abroad. In addition to his programming and advising responsibilities, he manages the scholarship process for summer programs and acts as an evaluator for the university's Fulbright Review Committee. He has led student service trips to Jamaica and Russia and has also spent time teaching English in Mexico. Tyson holds a BA from the University of North Carolina at Charlotte and an MEd from the University of South Carolina.

Kerri Staroscik Warren, PhD, is professor of biology and coordinator of the Roger Williams University Public Health Program. Her academic interests include environmental influences on health outcomes, authentic community engagement in undergraduate public health education, and the role of assessment in conscientious course evolution. Since 2009 Warren has led global health service-learning programs in Latin America and has worked with Quezada de Tavarez to develop interdisciplinary short-term study abroad experiences that incorporate fair trade learning practices.

Paul Webb is professor of marine biology at Roger Williams University, where he specializes in the physiological and behavioral ecology of marine vertebrates. He received his PhD in biology from the University of California, Santa Cruz and has been involved in field research projects in British Columbia, the U.S. Virgin Islands, Antarctica, and throughout California. At Roger Williams, he has been a member of the advisory board for faculty-led study abroad programs and the Phi Beta Delta Honor Society for International Scholars. He has led a short-term tropical ecology course in Belize since 2003 and a coastal ecology course in the Azores.

Brian Wysor is a marine biologist who specializes in the biodiversity, distribution, and classification of seaweeds. His research has ranged from the characterization of the marine flora of Atlantic and Pacific Panama to studies of green tide biodiversity in Rhode Island to the molecular systematics of green algae. Wysor earned his PhD in evolutionary and environmental biology from the University of Louisiana at Lafayette, during which time he received a Fulbright Fellowship to Panama. His work has since been supported by the U.S. National Science Foundation, which facilitated basic research and the development of field phycology courses in Panama for undergraduates, graduate students, and young professionals. At Roger Williams University, Wysor has served on the international advisory board for faculty-led study abroad programs, and he has been coleading one such program to Panama since 2010.

Min Zhou was born and grew up in China. She received her BA and MA in Germanic languages and literatures from Peking University in Beijing,

China, and her PhD from the University of Michigan in Ann Arbor. She also studied for two years at the Free University of Berlin in Germany and is currently associate professor of languages at Roger Williams University. The experience of studying, working, and living in different cultures has inspired her research interest in travel literature and in the images of the East in Western literature and culture. She is passionate about teaching modern languages to American undergraduate students and about helping them develop intercultural competency in the classroom.

INDEX

emphasis on recent studies that offer convincing evidence about what undergraduates are or are not learning; brings to bear the latest knowledge about human learning and development that raises questions about the very foundations of current theory and practice; and presents six examples of study abroad courses or programs whose interventions apply this knowledge

This book provokes readers to reconsider long-held assumptions, beliefs, and practices about teaching and learning in study abroad and to reexamine the design and delivery of their programs. In doing so, it provides a new foundation for responding to the question that may faculty and staff are now asking: What do I need to know, and what do I need to be able to do, to help my students learn and develop more effectively abroad?

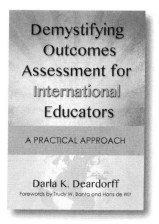

Demystifying Outcomes Assessment for International Educators
A Practical Approach
Darla K. Deardorff

Foreword by Trudy W. Banta and Hans de Wit

"In the service of international outcomes assessment, this book provides an accessible introduction to the uninitiated, reassurance to the intimidated, and new insights to the accustomed practitioner. An indispensable book for international educators who recognize the value in demonstrating the transformative results of their work to their campus constituencies."—*Dr. Harvey Charles, President, Association of International Education Administrators*

For many in international education, assessment can seem daunting and overwhelming, especially given that such efforts need to involve much more than a pre/post survey. This book is a practical guide to learning-outcomes assessment in international education for practitioners who are starting to engage with the process, as well as for those who want to improve the quality and effectiveness of their assessment efforts

22883 Quicksilver Drive
Sterling, VA 20166-2102

Subscribe to our e-mail alerts: www.Styluspub.com

Also available from Stylus

Working Side By Side
Creating Alternative Breaks as Catalysts for Global Learning, Student Leadership, and Social Change
Shoshanna Sumka, Melody Christine Porter, and Jill Piacitelli

Foreword by Tanya O. Williams

"I and many other champions of service-learning have long had our doubts about short-term service including alternative breaks. *Working Side by Side* speaks directly and authoritatively to these concerns. Its focus on authentic relationships, capacity building, and preparing students to recognize and address systemic oppression is both philosophical and eminently practical. This volume is an essential resource for educators and student leaders who seek to engage students in alternative breaks."—***Barbara Jacoby,*** *Faculty Associate, Leadership & Community Service-Learning, University of Maryland*

This book advances the field of student-led alternative breaks by identifying the core components of successful programs that develop active citizens. It demonstrates how to address complex social issues, encourage structural analysis of societal inequities, foster volunteer transformation, and identify methods of work in mutually beneficial partnerships. It emphasizes the importance of integrating a justice-centered foundation throughout alternative break programs to complement direct service activities and promotes long-term work for justice and student transformation by offering strategies for post-travel reorientation and continuing engagement.

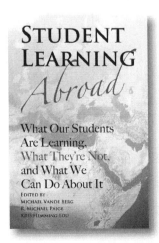

Student Learning Abroad
What Our Students Are Learning, What They're Not, and What We Can Do About It
Edited by Michael Vande Berg, R. Michael Paige, and Kris Hemming Lou

"The book is a good source for study-abroad professionals and has the ability to provide direction for programs needing new life breathed into them, particularly at a time when budgets are shrinking, calls for accountability are increasing, and students deserve, more than ever, to have truly meaningful study-abroad experiences."
— *The Review of Higher Education*

Student Learning Abroad reviews the dominant paradigms of study abroad; marshals rigorous research findings, with

(Continued on preceding page)